CHILDREN AND TEENAGERS WITH ASPERGERS

THE JOURNEY OF PARENTING FROM BIRTH TO TEENS

Anna Van Der Post et al

chipmunkapublishing
the mental health publisher
empowering people with Aspergers Syndrome

Published by
Chipmunkapublishing
PO Box 6872
Brentwood
Essex CM13 1ZT
United Kingdom

http://www.chipmunkapublishing.com

Chipmunkapublishing gratefully acknowledge the support of Arts Council England.

Acknowledgments

I am indebted to many more people than I can mention on the one page I have allotted myself.

I give heartfelt thanks to all the parents and carers who have so generously and bravely shared the uncensored accounts of their daily lives with us – what enormous respect I have for you all.

No words can adequately acknowledge the support that my mother and father gave me throughout, whilst researching and preparing this book.

To Good Housekeeping magazine, David Reid, the National Autistic Society, the American Autistic Society and the Canadian Autistic society for playing such a pivotal part in finding my superb contributors.

To John Vander Maten for his insightful comments and dependable efficiency.

Profuse thanks to Rachel for giving her time and expertise to set up and run the book's website.

To Sarian for making me laugh and for having the good sense to laugh back at my jokes - you kept me going during those rare (o.k. weekly!) moments of blind panic and self-doubt.

To my proof reader Ann Andrews, with thanks for working with such sensitivity and meticulous care.

To my readers Sylvia Redfern and Kath Ferry-Roberts for their invaluable observations.

To everybody at Chipmunka publishing for their vision; it has been a pleasure working with such patient and consummate professionals.

Anna Van Der Post et al

Dedication

To my mother and father with love, for believing in me and for their boundless support.

To my obnoxious, but much beloved, son and to all the other children in this book.

*

Anna Van Der Post et al

'Misery loves Company'

John Ray 1627-1705

~

'If you have met one person with autism,

you have met one person with autism'

Stephen Shore

Anna Van Der Post et al

Introduction

I am the mother of a teenager with extreme end Aspergers[1] and sometimes life has been such a struggle that I have questioned whether I wish to go on. During my dark times I looked, in vain, for a book that reflected my journey. All I could find were books which put a positive spin on things and as this view didn't even begin to match my experiences, I came away feeling even more desperate and alone. Something needed to be done. As a research psychologist by training, I decided to find out to what extent my feelings and experiences were unique. I placed various adverts asking for first-hand experiences and received hundreds of e-mails from extremely desperate parents. I soon realised that I was far from alone and that there was a huge gap in the Asperger literature. Parents were desperate to have their experiences and, at times, negative feelings towards their child validated. Clearly a book was needed which reflected what it is really like to raise a child with Aspergers. I wanted to discover what day-to-day lives were like for parents raising children with extreme behavioural problems and complex needs. What was the effect on them and the whole family? So I asked them and this book is the product of my questions.

After six months of research, communicating with over two hundred parents, I decided to compile an

[1] Aspergers throughout this book is used to denote Asperger's Syndrome, named after the Austrian psychiatrist Hans Asperger.

anthology of six cases written by the respective parents. The stories I eventually chose are representative of the parents who contacted me. They give an in depth picture of the huge variation in problems and family structures; however, they do share the common experience of desperation and, for some, despair. I hope that readers will find that some of the accounts featured reflect their own struggles and emotions. The families recount life from birth to the teens. This book is not about giving false hope but about confronting reality. Knowing that others battle and feel as we do, removes the guilt, isolation and inadequacy that many of us feel. Embedded within each family's story are their own solutions and ways of coping which are revealed as the narrative unfolds.

Although I have compiled this book principally to comfort parents, our chosen method of writing case histories is also the perfect medium for the professional reader. The uncensored nature of the information given may give them a deeper insight into the far reaching effects of Aspergers on the individual and the family unit. It may also shed light on which aspects of their behaviour are helpful and which are problematic.

The stories are hard-hitting and intensely emotional but because they are written with honesty and humour they are surprisingly easy to read. In sharing these experiences I hope that many of you will gain a deeper understanding of Aspergers and its repercussions and for those of you with such children that you will no longer feel alone.

Lilly's Story

Birth - Age Five ~ *"Me Love Mummy"* James *Aged two*

Nobody could have wanted a child more than I did. I had always known that I wanted to be a mother so when, on my thirtieth birthday, I conceived, my life was complete, right on plan, or so I thought! I had, at last, realised my biggest dream.

I had a normal pregnancy and birth. James was born screaming and had clearly enjoyed the whole process about as much as his mother had! Everything seemed normal and he was, seen through the rose tinted glasses of most new mothers, perfect. I soon discovered that James did not believe in sleep; he took short cat naps, and then only if I held him. When I attempted to gently transfer him into his pram, he usually woke instantly, over-sensitive, it seemed, to any changes in his sensory environment. This inability to sleep carried on until his fifth year, waking hourly through most of his infancy. Apart from his sleep problem, he seemed to be pretty much the same as other babies I had known - only much more demanding. Looking back it was obvious that he was exceptionally bright. I can be forgiven for failing to notice because before I had my son, I had been a nanny to three very intellectually able boys. As a consequence, my ideas and expectations of normal development were skewed, based as they were on an artificially high starting platform.

When he was just two or three months old James moaned relentlessly even when I held and talked to him. Like most parents I tried everything I could think of to calm him. I soon discovered that he could be reliably entertained if I walked him around the house pointing at objects and naming them. The other very bizarre action was to run round and round the dining room table as fast as I could. I cannot imagine what on earth made me do this with a vulnerable baby in my arms, but it worked. I spent an inordinate amount of his childhood doing laps around the dining room and as we had floor to ceiling windows and were over-looked by adjacent flats I'm surprised no one called social services or the local mental health team! [1]

Throughout his first two years it was a struggle to keep him amused and we were exhausted and irritable from lack of sleep. James met all his developmental milestones, including crawling and walking, pretty much on time. He was breast fed and showed little interest in solids until his second year when he ate a range of foods quite happily with no ill effects.

At one year four months, James saw his grandma cry; he kept looking at her, clearly concerned and then proceeded to cuddle her. I noted proudly in my diary 'James showed genuine sympathy today.' I have included this because his ability to empathise was short-lived and, as you will see, by his teens seems to have disappeared for good.

---

[1] Knowing what I now know about autistic children's penchant for rocking and spinning, this could have been seen as an early warning.

At one year five months I noted 'James loves jigsaws and can effortlessly complete eight piece puzzles. When playing in the garden he will often lie on his tummy and watch nature, focusing on tiny ants for long periods of time. He can now easily match 12 different shapes in his shape sorter. Yesterday he surprised me because his cash till broke and when I took it apart to fix it, he was absolutely transfixed and insisted on helping to reassemble the bits.' I am not recounting his interests out of maternal pride, but it seems to me now, that all of these activities require a very focused one track mind. This may have been an early hint of his later phenomenal ability to focus on a single task to the exclusion of all else.

When he was about 16 months old, I realised just how bright he was. One of his favourite pastimes was when I gave him a complex instruction, usually involving three or more sequences of tasks e.g. 'Go into the kitchen and open the second drawer, find a red tea-towel and bring it back to me please.' He loved this game and always obliged with the right colour tea-towel.

At 19 months I have recorded that he loved to feed dolls and cuddly toys. He was clearly participating in and enjoying imaginative play - which later he was to drop.

I also noted at this age how much he hated wearing clothes and was particularly resistant to shoes and coats. At the time I thought he was beginning 'the terrible twos' and just wanting to assert himself.

Knowing now how over-sensitive James is to tactile stimuli, I am so glad that I decided not to make it into a battle and allowed him to be naked at home and dress eccentrically when out. He would happily tolerate his pyjamas and it was not unusual for us to attend playgroups with pyjamas and sheep slippers. It was often embarrassing when James wore dirty old pyjamas in very cold weather and at the time I experienced it as quite a stress. But looking back it seems unimportant.[1] However, over-sensitivity to touch is another early indicator of Aspergers which now makes sense.

At 19 months, I was reading him a new Postman Pat book which, somewhat out of character, he ripped from my hands and threw on the floor. I asked him what the problem was and told him to pick the book up and show me. He pointed to the dog which I had correctly called a sheepdog. It didn't take me long to realise that he had been disturbed and confused by the word 'sheepdog'. He had felt uncomfortable as his understanding of the world was suddenly thrown into disarray; he knew what a dog was and he knew what a sheep was but there was not such a thing as a sheepdog. I explained that a sheepdog did not mean a dog that was also part sheep but that it was a type of dog that was very good at helping farmers to keep their sheep from wandering too far and getting lost. He smiled and we happily carried on with the story. This sort of misunderstanding became increasingly

---

[1]   Even now, some 14 years on, he still hates the feel of clothes.

common and began to trouble me.[1]

I think at this point that I ought to mention that in order to afford to stay at home with my son, I child-minded. I am extremely lucky to have a mother who totally supports me and is my very best friend. Together we somehow managed to care for James and, over the following eight years, he was surrounded by children of all ages. Like most babies and many under twos he showed only passing interest in children of a similar age, much preferring the company of older children or adults. However, in his case this propensity continued.

At around two and a half, I wrote, 'he has an imaginary friend called Bertie. His imaginary friend is a really tiny boy who has a tiny white car with yellow seats. James also has Dania the butterfly who is sometimes a bit naughty! His language is pretty fluent now but still unclear[2]. Lots of questions *How cuts get better - what happens in me body?*; *How does the moon stay in the sky*? Knows left and right hand, his alphabet and can count very well. He spends hours building spectacular models with bricks. James told me he loved me for the first time *me love mummy.*

*

[1] Most people with Aspergers tend to understand language on a very literal level – so this too now makes sense,

[2] James had very unclear diction for which he received three sessions with a speech therapist when he was five. Despite this, his speech has continued to be a little unclear.

Going Potty!

As a nanny, I had effortlessly potty-trained many children. So it was with utter confidence that I began to train James. He was willing and understood what was required of him, but when it came to the crunch he just couldn't seem to do it. I wondered if he found weeing in the sitting down position difficult, so I encouraged him to try weeing standing up in the garden, I also used star charts, rewarding every attempt - but nothing worked. I nearly gave up, wondering if he was a late developer. Knowing that he seemed sensitive to different textures I decided to line his potty with a nappy and this worked wonderfully, up to a point that is! James could only wee in his nappy[1] lined potty. Eventually he learnt to wee standing up but, having got accustomed to this position, he then found it impossible to revert to sitting in order to empty his bowels. There appeared to be an inflexibility in his learning. When it came to poo we had to wait many more years for success and the situation caused untold problems for us all (more on this in the 4-8 year section). All these difficulties are now explainable by an understanding of the inflexibility of many people with Aspergers. Having got used to doing something in one way it becomes almost impossible to change approach.

At his 3 year development check he played with stickle bricks and on one there was an image of a butterfly. It had a thorax with wings and a round smiling head on top. I asked him what it was and he

---

[1] Nappy is an English term for diaper.

confidently said a mouse. I asked if he was sure, to which he replied "yes." Smiling, I asked "so it's a mouse is it?" to which he replied "no it's a mouse on top of a butterfly." James once again took a literal interpretation. He knew that butterflies didn't have faces and when he saw a butterfly shape with a round face on top he understandably concluded that the face belonged to something else which was sitting on top. How easy it is to think that a child is failing to understand something when, in fact, it is we who fail to understand them!

Around this time (aged three) I recall in my diary that I had told James "I love you the whole world and more, as much as anyone can ever love" and he immediately responded with perfect logic "I love the universe a billionth of an atom more than you because without the universe and earth we couldn't be here." James has always seen flaws in statements and even at such a young age he spotted weaknesses in the simplest of remarks and felt obliged to comment (as he still does!) I have often observed that people with Aspergers tend to focus in on errors and only pass comment when things are wrong. James has explained this to me - there is no point in stating something is all right, as this is implied if nothing is said. If no change needs to be made, it is pointless to comment.

*

String Theory

Around the age of three James learnt to tie knots and from that moment he became obsessed with string. He tied toys to posts and most days whole rooms were literally covered in string. I had to precariously climb through his 3-D extravaganzas. James would do this for hours and any attempts to dismantle them were met with distress. Looking back it is easy to see how an outsider might think I was indulging a very spoilt child but in reality I knew that he had invested so much of his energy and reasoning in these projects, and that to dismantle them would be sabotaging a work in progress. In addition, things were further complicated by his anxiety, his need to leave things untouched and unchanged. I handled it, wrongly or rightly, by letting it run its course and patiently waiting until he was ready to start on another room. I acknowledge that it was comparatively easy for me to indulge James because of the absence of siblings. Some obsessions, I have learnt through time, are best tolerated and seem to need to become all consuming before they can burn themselves out.

Anxiety Rears Its Ugly Head

At the age of just three James began to get progressively more anxious. He became very upset and distressed if I threw anything out. I once threw out an old sock and by bedtime he was literally inconsolable and in a very agitated state, which rose to something approximating panic. He was also oversensitive about sticky fingers and would often wash his hands. This was all the precursor to OCD (Obsessive Compulsive Disorder) which I believe is often experienced by people with Aspergers. He refused to colour or draw at this time because he felt he couldn't do it perfectly enough as he inevitably went outside of the lines. This perfectionism has been a recurring theme and on many occasions has sadly prevented him from pursuing his interests but, paradoxically, this very same trait is what has enabled him to excel in other areas. In my diary of that time I rather sadly noted 'Other children of this age don't seem to be this self-critical or even aware that their pictures do not match reality, James sadly is.'

At the age of 4 James heard his grandma say that she didn't like milk. After hearing this he refused to drink milk, cheese, yogurts, chocolate, biscuits, anything which might have a trace of milk in it. He developed something between a fear and an aversion. This was a very extreme response to a casual remark and this tendency to respond excessively to flippant asides was evident in his pre-teens period.

One diary entry stated 'he has been causing me some concern recently (aged 4). He seems to have obsessive thoughts particularly at night when he is going to sleep and when he first wakes up in the morning. He will suddenly cry and may worry about: -

- a torn comic, card or drawing
- an envelope he can't find

- replacing a kite with a tangled string (although I had already mended it)

He wouldn't have a comic he really wanted in a shop because the balloon was taped on and this would mark the comic.' In order to help him cope with his worries I bought some 'worry dolls'. These are tiny little handcrafted dolls which are held in a small draw-string bag, the whole kit smaller than a little finger. The child is supposed to take the dolls out at night and tell a worry to each doll. The dolls are replaced in the bag and put under the pillow. During the night the dolls help them to solve their problems. This crutch seemed to calm James; it probably made him feel less over whelmed by feelings which were too complicated for his tender age to cope with.

Around that time (aged 4) I also wrote 'I have found James with tears streaming down his cheeks on several occasions. I tried to discover what was upsetting him but he wouldn't say. He often talks about what is alive and what is not and I wondered if he was contemplating the concept of death. My suspicions were confirmed this morning when he was sobbing his heart out at Bambi. I gave him a big cuddle and we talked, he soon admitted that he was afraid I would die. I reassured him that I was very healthy and that I would probably live to be as old as great uncle Steve. I told him if I ever died someone would always look after him and love him e.g. grandma, uncle Stephan or a friend.' At that time I wrote 'James keeps on getting tearful. Yesterday he cried because a drawing of a balloon looked sad and he kept on dwelling on it. Today he cried because some babies are not breast fed. I worry about this oversensitivity and just hope that it is a developmental stage.' We have both suffered from the effects of his anxiety as it has infiltrated, albeit in different guises, throughout his life.

Playgroup/Nursery School

James went to a total of three nursery schools before we found one that he could tolerate and sometimes even enjoy. He hated the noise and chaos, and wanted to play in a different way to the other children and certainly not with them. He seemed overwhelmed and uncomfortable which made him clingy and so genuinely fearful of being left that someone in the family always had to stay.

On one occasion James was using bricks and a railway set to design the strongest bridge he could. He set about the task by building a bridge and testing its strength. Based on what he observed he built another, and so on, until he had a design he was satisfied with. This project had a very specific scientific objective and was clearly not imaginative play and something that could be shared, so when, rather predictably, another child came along and pushed his train on James's bridge, James got upset. The play leader, oblivious of James's experiment, told him not to be silly and to share. This was not an isolated incident and I actually felt very sad for James because it was becoming apparent to me that the concept of sharing was often not relevant to his sort of play. Had James been painting he would not have been expected to share his picture, and this bridge was his picture. So often well-meaning and very kind staff either fail to observe or don't understand that sharing is not always appropriate. James seemed to play in a different way to other children, he was usually testing a hypothesis. This was to prove to be a recurring problem.

When I heard about a local Montessori school where the philosophy allowed each child their own space to play, undisturbed by other children, I jumped at the chance to enrol him. I thought it might be somewhere James could fit in. It was a small, quiet school with the order he seemed to need. I have to admit that by this time I was getting pretty desperate and felt he might never settle without me; moreover I was beginning to doubt myself, wondering if I was somehow to blame. In my diary at that time I wrote 'James went to a Montessori school today. Mum took him because I had to work and we felt he would cling more to me. He apparently went in reasonably happily but after break time he was too tired to participate. I found it very hard to concentrate at work, my thoughts were with James. I so want him to settle and be happy and I am so dreadfully fearful that he won't.' Sadly even at this very gentle school he was unable to settle and after some months of perseverance, the teacher kindly said that she thought James was happier at home. This was exactly the conclusion I was coming to.

It is interesting to note that from the age of one to

four James showed genuine feelings of empathy and love on a number of occasions. He also enjoyed imaginative play, albeit rather obsessively but, by the age of four and a half, almost overnight he ceased to exhibit these traits. I have often wondered why this happened. My take on it is that around the age of four his brain was pre-wired to accelerate on the logical side. This manifested itself by a sudden obsessive interest in numbers, chess, reasoning and debates, almost to the exclusion of everything else. This switch-over seemed to either over-write or supersede the empathetic side of his personality. The only other plausible explanation I have come up with is that because his imaginative play was acted out in an obsessive way, he somehow managed to pass through a whole developmental stage in a compressed time period.

*

Four – The Age of Reason!

At four years of age James suddenly became very logical and fascinated by numbers. I taught him basic maths, the four rules of number: addition, subtraction, multiplication and division and he so loved the exercise of mental arithmetic that he begged for "more sums" from the moment he woke up to the moment he went to sleep. My enthusiasm for this pursuit was somewhat less pronounced and, by contrast, I could frequently be heard begging him to stop, "No more sums James, *please*, mummy is tired now." At age four and a half a family friend, Philip, who is a secondary school teacher, upped the stakes by setting him mental arithmetic problems using different colours to symbolise different numbers, e.g. red = 1, yellow = 2 etc. He then set James some problems e.g. yellow takeaway blue times red. James got them instantly (usually before we had) and where appropriate, translated the answer back into colours. He became so quick and reliable that I was unable to work out the answers before he was asking for the next one. In the end, I was so confident that he was correct that I always said "well done." James cottoned on to this and deliberately answered several wrongly to which I said my usual "well done" and James, rather cross, correctly accused me of failing to check he was really right!

As James (aged nearly five) had been begging me to teach him chess I asked Philip to refresh my memory. James watched as Philip went over the basics and he instantly learnt the names of each piece and how they move. We then had a trial game where I discussed with him where the next move might lie and why. When we went home that evening James insisted on playing until nearly twelve o'clock and by the end of the evening I was struggling to win and to stay awake and James was deliriously happy having found a new obsession to torment me with!

During this period James would often draw diagrams and charts to explain things, preferring this medium of communication to writing. I also encouraged writing by sticking little messages around the house for him, sometimes with clues to a small treasure I had hidden and he would write me little messages back e.g. 'my cof is bad'.

Another of his favourite games was Dr Xargoyle. I pretended to be Dr Xargoyle and I came from another planet so I didn't know anything about earth. I used to say to James "what's that'" and point at something, James then tried to define it. I asked him a series of questions such as "what's the difference between men and women." James replied "women have boobies and men have penises and girls have long hair." So, still in character I asked "If I cut their hair will they be a boy then?" He laughed and said "no, just a girl with shorter hair." As the above examples illustrate his play had now become almost exclusively logic based. As James had always enjoyed my making up stories, especially if I managed to include him in them, I continued to fabricate ever more convoluted plots and encouraged him to add his own bits. This, I reasoned, at least encouraged some imaginative play.

*

Hindsight Is A Wonderful Thing!

Much of the information I have selected to write about in his early years, when seen as a whole, is highly indicative of autistic spectrum problems. However, at the time, I was so focused on coping from day to day that the abnormalities, when taken singly, did not unduly trouble me. I saw James as an oddball (plenty of those in our family!) and just thought it was because he was bright. The realisation that my child might be autistic dawned phenomenally slowly, not because I was in denial, afraid to face reality, but because the problems which I encountered, when seen in isolation, were often within the norm. However, when viewed in hindsight, as a whole, much like a jigsaw puzzle, the true picture only emerges when you have most of the pieces in place.

*

Ages Five - Eight ~ *"If you love me you'd kill me" James aged eight*

When James was about six, a diary entry shows very clearly how his interests continued to have the tendency to be all-consuming and how most of his hobbies were, disconcertingly, at odds with the 'normal' child of a similar age. He was, to put it quite bluntly, a bore! 'James talks endlessly about computers, modems, how to check that everything is fully operational and virus free. The only games he likes are Scrabble, Chess, Nintendo and Cluedo but he is so good at them that other children don't want to play with him and quite frankly, who can blame them! He loves classical music to the exclusion of all other types and enjoys reading and memorising the back of each disc box, including the time of each movement and the accompanying notes - lord knows why! He talks about Mozart (his favourite) and wants me to listen for up to 60 minutes in total silence; he then discusses how he would play and interpret the piece. I get bored and fidgety like a child and he sits still, totally engrossed! James observed to his grandpa that some music needs to be listened to without interruptions and others you could do things to whilst it was on.'

I remember James getting very upset during this period because he wanted to share his enthusiasm for computers or music with the other children in my care but, in true Asperger style, he talked at them, not to them, in a droning monologue, a stream of consciousness. In fact their nickname for him was 'the professor.' Poor James simply couldn't understand why they were not equally enthralled. Much of his distress around this time was caused by having deep thoughts which were conceptually above his emotional development and this caused conflict. This tendency to intellectualise is further supported by the following entry - 'He is less demanding than he was but still requires far more stimulation than other children I know. He is so very different at times to his peers and it makes me both smile and fear for him. He bores other children with his topics of conversation and the intensity of his interests and he in turn finds them boring and silly. He seems to have deeper thoughts than any other child I have known of his age and this does not make for a carefree child. Yesterday James suddenly looked at me and said *Mummy, the more I argue the less sure I am*. This so perfectly expresses what I feel as a parent, the more I observe, question, try to see things from his perspective the less sure I become about how to handle things.'

On reading my later diary entries I was happy to be reminded that he did have a few characteristics typical of an eight year old boy - 'He is quite disgusting at the moment, he likes to jump on me, pin me down and fart.' As a parent, you know you have problems with your child when such behaviour is cause for celebration - for once, your child is normal! He also had a voracious appetite for adventure books and having long ago devoured 'The Famous Five' and 'The Secret Seven' he went on to 'Nancy Drew.' I didn't have the heart to tell him - as he took out yet another batch from our local library - that they were written for teenage girls!

Another of his favourite pursuits during this time was debating and lecturing. Once a week we used to have an evening meal with my parents; on these occasions we would often pair off and debate opposing themes. One week he and my father defended vegans and the next they might take the side of confirmed carnivores etc. After dinner he was usually loathe to stop and would often start walking round and round the dining room table lecturing and pontificating in a very pompous style. "We currently believe that string theory is..." He carried on, oblivious as to whether his audience had fallen asleep, left the room or were transfixed by the brilliance of his argument! Usually, it has to be said, we'd left the room!

Word Count

When he was seven James became increasingly obsessed by adult Scrabble. He often beat us and memorised the whole scoring system. I thought that this was rather amusing and so very typical of my little boy. When I later noticed that he was muttering under his breath whenever anyone was talking, I no longer saw the funny side of his interest in Scrabble. It is no exaggeration to say that I was horrified when I realised that he was totting up the Scrabble score of my words. When he read a book, he did the same. It seemed to me that he had now moved from the realms of *quirky* to *disturbed*, as this was no longer a choice but a compulsion. I think it must be very hard for parents with neuro-typical children to understand what it is like to witness a child engage in such essentially 'batty' behaviour. What, on this occasion and many others, compounded my feelings of distress were the judgements, both spoken and implied, that resulted. If a child is odd, we have been conditioned by now (thankfully) largely outmoded models of psychology, to assume it is the parent's fault. The idea that much behaviour is inherent, wired in the individual's brain, is only now beginning to free people like me from the stigma of being a bad parent. In so many cases it is unjustly assumed that at best we are incompetent parents and, at worst, we must be downright abusive to have such disturbed and odd children. Nothing could be further from the truth and such an assumption is so deeply hurtful and has made me unbelievably frustrated on more than one occasion because their false contention cannot be disproved. It is at times like this that I take refuge in the very uncharitable thought of wishing such a child on their household! I would like to see how well their rigidly held beliefs about how to handle children would stand up to the challenge of children like James. I must confess that on one particular occasion, a member of the public felt entitled to pass judgement on me and my child and as I was particularly stressed and tired I was unable to ignore her. I am both ashamed and proud of my rather acerbic response which went something along these lines: although I admit not quite as fluent, I was after all having to think on my feet. "As you appear to have all the answers and the confidence of the inexperienced to go with it, I suggest that you become a foster parent and use these superior skills to good effect. I'm sure we'd all be most grateful!" Don't mess with a parent at their wits end!

*

Still Going Potty!

I cannot recall how old James was when we finally cracked his toilet training. For some unknown reason I failed to record the date in my diary. I guess that it was somewhere around six or seven. James, as I mentioned earlier, could only poo if we put a nappy on. He was terribly embarrassed by his problem and would only use this method at home. If we were out he simply held on. When we had to go away it inevitably turned into a traumatic occasion for us all. I knew that he was desperate to go and as a consequence, quite understandably, his behaviour deteriorated and was at times quite shocking and inappropriate for someone of his age.

People around, who generally did not know about his problem, were then very judgmental of his behaviour and, to add to our problems, were even more critical of my apparent inadequacy in dealing with him. I generally kept calm and allowed him to be rude and extreme because I knew that his behaviour had a cause and that my anger would be a cruel and pointless addition to his suffering. He was not badly behaved because he had no boundaries, he was badly behaved because he desperately needed the toilet. As time went on his inability to poo without a nappy on put us in so many intolerable situations. I couldn't explain to people about his problem because he was too embarrassed and I knew most people wouldn't understand why I had allowed it to go on this long.

At this point none of us knew he had Aspergers but I did know my child, and I did understand that for some reason he couldn't adapt to a different way of going to the 'loo. We had tried on numerous occasions to crack the problem but had always failed. It all came to a head when we took him to an open air picnic and concert. He had not been to the 'loo that day and I suggested that we cancel the outing. James really wanted to go and as we left I had a nervous stomach as I knew that after tucking into a large picnic he would be desperate for the 'loo. As I had predicted, after eating, James began to fidget and looked uncomfortable, I whispered did he need the 'loo to which he angrily replied that he did not. By half time he could no longer keep up the pretence of being alright and we hastily retreated. In the car on the way home he became increasingly desperate, I suggested we stopped to put a nappy on but he was understandably not willing to do this.

He then began to vomit profusely. I felt so bad for him and finally decided that it was cruel not to tackle the problem once and for all. My usual tactic of patiently waiting until he was ready to change had, on this occasion, failed. The next morning, while the stress of the night before was still fresh in both of our memories, ready to act as a motivating force, I explained to him what we needed to do and why. James was in total agreement. We decided to go cold turkey and that he would not be allowed a nappy. If he needed to poo he could use the 'loo or if he felt he could only go standing up (like in a nappy) then to approximate this he could do so in the shower (lined with kitchen roll), perhaps with some toilet paper around his bottom to help mimic the feel of a nappy. He tried so hard, but several days on (he usually went twice a day) he still hadn't been. Poor James was in such pain, he was distressed and understandably very irritable. I nearly gave in as I found it almost intolerable to watch the child I loved so much, suffer. I then did what every mother at their wits end does: I called my own mother. I explained that if I stayed at home any longer I would give in. We decided that I should make myself scarce for the day while she valiantly took over. Much later that day my mobile rang and she reported that he had managed to poo in the 'loo. I can't describe how 'relieved' I was. They had both had the most miserable time imaginable, James had vomited and cried in pain and my mum had somehow managed to stay strong enough to get them both through. It was not exactly plain sailing thereafter but a few weeks on he had it nailed.

Not a chip off the old block!

At seven I noted 'James really enjoys a computer maths game called Dr Brain. When he plays the games (some intended for sixteen year olds) he is very driven showing competitiveness, determination and a strong desire to succeed. It is quite comical because I am the least competitive person I know and as a child I gave up immediately if I wasn't instantly successful. I have only ever felt comfortable competing with myself. He is just so, so different from me.' From a very early age I realised that, unlike me, praise and competing with oneself was not a motivator for James. By contrast he liked to be challenged and could often be spurred on to complete a piece of work if I suggested he would not be able to finish it before, say, I had washed up. In the end we have to recognise that our children are sometimes quite different to ourselves. With Aspergers children, to an even greater extent than with neuro-typical children, the skill seems to be in recognising and acknowledging what motivates them and what distresses them and then to respond accordingly.

Programmed to Program!

On his eighth birthday James watched a friend's teenage son do some programming. He was instantly transfixed and that evening asked if he could order some books to teach himself visual basic, HTML and C+. I gladly allowed him to spend some of his birthday money and he carefully selected and ordered three books on-line. A few days later the books (of over 500 pages each) arrived and this, unknown to me, was the beginning of the end! He got stuck in straightaway and by the end of the day said "Now I have a purpose in life, now I understand the point." He spent the next few weeks working all day and late into the night and very soon had become proficient in programming. And - some seven years on - this is still central to his life. It is the perfect tool for the mathematical Asperger mind, it seems to satisfy him in a way that nothing else can.

I can't quite remember when James began to take a serious interest in physics but by age ten he had certainly read extensively on the subject and was fascinated by string theory. At this time, realising that I was out of my depth, I tried to find a physics teacher. This was a tall order because not just anyone would do. I needed someone very special who would not be put off by a child with a very pompous style. In common with many people with Aspergers James can see nothing wrong in correcting someone, no matter how eminent. It was thus essential that any teacher we employed would need to understand that James would correct him/her if he believed they were wrong or insufficiently accurate. Sadly, despite my best efforts the position went unfilled. I feel I let him down as there was no doubt that he had a genuine talent for physics and with no outside input it has been demoted to just a mere interest and not the passion it once was.

Throughout all this time James's love of numbers continued. He could often be found muttering to himself as he worked through and tested a theory. My father taught him percentages (aged 8) but it transpired that he had already worked them out for himself including a functioning formula. I mention this if I am honest because I find it astounding and can't help being a little proud. However, as time goes on it has become more and more apparent to me that giftedness and Aspergers when combined can occasionally, as in the above example, be a blessing but, as you will see later, it is sadly, more frequently, a curse.

*

The Panic Attack

It is hard to select the ultimate worst moment of being James's mother but I think the following example is easily up there in the top ten. It is relevant to mention at this juncture that James was unable to sleep alone until he was eight when, eventually, I felt obliged to force the issue. This inability to sleep alone is another example of his being unable to cope with and adapt to any change.

It is worth noting that many people with Aspergers are also significantly handicapped by an inability to adapt. Human beings are survivors due to their ability to adapt and change. A tree that can bend in the wind survives, one that can't is more likely to get into trouble.

My diary painfully notes 'Poor James had a panic attack yesterday. He had a rotten cold and was consequently vulnerable. He was in bed trying to go to sleep and suddenly burst into tears, complaining that he couldn't stop thinking about his Nintendo game. He was frightened because he had forgotten how to get to one particular bit. I tried in vain to calm him and take his mind off it. He then held his head, jumped up and rushed around the room screaming *I can't stop thinking about it*. He then said *I wish I was dead, I'd rather die than have this. If you loved me you'd kill me*. I eventually managed to hold him (as he generally hated cuddles and touch this was a surprise) and rocked him saying calmly and slowly, over and over again, that everything would be alright. I assured him that although it had felt horrible it would stop and he would be fine and said that he should try and accept the feelings and not fight them. Once he calmed down sufficiently, I took some rose and lavender oil and massaged his hands. I told him other people had felt the same which seemed to calm him further. I then explained the 'fight or flight' system and why chemicals made by a frightened body made him feel so bad and that a body cannot carry on feeling like that for long. I am still, a day on, feeling shocked to my core and cannot begin to describe what a mother feels to hear her child beg *Why can't you kill me?* I am confident that this was an isolated problem, he has had OCD episodes but last night was his first full-blown panic attack and I hope for both our sakes his last.' Soon after, I made another entry 'As a result of his panic attack, I had a really productive, deep and honest talk with James last night about his scared feelings and obsessive thoughts. I started to talk while he was lying in bed and we were both relaxed. I got him to answer some questions on an anxiety scoring test I had found. He listened carefully and thought before giving an honest answer, thankfully free from embarrassment or shame (I think the bed is a good place for us to talk as it is a bit like the car - he prefers not to look at me.) He seemed to enjoy it and I suspect the fact that someone had written something which reflected what he had experienced was very comforting. This gave us a starting point to discuss things.

I asked him on a scale of 1-10 where 1 is little, what score he would give his obsessive thoughts on a daily basis, he scored himself a 7. I asked if he wanted us to work towards getting an improvement and he sounded keen and committed. I explained that I felt we could do it alone but if we couldn't quite manage to get enough of an improvement we would need to consult the GP. He seemed fine with that. He said he had obsessive thoughts about Nintendo when he is stuck and doesn't know where to go next, he tries to use cognitive skills to challenge his thinking which helps but only a little. He finds that as soon as he is not occupied, the thoughts come back which, it transpires, is why his tolerance for boredom is so low. This really distresses him (me too!) He also has generalised feelings of being scared at nothing in particular and having a feeling that something bad will happen or someone might hurt/harm him. He knows it is not rational but he can't help it.'

In the above passage James mentions cognitive skills. I am a psychologist by training and many years ago encountered and used a technique called Rational Emotive Therapy. In essence it helps individuals to challenge and change rigid beliefs and unrealistic expectations in order to lower anxiety and help us to be more contented with our lot in life. I had always found it useful and believed that every child should be equipped with the basics to help them navigate through life (although it is not a cure-all and in my opinion is currently over subscribed). I had bought a book about Rational Emotive Therapy which I read and made some child-friendly notes. Then, as part of his school work, I proceeded to teach him the basics. He responded well and seemed to enjoy the exercises, so I was very gratified that he had tried, so valiantly, to apply them to his obsessive thoughts. (He later was to employ the same techniques with good effect to his germ phobia.) At this time I also changed his diet to ensure that it was rich in fish oils and B vitamins which may have contributed to the amelioration of his symptoms and we also took many long country walks.

*

Ages Eight - Twelve ~ "Even if you fail in your objective, you will already have learnt from your experience." James aged ten

How Nice - a holiday!

When James was ten we were invited to stay with my brother, Stephan, at his new house. I felt that it was important for us to go as he had recently divorced and needed our support. But I knew that the visit would be at a cost to James, who hated being away from home. By this point we still did not know that James had Aspergers. When we arrived Stephan showed us our bedrooms. James at this time had a dirt and germ phobia and instantly honed in on a tiny spot on the sheet which looked to me as though it was a grass stain perhaps from having been dropped off the washing line. James, unknown to Stephan, was absolutely freaking out, insisting we couldn't stay, or, if we did, he was going to sit up both nights - I knew that this was no empty threat. I told him we could ask for some new sheets or I could dash out and buy some but now the germ fear had generalised to the whole house so this was not acceptable.

I suggested that we 'come clean' and explain his phobia to Stephan and we perhaps cut our trip short and find a hotel for the night but James was too embarrassed and insisted that Stephan wouldn't understand. Sadly, he was right. In my experience most people are very judgmental. I think they often believed that James was indulged, unaware of what was usually going on behind the scenes. Stephan would probably have said that if James won't sleep in the bed then tough, that was his look out. Had I taken that route, and I did briefly consider it, James's phobia would have got worse and the high levels of stress hormones could have caused new problems or induced a panic attack. He certainly wouldn't have learnt how to cope with and control his germ fear under such conditions. So, as on countless occasions previously, I had to think on my feet, and when one's child has endless problems, destructive secrecy becomes a way of life. When people judge aberrant behaviour then aberrant behaviour goes underground.

I became very adept at creative thinking. I told Stephan that James and I wanted to pop out to the local mall to take advantage of the excellent shopping opportunities. We rushed out, leaving Stephan preparing supper. I tracked down a camping shop, and spending money we didn't have, bought a two person tent, camping mattresses, sleeping bags and pillows. Back at Stephan's house I feigned immense excitement, having found (I lied) a camping set on sale. Then, despite being exhausted from the journey and James's earlier distress, I pretended we were impatient to try it out and, as we hadn't got a garden, could we please borrow his? Stephan agreed but seemed rather taken aback, particularly when it started raining and I insisted that this was even better because we could test it under real conditions and what is more I simply loved the sound of rain on the tent! A bit of rain and gale force winds were not going to deter me putting the tent up I jovially laughed! I have to say that this was one of the most stressful weekends I have ever experienced and I am only now, some five years on, just about able to see the funny side.

Sleep - How can something so easy be so hard!

At 11 (until about 13) he suffered dreadfully from insomnia; his sleep deprivation was compounded by all-night sessions on his computer. As a result of his tiredness, and possibly from pre-adolescent hormonal surges, he became very bad tempered and aggressive and his basic background mood was one of irritation. I wrote, before we had a firm diagnosis, 'He has a great tendency to misinterpret what is said leading to anger, frustration and feeling victimised and hard done by. As a consequence I am in the firing line and am blamed for everything. Whatever decisions I make I am always wrong - I simply cannot win.'

*

Greenpeace Turns to War!

James became obsessed with saving the environment. His beliefs and fears affected every aspect of our lives. He began to worry about using his computer and me using the car, to the extent that he tried to physically bar my leaving the house if he thought I was going to use it. We recycled everything including stray bottles in the street (this helped to offset a short period of computer usage.)

On one occasion he caught me throwing away an envelope (as they could not be recycled). Furiously he lugged the dirty external bin indoors and proceeded to empty the contents onto the floor, totally ignoring my remonstrations. He sifted through the detritus until he found the envelope. Carefully James removed the parts which could be recycled. On this occasion he seemed incapable of listening to reason and insisted that what I had done was unforgivable and that his very extreme response was appropriate and necessary to save the world. He was seriously afraid about the environment and fear can so often lead to anger particularly, I have found, in boys. He increasingly became physically aggressive which was a great shock as I had never smacked him and we are not an aggressive family, so I couldn't understand where such behaviour came from. In James's case his obsessions take hold and he then justifies them by a series of logical statements. There seems to be no way to get him to take a more moderate view. Anything which gets in the way of pursuing or achieving his obsessions, is met with either extreme anger or fear. It is like trying to argue with an extremist, there is no compromise because extreme beliefs do not allow for a change in position. As he is not generally interested in my or anyone else's happiness he is not motivated to compromise.

From this point on James blamed me for everything and rarely had anything pleasant to say. Like most mothers, despite the abuse, I continued trying to be decent - a good role model! I hope I am not giving the impression that I am a wet blanket, unable to set limits or unwilling to be unpopular with my child, for that is not true. As I am disliked whatever I do, I would be unlikely to let a fear of losing his approval effect my parental duty!

*

Anxieties and Obsessions

Between the ages of 11 & 12 James suddenly became very anxious about his health. It should be noted that he had always been very healthy and had never suffered more than an odd cold and one or two diarrhoea and sickness bugs. But suddenly he became fearful of having a heart attack. No one in the family has heart problems so I don't know from where that particular fear originated.

During a particularly hot summer I noticed that he hardly drank. I said that he ought to drink a bit more in case he became dehydrated and, as so often, I later regretted my well meaning advice. James must have gone on line and read up on dehydration and subsequently began to drink obsessively before bed as he had now become over-fearful of dehydration. When I suggested that he was going a bit overboard he snapped at me and said that I didn't know what I was talking about and continued to force himself to seriously over drink. Most of my advice was ignored by James but often the more casual remarks from me or family and friends could suddenly provoke some very obsessive behaviour. With time I learnt to predict likely triggers and to be guarded in what I said. Many was the time when someone said something and my stomach sank as I knew it could possibly lead to months of a new problem.

A Family Night Out!

I have been publicly humiliated by James more times than I care to remember but perhaps one of my most embarrassing experiences was when James was nearly thirteen. A local senior school sometimes hosted free science lectures which were presented by quite notable scientists. A lecturer with an expertise in nuclear physics came to talk and James wished to attend and to ask some questions. The lecture took place in a large theatre, reminiscent of a university lecture hall with a stage, podium and many rows of tiered seats. It was full to capacity of mostly adults and a few teenagers. James loves to find fault, weaknesses in things, and he sat through the first half shaking his head in disapproval and rapidly scribbling illegible notes. When his attempt to keep track of his thoughts failed, he started whispering things for my mother to jot down.

We told him to stop whispering and to listen because he was disturbing the lecture. He was beside himself with fury because he was desperate to challenge the lecturer and correct the inaccuracies he thought he had spotted, and that was all that mattered. James is not bothered by what others think so the usual embarrassment or concern for others that might curb an older child's outbursts, did not act as an inhibitor. Without suitable notes James could not contest the content of the lecture. He persisted in loudly whispering a stream of points and would not stop. By this time people were staring, the lecturer was looking bemused and I was at a total loss what to do. I was close to tears, as I so often am. I did what I usually do when faced with public humiliation, I go into an automatic shut down.

I stare at a chosen point and sort of filter out everyone around and ignore their responses. I then have this very sharp tunnel vision which enables me to focus on James, and James alone, until we can escape. On this occasion James refused to budge and I didn't feel that I could leave him because he was quite capable of hijacking the lecture and shouting out his criticisms and I couldn't subject the poor lecturer to that. The trouble is that because James and other children with Aspergers look normal, their behaviour can be so at odds with that which is expected of a 'normal' child of that age. During half time we were given five minutes and any questions could be written onto a small postcard and the lecturer would pick out and answer a selected few. James took a handful of cards and was yelling urgently for my mother to write out his question. Bear in mind we had a small card and needed to be succinct. James proceeded to take an inaccuracy and then explain at great length why the lecturer had been wrong and misled his audience. My mother duly started to write what he wanted but she soon realised that it would not fit on a card and that due to the length and complexity of James's point, it was not an appropriate time or place for his attack. James would not be sanctioned or accept that the lecturer couldn't possibly read out such a long point. He started talking loudly, totally unconcerned by the fact that the whole audience were now staring. He insisted that any true scientist would welcome an opportunity to defend their position and if he was competent he would not be threatened by such a challenge.

He then snatched the pencil and card and in the handwriting of a four year old, managed about four words to a card and these were illegible. James proceeded to march up to the school head and hand his cards in. I was trying to stop him, embarrassed by how unbelievably bad his writing was for his age and concerned about how awkward the lecturer might feel when confronted with seven cards each with four unreadable words on them, it looked like the ramblings of a mad man, not a highly intelligent teenager. So often during these types of outburst I find myself torn between understanding why my child is reacting as he is, trying to calm him and to explain how others see the situation. At the same time I find myself trying to protect other people from the shrapnel produced by his fury. The remainder of the lecture continued much as the first half and at the end James wanted to catch the lecturer and go over all his points. I said he couldn't because I knew that James wouldn't just politely ask a question or two and gently challenge his response. James was ready to give his own lecture and to take the lecture apart point by point. He now refused to move or let us pass and he was physically blocking our way out, crying with anger and frustration because he felt it was essential to correct a wrong and as we were the only obstacle in his way he began to verbally attack us. My mother was losing her temper, mainly through embarrassment and fear of how we must be looking from the outside. I was trying to prevent everything escalating even further and was focused on how to get James to agree to leave as quickly as I could. Because I went into one of my trances, a shut down state, I really can't remember how we got out and how, by then, people were reacting. I do remember that we all sat in stony silence on the journey home. I also remember feeling so angry with him for having such an outburst and for failing to see reason. I went straight to bed and wept, howling in utter despair, shouting in my head like a seven year old 'I hate him'. But deep down I knew that he couldn't help himself so how could I be cross? Yet another place where we won't be showing our faces again!

*

Home Education

When James failed to really settle in any play school setting I asked him what he didn't like about it and he told me that he didn't like being in large settings of just children and much preferred to be at home with me - "other children mess things up, I can't think and I become disorganised." I had put his name down for the nursery section of a local school, so when they wrote to say he had a place I felt very ambivalent. It was clearly obvious that he would not settle without a considerable amount of help. I rang the school and arranged to meet the teacher to run over his problems and ask if I could attend as an unpaid helper, so that I could be a presence without undermining his chances of integrating. The response was both predictable and understandable. She said if I left him he would soon settle as they all do, he was no different from others (considering she had never met him this was a quite extraordinary statement. It is amazing to me how often and quickly professionals make judgements about our children). As she would not let me attend I knew I only had one choice. I chose to listen to my son. He was clearly not ready for formalised school or to be separated from me. I have always felt that, in an ideal world, children should be allowed to become independent at their own pace, it is they who should push us away and not the other way round.

As I had been raised abroad I knew that many European countries did not start formal school until seven or even eight. So I decided that I would home educate him for a few years until he was ready. I felt that for some children, the institution of school is unnatural. They offer a one- size-fits-all approach, principally arranged around age. For the majority of children this works quite well, but schools generally fail individuals who substantially deviate from the norm. The classes are usually too large to really accommodate the individual's needs and personality and are unable to respond to the child's mood and personal interests. The curriculum makes it hard for teachers to go off at a tangent if a particular child is interested in some idea sparked by a class topic. James hated noise, chaos and only enjoyed certain types of play and only then if the rules were rigidly followed. He was uncoordinated and would have been totally lost in the playground jungle. In addition I had observed that he had next to nothing in common with the average child of his age. He liked to play chess, to contemplate large numbers and to debate many topics i.e. could God exist.

Schools are not always experienced by the individual as a positive model of learning, offering a happy and protective microcosm of society. They are structured to suit the norm (say, IQs between 90 and 125) and by and large they do a good job. However, they do not generally cope well with the exception and the exceptional. Because I knew that James could not cope with school and because I only saw home education as a temporary step, I was not as scared as you might imagine. I was therefore cushioned from the panic I might have felt had I started out with the intention of taking responsibility for his entire education. This would have been over-whelming. Home education does not have to be a decision for ever. Taking it a single step at a time was the only way I could cope with it. I found a lot of support and information by joining a home education association and we attended a local group. James and I were fortunate to meet one particular family who are now life-long friends.

We used to get together for outings, fun and educational activities. For educational material I often went to boot fairs and jumble sales[1] to pick up books including an entire Ladybird reading scheme. I used on-line resources and ordered a book on teaching children to read phonetically. I sometimes ordered books and resources off educational sites used by schools. In response to his interests I made cards and games to reinforce whatever he was currently learning.

I decided to inform the LEA of my decision to home educate James and kept a diary of what we did each day. To begin with I behaved as if he was at school as this was the only model of education I knew. We made a small box room into a classroom and kept school hours but I soon realised that this was totally unnecessary and that I could be led by James. He was so interested in life and so motivated to learn that when I followed his lead we would have periods of non-stop learning followed by lulls when he seemed to be consolidating what he had learnt. Much of his learning was through play. On his first school inspection (aged 5) the inspector stated 'James frequently questions ideas or facts which makes it a very tiring time for his mother,' and it was, but I cannot express how very, very privileged I feel to have had the opportunity to observe how easily a young child can learn when you don't force them. I sometimes feel that too many children are forced to learn things when the curriculum dictates, irrespective of whether they are developmentally ready, or in the correct mood to

---

[1]   Jumble sale is an English term for a rummage sale.

focus. I soon learnt that If I chose the right moment to teach something, James would pick it up instantly and if I pushed when he was not in the mood we got nowhere and he quickly began to hate whatever we were doing.

By the age of seven James was clearly very advanced in all areas of learning except for the mechanics of writing, which was indescribably bad and consequently interfered with his creativity. We overcame this by doing short bursts of handwriting practise but the rest of the time he dictated to me or used a keyboard. He continued to learn a lot through games and James played Scrabble at an adult level, nearly always winning against us all. By the age of eight I had a crisis of confidence. James was suddenly resistant to do any formal school work although we generally only did an hour a day[1]. I was undecided how much to push him, particularly regarding his handwriting which I felt might be part of the problem. I took him to an educational psychologist to see if there was a reason for his resistance. She felt he was dyspraxic and that he would be better served by concentrating on learning keyboard skills. I bought some software that taught touch typing and from then he took off again. She also said that at the age of eight he had number skills equivalent to a 15 year nine month level, reading to a 14 year old level and an IQ of 147. So I knew then, that it was unlikely he would ever go to school again, for where would he go? By

---

[1]   I found that an hour of work, when he was in the mood, was extremely productive and he generally covered a days school work in this hour.

the age of 10 he had covered most of the GCSE[1] maths syllabus and easily scored an A grade but, wrongly as it happens, I decided he was too young to sit an exam. This decision was a mistake because he regressed and lost interest and when he took the exam at 13 he refused to study and deliberately answered ambiguously phrased questions wrongly and got a B.

I had always been careful to say that if he ever wanted to go to school I could soon arrange it, but he never showed any interest. When he was eleven, a boy we knew got 13 GCSEs[2] all A*s and James, always a perfectionist, decided that he needed to do the same. I tried to explain that this was not necessary but he became obsessed and felt the only way to meet this objective was to go to school. He did not want to go to school but it seemed to be the only route. From that moment on I did my best to support him in his decision, but I also felt he needed to be aware of what he was buying into; he needed to have realistic expectations about school. Judging by how he reacted to other children I had numerous concerns about his ability to cope. I spoke at length to a good friend who teaches excluded pupils and I said that I wondered if his oddities were more than just anxiety and giftedness and that I had sometimes toyed with the idea that he might have Aspergers. She then confessed that she had often wondered

---

[1] General certificate of secondary education, an exam usually taken at age 16 in the UK.
[2] The UK government target for this age, is to obtain 5 GCSEs at levels C or above and must include maths and English.

too. So, that afternoon I logged onto and later joined the NAS[1]. It took an afternoon of concentrated reading for me to identify that James fitted all the criteria like a glove. I isolated no less than seventeen traits that were typical of Aspergers. I cried so loud, making a sobbing sound which appeared to come from somewhere else. I cried with sheer relief. I was not, as some had made me feel, an ineffectual, bad parent that had somehow encouraged or facilitated my child's weird personality. I decided there and then that if James was going to attend school and survive, I needed a formal diagnosis. I was not going to trust this one to the state[2] I withdrew savings and made a private appointment to see a professor of psychiatry, who had a life-time's experience in autism. He was truly a wonderful man and after spending a good three hours with us and relaxing James so sufficiently that he behaved relatively normally, we had our suspicions confirmed, with the additional diagnosis of OCD. The best advice I have ever received regarding managing Aspergers was at this meeting. He advised "you need to adapt because he can't, and you need to learn to communicate in a very precise and accurate way." It sounds so easy but is surprisingly tricky, I have often said to James that I need an English-Aspergers dictionary!

---

[1] NAS – National Autistic Society - a British charity

[2] I was advised by people who had not met my son, that he did not need to be statemented (a document which states the child's special educational needs.) Under-diagnosing or misdiagnosing is common and many parents feel that budgetary constraints often override the Local Education Authority's' (LEA) responsibility to represent the child's best interests.

James took a school entrance exam and based on his exam results was offered a place in the accelerated learning part of the school. We selected this particular comprehensive school because they also had an Asperger's unit. I then set about trying to secure him a place in the unit, but because of insufficient capacity, they were unable to take him. By this time, James was having second thoughts, having experienced some of the other children at the exams - "why are they all so silly and noisy?"

By the age of 12, James had become (in his own words) 'an autodidact', i.e. self-taught. He was, by now, more advanced in many of his studies than the tuition that I was personally able to offer. My parents had both had a considerable input (I would have found the process hard to do totally alone) but even their efforts were now rejected. I provided the materials and he got on with it. Now, in his teens, he has rejected the state sanctioned curriculum and exams but nevertheless continues to absorb information and teach himself at a phenomenal pace. I appreciate that this route is not for everyone but I think it worked pretty well for him.

The Teenage Years

Where Are We Now
"I will not be socially engineered by a dog" ~ James aged 15

This is a very honest account of what life is like at the moment and how I sometimes feel. I hope, for those of you struggling like I am, it is not too demoralizing. I write in the belief that in being totally honest, without the usual self-censorship, my vulnerability and imperfections might provide strength and comfort to others.

Because James's intellectual development has always been far more evolved than his emotional development, James was, and still is, totally ill equipped to handle emotions. He tries to apply logic to them which can only ever work up to a point. He seems to have a fear of emotions and when he has outbursts, does not appear to reflect on them. His ability to see himself realistically or to admit fault seems to be considerably more impaired than his 'normal' peers. It is always hard with teenagers to cope with their extreme and yo-yoing emotions but all the normal problems, for us, are compounded by our children's disabilities. All teenagers are self-centred but usually have some, albeit intermittent, capacity to comprehend and care about others' emotions. This helps them to control some of their own outbursts, whereas the Asperger teenager lacks the ability to judge how someone else may feel and to modify their response accordingly. Social interaction is always tricky for teenagers but children with Aspergers have communication problems as their base line, so the problems they, and we, face increase exponentially and it seems that compromise during this time becomes unobtainable.

It is often said in jest, by parents of teenagers, "only his mother could love him." This statement affectionately recognises that at times their child is moody and difficult, but the parents are nevertheless proud of their child and in reality enjoy the positive things that others have to say about them. I, too, say about my teenage son that he is so unpleasant "only a mother could love him" but I am not joking. As his mother I sometimes struggle to love him. currently I do not like him and I have enormous trouble coming up with a list of positive things to say about him.

Of course I do really love my son. How do I know this? Because I lie awake night after night worrying about my child. Because when he is ill or occasionally seems so very, very vulnerable and alone, it is then that my need to protect him is there as strong as ever. But what I now feel is not the warm, easy and rewarding love I felt in his infancy, it is the heavy, burdened love of a mother afraid for her child's future. But it is love, of this I am sure, because it hurts so very, very much.

I loved my son, unconditionally, even before he was born. When I took him home from the hospital I was unable to sleep for days because I couldn't take my eyes off him. My body was literally swimming with love and bonding hormones. I couldn't believe that I was a mum and that this indescribably beautiful scrap was mine and had come from me. If someone had said that in years to come I would struggle to love him, I would have been incapable of accepting such a scenario; nothing, I would have adamantly asserted, could ever stop me loving my child. To me, the love of a mother is sacrosanct and is the only constant in life. Your mother is someone who truly understands you when others cannot, it is the only thing which is guaranteed. The unwritten rule is that you never, ever, give up on your child and the mother that fails to love her child is an aberration, it is incomprehensible and unforgivable. I was the last person I would ever have believed, 16 years on, would be struggling to love her own child. I do not need my child to be academically successful, socially popular, artistic or sporting. I will truly be thrilled if he lives nearby in a clapped out caravan, pursuing his all consuming hobbies, but even this poignantly modest dream at present seems too much to hope for.

I am so worn down and worn out that I seriously question whether life is worth living. My son's early years were difficult and intense, he rarely slept and moaned unless I continually entertained him. I was constantly worried and felt that others blamed me for his eccentricities, but at least then he seemed to love me, he needed me in an obvious way and, although I was exhausted and overwhelmed, his vulnerability energised me. What was needed of me was clear cut and I knew what I had to do to make his environment comfortable, to make him happy. Later - as his teenage years approached and hormones kicked in and he just wanted to be left alone - he resented any show of affection or any normal parental concern. I pulled back, accepting that he was growing up and just wanted more autonomy but before long I was just a skivvy, shopping and cleaning up after him. He despised me and was disgusted by me. The slow trickle of abuse and the endless list of things that have to be controlled because of his obsessions and belief systems means that I no longer have a life and that the life we now have is so abnormal that I cannot any longer be a normal part of society. He challenges everything and the very foundations (on which most of us base our lives) have been removed. The social rules, which do not stand up to logical analysis, no longer apply. I am floundering and exist bathed in despair, as we live a problem to which there is no acceptable solution.

The Daily Grind

I've been awake again most of the night, computers humming and endless clattering from above. Fifteen year old James is working through the night on whatever his current obsession is. The wind is howling and the rain is once again pelting down through the open skylight onto the landing. I have closed it on six occasions through the night and once again heave myself out of bed to shut it, slipping on the rain drenched wood floor and shivering in the icy damp air. I use a long pole to tap the lock down to close the window; it is tiring and unpleasant at three in the morning to be doing this. I then proceed downstairs to check that the kitchen window is still closed after I shut it at 2am, when James prepared his evening meal. More recently he has started leaving the front door wide open too.

This open and close process is not a power struggle between us; he has always over-reacted to sensory stimulation and at the moment cooking and cleaning smells are intolerable to him. So even on the coldest, wettest day, our house is well-aired. Cooking takes around a third longer than it should as the cooker struggles to maintain temperature with the cold air coming through the open kitchen windows. Not only is this uncomfortable, it also disturbs sleep as I fear that burglars might gain entry through the constantly open ground floor window or that the hall landing will be damaged from regular dousing from rain water. I also fret about the extremely high gas and electric bills from very long cooking times and 24 hr multiple computers running (well over 15 of them).

In addition to checking the windows many times a night, I also have to spend around 2 hours a day cleaning the kitchen after he has cooked for himself. He sees me as contaminated and is consequently repulsed by my presence and will not let me cook for him. Because he is also dyspraxic and a teenager, the mess created at times looks like I have given free reign to a couple of budding six year old cooks. So, at least twice a day or night, in addition to my own cooking I have to wash up, clean surfaces, clean cupboards and wash the floor. This is further complicated by my extreme disgust at hairs near or on food and my son regularly drops hairs all over the kitchen.

James has not washed, showered or bathed for two years now, he hasn't cleaned his teeth or washed or brushed his long hair and, as I am not allowed anywhere near his room, it has not been properly cleaned for years. He has an en-suite bathroom and the 'loo, I know, is black inside and out, as it has not been cleaned for over two years. His sheets likewise have not been changed in this time and he refuses a pillow. I don't know, but I think he sleeps in his chair with just one grotty old cellular cotton blanket. He will only wear two of his t-shirts both dirty and hair ridden and two of his shorts, even in the winter. He only owns one pair of broken sandals which are also worn in the winter. He will not wear anything warmer, even when he is physically shivering and he never wears underwear. He hates the feel of clothes on his skin and layers constantly irritate him.

Although as a rule I am past worrying what people think anymore, I do worry that people will think he is neglected. Neighbours rarely see him as he only occasionally ventures out (more on that later) and when they do see him, he is in the same holey clothes and sandals, with no coat in winter and he has long, knotted hair and looks thin and stooped. I also spend a lot of my day worrying about just how cold he must be with thin clothes and just one blanket at night. But there is nothing I can do. I have spent hundreds of pounds on super soft and light but warm clothes, urged him to order things for himself on-line, I have provided blankets and heaters but he so hates the feel of cloth on his skin that he prefers to shiver. Because he hates smell and windows are open, it is pointless heating his room. His refusal to wash is based on it being a waste of time and he also believes that it isn't necessary and that we have all been brainwashed by those who sell cleaning products. As is so often the case with James, he has a valid point. He actually doesn't smell bad, his hair isn't greasy, he has never had a spot and he rarely gets ill. His clothes do smell pretty rank which is socially inconsiderate and the smell that emanates from his room is not a pleasant one and if the windows were not open so much, our home would smell unclean.

I am no longer happy to invite new people back. I am also restricted in what products I can use on myself and in the house and I generally try to bath and wash my hair at my parents' house because James gets cross and upset by the smell of soap and shampoo. So, if I feel tired and stressed, I am denied the luxury of a long soak in a beautifully scented bath in a warm bathroom. This cleanliness issue also worries me because, if it is not just a phase, it will make it impossible for him to apply for jobs (in the unlikely event that that this will ever happen) or to attract potential friends (also unlikely). So as you can see, I am constantly worried and aware that he might be cold and suffering. If I try to help alleviate his problems, he regards it as meddlesome and controlling. He fails to receive any help or advice in the spirit in which it is always intended, which is one of love and trying to make things better. I have had to learn to shut my mouth and never say "shouldn't you wear a coat and take a torch?" as he leaves the house at 1 am for a night-time stroll in his t-shirt and sandals in a December rainstorm.

If I ever make suggestions, which I now rarely do, he gets furious and is likely to deliberately do the opposite. He believes, with an intensity beyond any I have known, that he is totally responsible for himself and that I have no right to make any unsolicited comments on his life choices. If he makes a mistake and gets himself into trouble, that is his look out and responsibility and I have no right to interfere without his consent. I also have absolutely no right to know what he does with his time even if my interest is purely one of social curiosity. I have tried to explain that purely in terms of the law, never mind my own motherly concerns for him, I am responsible for him and have explained that I could get into a lot of trouble if he got harmed and I failed to guide and protect. He argues back that just because the law states something, if it is ethically wrong, i.e. just because one child of 15 is not sufficiently developed to take full responsibility for themselves, this does not mean that another child can't. I should not blindly follow a law that is essentially arbitrary according to chronological age. He, as a free individual, does not want to be controlled and is angered and insulted at others deeming their decisions regarding him as better than his own.

Besides computer programming, James is obsessed with Civil Liberties. Most of the difficulties I have with him stem from one core belief system, that he should be entirely autonomous, a totally free individual without any external or government control. This belief informs nearly every aspect of our life. He is extremely fearful of his biometrics being taken. The threatened introduction of ID cards has led him to plan running away from home within a few years. He plans to leave without papers, money or even basic survival gear and disappear into another country. He has stated that he will never contact me again, as to do so would compromise his anonymity.

I have explained that I would then be left to live in torment, not knowing if he was alive, hungry, safe, well, happy etc and he simply replies that it is my free choice to respond like that and that I can always commit suicide. This is probably the scenario that causes me the most distress for I cannot bear the thought of not knowing if he is alright and not being able to try and help him. I am terrorised by the idea that he could be anywhere in the world. I would have no clues and no way of ever finding him; how could I live in a constant state of the unknown, especially as the probability of his being alright is so small as to be almost impossible. I cannot think of any 'normal' adults who could survive unscathed in a foreign county without identification papers or proof of qualifications, with no money and just the clothes on their back. Imagine, therefore, my concern about my obsessive, socially impaired and inexperienced son.

As I said, James is paranoid about his biometrics being taken. He won't cut his hair unless he can dispose of it, in case it is collected; he wears a full cover balaclava whenever we go out in the car to avoid CCTV cameras; he cannot go to shops, museums etc because of security cameras and will not talk if a mobile phone is on standby or when anyone is talking on a regular phone. I have no photograph of him since the age of 12, because he won't let me take one, and if I were to try he would attack me and break the camera. If he were to disappear I have nothing to show the police and on a personal level no sentimental record to enjoy in the future. I am not supposed to talk about him to others because he says that it is an intrusion into his right of privacy and so I write this under an assumed name.

Any time I make even a minor transgression regarding areas he perceives as his right, I am then severely chastised, sometimes aggressively pushed with the consequence that he trusts me a little less each time - he never forgets what he perceives as a betrayal. I once threw away some rotten meat of his and this is still brought up as I apparently had no right to make the judgement for him that the meat was rotten. He bears a grudge and trusts no one. It would be impossible to live up to his expectations but, none-the-less, I try. I feel it is somewhat akin to living with an abusive partner. The level of perfection expected can never be achieved or sustained, so failure is inherent. And such failures, even when impossible to avoid, make him angry and verbally cruel, as when he yelled at me "I hope you die a painful and lingering death."

James sees the world in terms of what is wrong and not what is right. He therefore never has anything positive or kind to say, because in his mind there is no point in saying it if something is alright. If nothing is said, it implies that everything is alright. Consequently I am always on the receiving end of abuse and negativity without any affection whatsoever. He has not touched me or allowed even a pat on his arm for years. This means that there is rarely anything to reinforce my desire to have a relationship with him, or to love him. My only reward is trying to lessen his distress or unhappiness.

Another major problem resulting from his civil liberty belief is that because I have said that I will call the police, against his wishes, should he run away before the age of 16, he considers himself imprisoned by me. As a result of this, he does not care about how much electricity he uses, wasting food etc because he is being kept at home under duress. I have said that I am not stopping him leaving, I just don't want him to leave without my knowledge of where he is and that he is safe. If I ask him not to do something, or ask him to be quiet at night, he once again plays his trump card – saying that as he is imprisoned against his will he is at liberty to ignore me. He refuses to respond when he believes a question to be intrusive or irrelevant.

Civil liberties also effect his diet; because animals are reared and held in captivity he refuses to eat any farmed meat or dairy products. I therefore have to buy wild game which is phenomenally expensive and he only eats organic food so I buy a vegetable box, three quarters of which he throws away. I am extremely worried by the nearly total absence of calcium in his diet and my attempts to explain and justify my concern are met with arguments about my being duped by the dairy industry propaganda.

He won't drink tap water because he hates the taste of chlorine nor, for some reason, will he drink bottled water. James will only drink when we have water that he has personally collected from a well forty five minutes drive away (inevitably petrol costs worry me). The well is owned by a local tea room whose goodwill we rely on and I worry that one day they could ask us not to disturb the tranquillity of the establishment, as we yet again traipse through with a tramp-like teenager and 12 clunking bottles of water. When he occasionally gets a diarrhoea and sickness bug I am besides myself with worry and cannot even get the normal reassurance from him because it is intrusive and none of my business. Sometimes he doesn't come out of his room for over 24 hours and I worry. Has he eaten or drunk? Could he be hurt or really ill? - because he won't answer me and I cannot enter his room, I am left fretting until I hear or see him. If I were to ever enter his room fearing for his life and he was alright, he would never forgive me and would become more paranoid about his privacy and would quite possibly avoid going out altogether to ensure his room was never left unattended.

He refuses to take exams because he would be tracked by the system and it would increase their profile on him and because, in his opinion, exams are inaccurate and ambiguous. He is probably the most knowledgeable and brightest person of his age I have ever come across but with no exams there is unlikely to be a job. He is adamant that where he is going, he won't need exams and that he would never work for a company where he had to be in the system. Tax, after all, is theft when you are a capital anarchist!

So I worry endlessly. I try not to play out the nightmare scenario of James leaving without telling me where he is going. I try not to give into the rising panic I feel as I visualise how he would survive with no money, papers or qualifications. I also worry what will happen to him if he stays. He is currently unemployable and would be unable to accept a job because of his fear of the system and being tracked. This would just about be alright if he would accept benefits but that means he would have to be part of the system which he is taking such pains to avoid. James also sees benefits as theft because others are having to pay taxes against their will, to support him, and his ethics will not let him take the money. So if James runs away I am damned for life, doomed to live in a perpetual state of panic about what is happening to him and if he stays I may have to financially support him forever. Without any carer's allowance I cannot possibly afford his special food, excessive electricity consumption etc and quite frankly the thought of his dirt and chaos for ever more fills me with despair.

In addition to all of the above, we have regular communication problems. His inherent tendency to over-analyse infiltrates into casual conversations. James cannot abide any communication that is incidental as he experiences it as pointless. Simple suggestions are interpreted as controlling and most questions are seen as intrusive and unnecessary. Communication difficulties often lead to verbal aggression and frustration for us both.

The combination of Aspergers and giftedness is lethal, for when obsessiveness and an over reliance on logic and brilliance merge, they all too often result in extreme views and a total intolerance of others. James is unable and unwilling to communicate in the average world; to him most people are imprecise, manipulative, inane and tedious. Normal social niceties are rejected as they are manipulative and dishonestly socially engineer another person for one's own gain. Strictly speaking he has a point but James takes his view to the extreme and will not even stroke a friend's affectionate dog when it jumps up to be petted and the following quote is verbatim *"I will not be socially engineered by a dog."* His ability to argue his position from a point of logic, albeit frequently founded on a false premise in my opinion, means that he wins every argument. James is dangerously good at arguing as was expressed in a report written by a math's tutor we employed when James was 13 "I was able to engage James in levels of conversation above those I experience with most adults. I used to pride myself on my reasoning ability and found that I could not out-reason him. .... I knew that I was right in some of the arguments we went through but could not justify my belief at the same level he could justify his own." The problem arises because James can easily out-argue us all, he continues to hold false or extreme positions which he has ostensibly proven through logic so, because he is far brighter than I am, I cannot adequately defend my position and he always wins. This makes parenting extremely difficult because he will not follow any advice unless it can be proved; blind obedience runs counter to his principles.

This inherent tendency to over analyse even infiltrates into casual conversations. James finds factual defects or ambivalences in even the simplest of statements. A normal conversation is not possible. Every word in a sentence has to be defined, qualified and used precisely as he is totally unable to infer from the context.

All of the above problems can change at any time. Obsessions seem to slowly arrive and steadily get worse before they peak and then wane only to be replaced by another. It is hard to reconcile the filthy James of today with the little 10 year old obsessed by germs and dirt.

I am wondering whether I ought to end with some note of cheery optimism or to make amends to James, by including a list of his more endearing qualities but to do so would, I feel, negate the purpose of this piece, which is to show just how bad things can get. Life is not fair and does not often have fairy tale endings. I am making myself vulnerable in sharing the raw, brutal unadulterated version of my life; in the end I believe this is more supportive than the pretence of coping and the false and empty promise of 'it will all be alright.' I have no relationship with my own son and yet I am forever related to him. I am imprisoned by the very act of being his mother, for even if I were to give up, and I very much hope I never will, I would be consumed by guilt and worry. There is, I realise, likely to be no escape, no 'happy ending' and that is, for very many of us, life.

*

The Confessional

When I read books and articles written by psychologists they always state the importance of keeping the doors of communication open with your child, and stress that this is especially important during the teenage years. This sage advice is useless if you can't see the door and quite frankly in my case, the door analogy is a bit of an exaggeration; the cat flap is nearer to the truth and it is well and truly locked. My trouble is that James sealed the cat flap by age eleven when he no longer needed my protection and had essentially outgrown me intellectually.

Sometimes I take out the proverbial key, dust it off

and try the flap again but even when I oil the lock and manage to turn it, there are multiple bolts strategically placed well out of my reach. The truth is, my son doesn't want or emotionally need a relationship with me. I have spent hours reflecting on whether I am partly culpable for this lack of relationship but I truly believe that I have not done anything so wrong to merit this response. I sometimes worry that because we have no relationship he doesn't realise how I feel about him, so every so often I say "I do love you, you know that don't you James and I am so terribly proud of you." He responds with anger and irritably asks "why do you tell me these things, don't you get it, I don't want you to love me or care for me because then you won't let me leave the country." He hates me because my love gets in the way of his freedom to live his life with absolutely no, and I mean absolutely no, parental input. So as I am unable to have a relationship with my son and find myself with numerous problems which we are unable to resolve I become frustrated and sometimes I am the one to experience 'a mummy meltdown'!

I have debated about how to tackle the next bit. In my pockets and on my bed side table are scraps of paper covered with half formed ideas, frantically scribbled with what at the time seems an inspired thought. I am struggling because I want to confess to some of the horrendous things I have recently found myself saying to my son. This only happens when the possibility of a compromise seems impossible and I am backed into a corner by his arguments to which I can find no answer and when he is verbally aggressive with a fixed look of absolute disgust. I really do not want to write about this because in the heat of the moment I can understand my response but on paper, with no stress chemicals circulating in my blood, I know that the horror of seeing my words before me will intensify the guilt I already feel. I don't want to share my nasty, less considered side and yet I am ethically forced to do so, otherwise I believe I am betraying the whole premise on which this book is based. If other parents have to live with the knowledge that they have said and done things which can never be taken back, then I want them to know that they are not alone. So here goes.

I am backed into a corner metaphorically and physically and he is yelling. I dared to make myself a cup of tea and he accuses me of making an unbearable smell. Yet again I explain that I already limit what and when I cook and so many other things so that he does not get exposed to unnecessary smells but that I won't give up absolutely everything otherwise I would no longer have any quality to my life. He totally refuses to accept that I couldn't have taken any more measures to avoid the smell. I have run out of responses and he is standing angrily waiting for a response; we have been over this hundreds of times and I know that it is leading nowhere and yet he wants to push on forcing me to admit that I am somehow wrong. I now find myself saying (yet again) "I suggest that you start trying to be a bit kinder because once you are sixteen you can bugger off if you carry on like this or if I am so awful

I can ring social services and they can find you somewhere *better* to live."

There are two motives behind my statement, one is that I am angry and frustrated and spitefully want to hurt him back (can't say I'm too proud of this one.) The other reason is that I am trying to get him to understand that once he is sixteen he is legally free to leave and therefore cannot accuse me of keeping him at home against his will. If he is living at home by choice he will become a sort of guest, here at my discretion. In other words, treat me with the same degree of kindness and consideration with which I try to treat him. But my attempts to say this in plain English, rather than ranting mode, fail and seem to fall on deaf ears, so I rant. Later on I move into guilt mode and then spend the rest of the day crying with my hair shirt on. I realise that if he were to suddenly leave home, I would have indirectly given him the message that I didn't want him at home. Would he know that I do truly love him. What if I never have another chance to tell him.

Before I had James the extent of my emotional repertoire was limited. Rarely, if ever, did I have to contend with multiple and conflicting emotions. I truly did not understand how it was possible to hate and love someone at the same time. It was generally easy to control myself and when necessary to keep a lid on things. Since James has hit the teenage years I have often had to cope with the discomfort which comes from the coexistence of multiple and conflicting emotions. Sometimes in the heat of the moment I let rip and later, on reflection, feel very differently. Emotions are often transitory and only now am I realising that I just have to accept that this is how it is.

On the positive side when I analyse our lives together, we do actually, for the most part, live companionably, albeit in separate worlds within our shared space. Almost invisible to each other, which is how he likes it. The main issues of contention are all, in fact, linked to one area; his hyper-sensitivity to smell and the repercussions of that. Aside from that, we rarely argue and he seems to exists in a state of self-contained contentment. So perhaps I have met his needs better than I realise and perhaps I have adjusted my approach and his environment.[1] Maybe we should all blow our own trumpet occasionally!

Friends, Family and Aspergers

Well my parents have been faultless and had it not been for my mother's daily, sometimes hourly support I'd have caved in years ago.

I feel that many, many friends (and some family) have really let me and James down. Of my old friends I consider only three have actively

---

[1] I and probably most parents, have instinctively employed what is called the low 'arousal approach' by avoiding confrontational situations and always looking for the line of least resistance. This, in my experience has worked well.

supported me. The remainder I describe as dormant. I feel temporarily estranged from them. I only have one friend in this area who I see reasonably often (Carol) but I am not even sure whether she sees me out of pity. We go for walks and talk and she has been a brick – kind, understanding and has not judged me. How sad is that, one friend!

I don't fully blame friends, for much of the time I am not fun to be with and frankly if I could have a break from myself I would too! I am tired because I rarely sleep more than two hours, I'm emotional, depressive and intense. But I am worth sticking by. Like everybody I have some good traits too – I am loyal and on good days I can actually be very funny, I can take a secret to the grave, I see things differently to others, I am a deep thinker, I accept oddities without judgement and for the people I love, I will always be there, even if that is all I can do. So I would stick by me even if they don't. I know that I sometimes over react but that is because I live on the edge. But I feel my reactions are understandable and forgivable. They are usually responses to someone yet again failing to understand something about me or my son. Being judged unfairly is the theme of my life and yes, I am angry and I think I always will be unless that is, I have given up. The day I stop being angry is the day my son will lose his mother. Anger is the only thing that allows me to keep going, it is my fuel, my fight, so don't bloody knock it!

Professionally Speaking!

I have put off writing this section until the very last. For me it is the hardest part to write and, perhaps the most important. I simply do not know how to approach it and nor how to recount my experiences and extrapolate the really important bits without being a dreadful bore. I feel I must acknowledge that I am inexpressibly angry about the approach, ignorance and harm done by some professionals but I am even more perturbed by the inordinate and dangerous power their opinions are sometimes given. I really want this section to count and I do not want it to become an airing place for my personal grievances. I will therefore try to keep my feelings in check and shall don my psychologist's hat, and offer my assessment of the parts of the system I have experienced. In the light of my observations I will then endeavour to offer constructive suggestions which could easily be achieved.

The power of a professional to transform one's life for better or for worse, cannot be understated. When this transformation is a positive one, and the professional has done their job well, the good they do cannot be overstated. The life-long gratitude we feel often remains unexpressed because it is simply impossible to find any words that adequately reflect the impact they have had; so, a polite but grossly inadequate 'thank you' often has to suffice. When professionals are unable to help I prefer them to be honest and say so. They need not feel impotent because to really listen and show genuine compassion is sometimes enough. I certainly do not expect 'experts' to have all the answers and do not fault them for being at a loss, but I do expect that if they cannot do good, they at least do no harm.

Before I move onto the flaws in the system I want to blow the trumpet for the psychiatrist who diagnosed James and to say my 'thank you!' Professor S had a life-long interest in autism and if I could have chosen the person best suited to James, he would have been the one. Professor S clearly had an intellectually playful mind; he was open, relaxed, and lacked the arrogance one often experiences. Prof S initially spent about half an hour talking with us and there was no sense that we had a time limit, it felt leisurely and informal. He spoke to us all equally and on the same level; above all he did not patronise James. James relaxed sooner than I have ever known; we were after all in a strange place with an unknown man. I too relaxed and did not feel on my guard or defensive or as if I was being judged, as can all too readily happen. James soon began to join in and challenge what was being said and Professor S perfectly judged that he could now begin the real work, getting to know James. He asked him a number of questions, showed lots of photographs with various expressions and managed to gain his confidence so much that James was even happy to volunteer that he washed his hands up to 200 times a day (which was news to me!) By the end of the meeting I felt utter confidence in him and knew that his diagnosis would more than likely be one I could have confidence in as it would be based on a thorough examination made at a time when I could see that James was being himself. It took well over three hours to confirm what I had suspected for some time; James had quite a severe case of Aspergers and tendencies to OCD.

I was relieved because everything we had both struggled with made sense and I had a clearer idea of what I would need to do for James. Prof. S gave us a few sage words about learning to communicate unambiguously, using language accurately and with a great deal of forethought. He also advised that the family would need to change because James couldn't. The quality which Prof S had, that no one since has managed to demonstrate, was to conduct a professional meeting in an ambient atmosphere of complete equality, free from arrogance, and to somehow feel like a jolly good, old family friend. He did not have pre-determined ideas about how a child of 11 should interact nor was he nonplussed by James's propensity to talk to adults as absolute equals. James believes that if someone is wrong, irrespective of age, he has the duty to challenge them. This is not intended to be rude and I have since noticed that both gifted and Asperger children will do this, with absolutely no malice intended and it is extremely hard to get them to curb this propensity. In this consultation we did not, as we have since, start in an environment of hostility. Previously the tendency has been for the professional to view James's need to challenge as rude, disrespectful and lacking boundaries rather than the natural consequence of a bright mind obsessed by the need to be accurate and precise.

I once met an experienced social worker who had a specialist interest in Aspergers. I briefly told her about James and after listening to me for a couple of minutes, I was shocked when she offered me unsolicited advice and made an imperative statement "He really should be socialising more." Desirable as this might seem, it is not something within James's understanding. The normal social niceties irritate him beyond belief, he does not understand flippant chatter and does not wish to engage in it even if it were to give him certain advantages. When I explained this to the social worker she persisted, unable to accept that socialising is not a benefit to everyone. She suggested that at college James might want to go for a coffee and might not know how to handle it.

I further explained that James communicates to obtain or issue information of a domestic nature or to further his knowledge or arguing skills; he would take no pleasure from unstructured chit chat over coffee. James does not understand the complex rules of casual social interaction, he does not know the nomenclature that most of us effortlessly pick up. Therefore her imperative in this instance was misplaced. I have mentioned this example because it is one of many I have experienced which run along similar lines and I feel that it perfectly exemplifies the general tendency of experts to generalise a belief. The primary belief in this instance is that social skills are lacking in Aspergers and they are key to a happy and independent adult life. They therefore deduce that all those with Aspergers must learn social skills. In the space of perhaps three minutes she had made a dictum that my son needed to socialise more, without ever having met him.

She applied a general rule that it is preferable for many people with Aspergers to develop social skills to a single very individual case and consequently gave an ill advised opinion. The milder cases frequently wish to learn and respond well to techniques which aid mixing with their peers. In James's case, he actively chooses to reject being changed in order to better conform to someone else's view of normality. The teaching of social skills would be a pointless exercise. James would resist such lessons and would no doubt sabotage any attempts to coerce him into participating. He rejects social niceties as they are, in his opinion, ultimately about social engineering which is both manipulative and dishonest. He is, he says, happy as he is and does not wish to change anything about himself. He finds most people boring. When someone is sufficiently interesting he is quite sociable in his own way. To pressure someone at the extreme end of Aspergers to behave in a way which is essentially at odds with their personality and brain type is potentially cruel, sometimes misplaced and may, quite frankly, be pointless. *So my first observation/recommendation/suggestion is: – do not attempt to draw a definitive conclusion nor offer specific advice after one meeting*

James has seen a total of three educational psychologists. When he was eight because I needed to find out if there was a reason that he was resistant to writing. The second took place when he was eleven and we applied for James to attend a heavily over-subscribed Aspergers unit attached to a local school. His final one was at the age of twelve when he wanted to take GCSE maths and we needed evidence of his dyspraxia. The first psychologist totally failed to pick up Aspergers and clearly felt that he was rude because he interrupted what she said and challenged her statements. She later took further offence when he gave unnecessarily complex and lengthy answers to simple questions and she interpreted this as showing off how clever he was. There is no doubt that she disliked his pompous manner and clearly felt it was the result of a child with lack of boundaries. It has to be said that there is no scientific basis for such a finding, it is merely an opinion to which society gives undue weight. In the light of his Aspergers diagnosis, his challenging statements and his verbosity now make perfect sense. It was not the result of rudeness or poor parenting.

The second (LEA)[1] psychologist had no real experience of Aspergers and the one hour assessment took place in a dingy office. James was not sleeping at the time and had refused breakfast. The psychologist was informed of this; he nevertheless proceeded to test his IQ. This was

---

[1] Local Education Authority is a local government agency who oversee matters to do with state education.

an unnecessary imposition, firstly because James had already secured himself a place in the schools' accelerated learning unit and secondly his right to attend the Asperger's base was not contingent on IQ. He appeared on autopilot and got out his set of little tests, which seemed to have no relevance to the task in hand i.e. in what way would James benefit from a specialist unit. James being exhausted and tetchy from a lack of sleep, was understandably foul; he was rude and moody with me and appeared objectionable. I could not believe how incredibly thick he was at some of the tests, he was clearly not in the right frame of mind or health to proceed.

I doubt very much whether most educational psychologists would be happy for their children's future to be decided by a test taken when they hadn't slept more than a few hours for many nights and hadn't eaten breakfast. A child that is autistic has an added problem, as do very anxious children, and James is both. They cannot be expected to perform well in a new setting relying on face to face questions (not a comfortable medium for Aspergers) asked by someone they have never met before. The reliability of IQ tests when taken by an extremely anxious person has not, to my knowledge, been properly tested. I have heard of numerous cases where children are removed from lessons at school without prior warning or parental consent and tested. Psychologists should, frankly, know better; a test carried out on a shy, tired, hungry or anxious child should not be relied upon to determine the child's future. *So my second recommendation is:- go to the child's environment to test them. Make time to get to know them and their family, perhaps showing a few sample questions so that they know what to expect. Many children with Aspergers would perform better if the tests were written and not verbal. Do not test if the parent's feel that the child is not ready or is in the wrong frame of mind. I feel very strongly that psychologists need to be more accountable for the accuracy of their assessments and tests; perhaps if their professional conduct and abilities were subject to external inspections (like teachers' performances are) they would take more care.*

The state psychologist clearly had no understanding about how to communicate with Asperger children or of their special needs. He asked James to 'read this.' James dourly sat there staring grumpily at the page and the psychologist began to look irritated. I realised that James was indeed reading as he had been asked, he had followed the orders exactly. When I laughed and explained "if you want him to read out loud you need to say so" he failed to see the humour or I felt to understand why he had been at fault and not James[1]. This man was in charge of writing a report which would heavily influence whether James got a place in the Asperger's unit and yet he didn't even appear to have a rudimentary understanding of the condition. *My third recommendation is:- make sure that the psychologist is properly qualified and trained to assess specialist problems and that the*

---

[1] People with Aspergers tend to understand language in a very literal way.

style of testing is adapted to suit the child i.e. use written IQ tests and communicate precisely etc. Finally do not inflict stressful IQ tests on children that serve no purpose just because that is what you normally do.

My response to the final psychologist was a little frosty in the beginning as I was put on the defensive within seconds. After years of covert and overt criticism, my radar soon picks up even the smallest criticism and I could see her hackles rise at James's assertion (unspoken) that he be treated as an equal adult. I confess that when a typical child expresses unformed and untested opinions in an overly forthright way I, too, struggle not to feel affronted. But James is intellectually like an adult and has well reasoned ideas. So this session could so easily have degenerated into an extremely expensive clash of opinions. In her favour, she listened and in the light of my explanations, changed her assessment and opinions. Initially, she had thought James was rude, because he interrupted too much and challenged adults in an unacceptable way. She had also felt that he should learn more social skills to prepare for university. Like James, if I feel someone is mistaken, I like to put them right, hopefully with a little more tact! Again she listened and by the end of the day she clearly really liked James because she no longer wrongly interpreted his manner as rude but instead saw that he was just an extremely independent thinker with an adult mind in a child's body and that he could indeed always justify his position. She was also impressed that he was not influenced by consumerism and had very high ethical standards. This psychologist made an instant false judgement but rectified her start position because she was willing to listen. *So my fourth suggestion is:- be aware that your hour's assessment can determine a whole future, so don't get it wrong! If you don't listen to the parents you miss a life time of relevant experiences. Would you like someone to judge you in an hour, possibly when you were out of sorts, and to make a wrong opinion which you cannot contest, will be shared with others and which affects your whole future?*

I have so much more that I would like to say and I could easily fill a book on this subject alone but I will confine myself to the few above mentioned examples. However, after my experiences with James, I wrote a comprehensive list of things which I felt my LEA and Educational Psychologists needed to consider in order to make their service less stressful, more accurate, and fairer. The Senior educational psychologist was kind enough to meet me, but I feel I wasted my time as not one of my recommendations has been implemented. I am left wondering If I am the only parent to complain and they therefore assume that they are generally doing their job to a very high standard and their conscience is clear. But when I have talked with other parents about the assessment process they have to endure when applying for a special needs place, they are generally dissatisfied with the care they received, so maybe we have a communication problem. I am concerned because unlike all other areas in education, no significant improvements or changes appear to have been made by educational psychologists and as far as I know they are not assessed by inspectors or accountable to anyone for the accuracy of their assessments.

In the end our experiences are only as good or as bad as the individuals we deal with. I don't want to end on a negative note or to demoralise all the professionals that give their absolute best and work so selflessly to try to make things better. If you do your job well and, hand on heart, would be totally satisfied if you or your child were at the receiving end of your care, then know how much you will mean to us and how indebted we are.

*

Lilly's Concluding Ruminations

All the examples I have used in my story are just the tip of the iceberg. Each part is perhaps just a single representation of what were in reality a myriad of problems. I think it is a general truism in life that no one will ever love you as much, or so effortlessly and be so readily on your side, as your mother and father. So if I sometimes struggle to love and like my own child, what chance has he ever got of being loved again, and what is life in the absence of love. I struggle daily with this one. It seems to me this is the essence of caring for children with Aspergers. We have to learn to live with pain and sometimes with insolvable problems. We have to be hyper-sensitive to the tiny cues which can warn us that all may not be well with our child and adapt before they explode. We have to learn to accept that someone else may feel in a way that is totally outside our experience or imagination and take them at face value. We must allow our children to be different, accepting who they are and not trying to make them who we, or society, might like them to be.

In the end how do any of us know if we have been successful, if we have done the best by and for our children, for we can't possibly judge how they would have turned out had we made some different choices. If our children are pre-wired to be different, provided they have a balanced diet, are loved, nurtured, stimulated and protected, they will turn out the same irrespective of what interventions we do or do not make. But for me the journey to adulthood can be made a happy or miserable one and I have tried to make it as happy and carefree as James's nature can allow. I suppose on reflection I believe that I have genuinely done the best for my son with the resources I have. None of us can be perfect or offer more than our own personality, health, ability and finances permits. Of course, when I have been tired or unwell or James has been unbearably challenging, I have been bad tempered and said things I shouldn't. But on balance, I have always tried to understand and accommodate James's needs by offering a quiet, ordered and, as far as practicable, a consistent environment. If something different is required of him or I need to interrupt him, I try to give sufficient warning. I often write to him as he finds this medium of communication easier because written messages are not complicated by body language and I am forced to be more succinct, perhaps taking greater care over my choice of words; this reduces misunderstandings between us. It also means he can attend to my notes at a time that suits him. As a consequence of his requirements, our life is a little eccentric compared to the norm but as we are not the norm this is hardly surprising; it is however our norm and I say 'Vive la difference!'

~

John's Story

They call me John - (pardon my love for Moby Dick) - who waited until the age of 63 for my first real close encounter with an Aspie. My storied past began as a secondary educator in English and Theatre. For ten years I owned and operated a residential group home where the county placed children for therapeutic care. I am currently working in an experimental foster care program (doing residential work in a foster care environment). Doing what I do, having reached the age of retirement, has caused my family to diagnose me somewhere between early and middle stages of Dementia.

For confidentiality reasons, I will call the young man Sam, although he would have no problem with me using his real name. Sam came to me two years ago at the age of fifteen after spending four unsuccessful years in different residential facilities. He had been shifted from social services to the department of corrections due to his incorrigible and bizarre behaviors. He spent all but one month on entry-level status during those four years.

He came with the diagnosis of Reactive Attachment Disorder[1], Bi-polar Disorder, Conduct Disorder and a suitcase full of medication. My previous exposure to an Aspie was very limited and never intensive. I began by making a false assumption the current diagnosis was going to be accurate. The school

---

[1]   Reactive Detachment disorder – an inability to bond emotionally to others or have a sense of empathy towards others, very self-centred. It's generally believed to be the result of neglect or abandonment.

year had already begun when he arrived so I took his Individual Education Program (IEP) the previous school had created and the school plugged in the adaptations that had been formulated. To my dismay, it was a disaster. Schools are hesitant to accept the "Aspie" diagnosis because of the increased level of services they will be required by law to offer - they do their own testing and will follow only their results. Since the criteria is so nebulous for Aspergers, that gives them a lot of latitude.

Once he had moved into my home, I was intrigued by his lack of "appropriate social graces" which included his interactions with my other two foster kids (boundary issues), hygiene (extremes of multiple showers to no showers), and eating protocol (had to drink from the faucet because he would gag if he drank from a glass). One other young man in my home had limited executive functioning due to a difficult birth process and I was struck by the similarities between the two and I began to look more closely at Sam's diagnosis especially as there was no history of any head trauma or birth difficulty.

In the meantime, with school in rapid deterioration and little progress at home, I began to significantly ramp up the consequences to moderate the behaviors. To my surprise, it didn't change a thing - his performance stayed consistent. His correction agent and I even went to the level of sending him to a correctional facility[1] for two weeks as a "wake up"

---

[1]   A juvenile prison – 75% punitive, 25% rehabilitative.

call. The day he returned he was the same as the day he left. I should add that with extreme consistency of moderate consequences, and the passage of time, they are having some positive effect on his performance.

During this time, what I considered as bizarre behaviors continued and here are a few examples. Sam would take a couple of sips from a bottle of pop and then put it in the fridge. A few minutes later he would come back for another sip and have a fit that someone had messed with his pop because it tasted funny and would throw it away. Food also tasted differently to him than to others. He would also complain about smells and odors that none of the rest of us could detect. Presenting as being quite intelligent, which he is, it was puzzling when trying to rationalize the "cause and effect" of choices and behaviors with him, when consequences that were being administered were generally unsuccessful.

I view Sam as living in a parallel universe to mine. Just as his universe makes no logical sense to me, my universe makes no logical sense to him. Somehow I have to get him to be willing to time warp to mine when socially necessary and then he can time warp back to his own when he is by himself. It would be unrealistic of me to expect him to totally leave his world for mine just as I would be unable to leave mine to live in his.

Having come to the conclusion that what I was doing was failing miserably, even though my techniques were time tested for me and it had generally worked before with other RAD, Bi-polar, and Conduct Disordered kids, I began researching back though my memories and stored materials and came up with Asperger Disorder. My previous encounter with an Aspie was limited and many years before. What struck me most significantly was the difference in the reality base for Sam and what is typically acceptable. Sam preferred to live in the world of fantasy anime[1]; while reading anime books and viewing anime videos on line he was calm and happy. I had had other kids with an interest in anime, but never to this level. The tipping point for my decision to get him re-evaluated was based primarily on when we would sit down to process incidents. His view on the incidents and its results were miles apart from mine and what would be considered society's norm.

I got him scheduled in with a psychologist that I always have respected. After the initial interview and as we were walking, out I was informed "you have a poster child for Asperger Syndrome here." It was at that point that my education began in earnest. I was fortunate that I could email the psychologist anytime I had a question and get a response within a day or two. I also spent hours on the internet and researched the local library and university for any information I could find.

I was, and still somewhat am, confused how Sam could have spent four years in intensive residential

---

[1]   Fantasy anime is a highly stylised and colorful animation usually with adult themes, originally developed in Japan.

placement and the concept of his being an Aspie never surfaced. Possibly the primary reason is that the diagnosis is relatively new in the mental health field. It is only recently that there is significant research being done and its results are still sketchy. Workers in residential facilities are often young college students who wouldn't have the background to recognize an Aspie or know what one was. This does not excuse the professionals who supervised the facilities and who missed the diagnosis but can help explain why it was missed.

A professional's conclusion has to be based on the information they receive; at the most they will only see the child a couple of hours a week and we see the child 24/7. I guess it is a natural instinct to look first at traditional diagnoses based upon surface behaviors rather than looking for underlying reasons for the behaviors. Typically, residential and professionals will look at moderating existing behaviors as a band aid to maintenance and then explore deeper if it is needed - unfortunately that does not work with an Aspie because the behaviors do not go away, they remain front and center and the total focus. It then becomes an easy step to move from any preliminary diagnosis up the ladder to a Conduct Disorder and possible Anti-Social Disorder. Once that is in place there is little need for them to look deeper unless the child has a very strong advocate. In my area the Aspergers diagnosis seems to be the new 'in thing' just like ADHD and Bi-polar had their time in the sun. This is just as unfortunate as when Aspergers was ignored. It has the potential to be watered down to the point where the true Aspergers do not receive the focus and services they should have - it can simply be a dumping ground.

My fear is that it is going to become a medicated diagnosis, which in my mind is a total waste. Sam's performance med free is only a minimal change from when he arrived loaded with the anti-psycotics, stimulants to "help him concentrate," and anti-depressants. Without the medication he is more argumentative and manipulative, but the basic behaviors have not changed. Unfortunately the pill has become the easy solution to so many situations where the real solution is patience and knowledge and skill.

In thinking back, I don't really know what or when I started doing things differently or how much I really changed operations. It was more of an acceptance of the diagnosis and an understanding of why things appeared so absurd and bizarre. Acceptance reduced my levels of being reactive and frustrated. They didn't disappear, but they did start to moderate. Maybe it was also part of my inherent fatalistic personality that things are generally going to be the way they are and I just have to deal with it as best I could.

I think the biggest adjustment I made in the home environment was allowing Sam to complete some chores and expectations in his own manner - occasionally. It still had to meet my expectations but I allowed him to create his own process hoping he would see that my process was more efficient (once in a while he would actually admit that my suggestion was better). The second would be the education of Sam into what an Aspie is. The third was the reduction of his medication to where it is now - only Melatonin to help him get to sleep at night. The fourth was establishing consistency, consistency, consistency and routine, routine, routine. I learned the fourth one after numerous battles over wording and the validity of the intent of statements. Sam attempted to make everything a negotiation if it wasn't going his way.

The education of Sam into the characteristics of an Aspie, which is still ongoing, was very carefully performed with the major emphasis that being an Aspie is not an excuse to do whatever he wanted however he wanted. It got to the point that as I approached the point of making the statement, he would beat me to it. Everything was framed with the attitude that he would have to conform to society's standards and even if he did, that did not have to change who he was inside. He would be allowed to be who he was regardless and he should take pride in being who he was. His alteration of performance was merely a utilitarian process on his part to help him be who he is and help him in achieving his needs and wants.

Sam moved with me to a different state and this new program - the state was more than happy to do the interstate compact for transference. We are going to abort his high school education and enrol him in the GED program.[1] I do not anticipate him having any great difficulty with the GED. Upon completion he will be enrolled in a two-year college that is only 6 blocks from home and we are attempting to secure funding for an "aide or mentor" that would attend college with him and support his process. The difficulty is what to put into place after he ages out of the program. He has had no family contacts over the last couple of years and all attempts to implement it have been rebuffed. All parental rights were terminated many years ago and the extended family has no interest.

Sam is now 17 and can remain with me while he attends college, so that has become our time frame to see what is available and what services Sam is willing to accept - the acceptance is going to be our most significant hurdle. I want to be optimistic for Sam, but it may not be very realistic. Given the fact there is not a single biological family member as a fail safe that has involvement with him, the fact I will legally only have 2 or 3 years at the most involvement in his life, and the fact he is an Aspie does not bode well for his future.

I suspect Sam will not search me out in the future for supports given the Aspie characteristic of an inability to form deep relationships. The relationship Sam and I have is more based upon supplying his needs and especially his wants, which are also

---

[1] The General Educational Development program leads to a General Equivalency Diploma – an alternative to high school diplomas, a two year college course leading to traditional college by passing competency tests.

needs in his eyes. I don't know if they occur within the biological unit or not because I don't have that level of experience, I can only speak for my environment. It took a year before he would accept my hand on his shoulder or for him to place his hand on mine (and then often it was because he wanted something from me). For Sam it appears that friendships are to be utilized to fill a want, not a need—in every situation "wants" trumps "needs." I can help with the needs, but not the wants. It is very, very difficult to remain optimistic for his future.

I don't know how I would handle it if he was my son and I would be responsible for him for the rest of my life. For me, I know he will age out of the system and another young man will take his place with significant needs that will require my focus. After so many years of seeing young men come and go, I have become a little hardened to the process, but the Aspie is carving out a very significant portion of my heart and will be memorable. I do hope he will become one of my flock that sporadically stay in contact.

*

Kitty's Story

Prelude

I had a fairly normal pregnancy – the hospital had picked up the fact that the baby had a club foot on the scan but I regarded that as a minor problem and was reassured by the consultant orthopaedic surgeon that this could be put right over time with surgery and physiotherapy – as indeed it has been. So my son spent his first seven months in a tiny plaster cast, having undergone surgery at three months. Subsequently, it was my job to give him his physiotherapy half a dozen times each day to ensure that his foot developed as well as possible. Apart from trips to the hospital, he was a happy, curious baby – breastfed (of course) – and I put his restlessness at night and his inability to sleep for more than forty minutes at a time, down to the plaster cast at first.

In fact, he used the plaster cast to his advantage and would swing it from side to side until its extra weight gave him the momentum he needed to roll onto his tummy and start to crawl. He was crawling before he was six months and took his first steps at ten months. Words started coming early too and he was at his happiest when we were looking at a book and he would use my finger to point at objects and name them – or when we would walk round the room naming the pieces of furniture and the ornaments. Naming shapes and colours came just as easily. He took such an interest in what was around him and in me and whatever I was doing that I felt I just had a very bright, happy baby, who hardly ever slept, on my hands.

And, of course, whenever I mentioned to relatives or other mothers that he hardly slept, all I got back was "Oh, my baby never slept at all for years" or "Well, it must be something you are doing wrong at bedtime then." So I tried different ways of putting him to bed (none of which worked, thank you Nanny-Know-it-All) and did not really worry about it much (probably too tired to).

Of course, life is never that simple – during the first two and a half years of my son's life, my brief marriage to his father ended, my father died of cancer, my mother died after bungled surgery eight months later and I took on the responsibility of caring for my severely disabled (with Multiple Sclerosis) terminally ill brother. So when my son seemed restless, was most unwilling to be separated from me (even when I was just in the next room), seemed to have strange attachments to objects or found comfort in them being placed in a particular order – I could find lots of reasons for him to feel that way. Also, as he was my first child and there is, as far as I know, no history of autism in my family, I was not looking for problems and, consequently, found none.

The truth began to dawn slowly. There were terrible problems when my ex-husband decided that he wanted to have contact with his son, when he was about two. At first we had to travel to a contact centre, ordered by the Court, about ten miles from where we lived which was a bit of an ordeal when the weather was bad as we had no transport. So when they would meet, my son was already tired and was not very keen to be left (which his father insisted on) – although he did enjoy meeting the other children at the centre and I was, in fact, complimented by the manager of the centre on how well socialised he was – sharing and being friendly and talkative with the other children. However, his father soon began to complain about his behaviour and that he would not speak to him – spending entire sessions of an hour or so simply asking for his mum. When he was with me, he was chatty and sociable – even to the extent of "picking up" a gentleman on the train (we've been together for fifteen years now).

Difficulties also arose when I enrolled my son at the local playgroup – at around the same time. He went reasonably happily – until it was time for me to leave. I followed the advice of the playgroup leader – settled him down to play, said I was going and went. At the Christmas party, when Santa arrived all the other little ones sang "When Santa got stuck down the chimney" (as rehearsed) and my son stood on the stage, threw his arms in the air and sang "Joy to the World the Lord is Born, Let Earth receive her King." I was embarrassed but secretly also quite impressed. A few weeks later he was asked to leave, as the leader felt he was just taking up too much of her time as he needed one-to-one attention.

I thought, well, if that's what he needs at the moment, that's what he shall have. So I spent the next months taking him to soft play sessions, swimming classes, the library, play dates with local children his age, trips to the park – no real problems to report, in fact he tended to behave rather better than other children but always took an interest in what we were doing. He knew his alphabet before he started at the school nursery – sounds and names of the letters and the order they should come in. I remember him pointing out to the health visitor at the clinic (when he was around three and a half) when she asked him if he knew his alphabet, that her files were in the wrong alphabetical order. I also remember being quite bemused that my bright little boy had trouble telling me which was the longer line, in a puzzle in his comic.

Why should something so simple and obvious be a problem? Of course, now I know why. Sort of. "Long" and "short" he had no problem with but "longer" and "shorter" he found very hard concepts to grasp. I think it is like when my husband asks me whether a building or road is on the right or the left and all I can think of to say is "well, it depends where you're standing". My son always has problems guessing or even choosing unless the choices are simple and clearly explained. For example, if he has to choose between two movies – will he ever have chance to see the one he does not choose now and if so, when. If he won't, he simply cannot choose between two things he wants to do and I can understand this too – until he has done both how can he possibly know which one he will enjoy more? He just does not have enough information to make a decision. Same with the line, in a way, if the "longer" line is then placed besides one that is even "longer" it becomes the "shorter" line, even though the length of the line itself has not altered.

Following a family outing to a dinosaur park (for by now he had a little brother), he developed a passionate interest in dinosaurs like many other children and I would tell other parents that he knew the names of all the dinosaurs in the encyclopaedia and they would always say "Oh, so does mine" but mine actually did and could spell them, and knew when they lived, where they lived, what they ate and how big they were. All of them.

Around this time, relationships with other children began to be difficult. My son would lash out or hit another child with no apparent provocation. I know that many children go through this phase and that's basically what we were told it was. But I started to feel uneasy about him being with other children, unless I was there to supervise the situation. He seemed to behave so much better if I was around. I had, I don't know when, started to talk him through social situations, explaining what other people wanted to say or do and what was expected of him. I gradually found that he would ask me what was happening around him more and more, and found myself interpreting the world for him most of the time – I still do. I find he still uses me as something of an anchor or perhaps a compass, to stick to the nautical metaphor. If someone asks him what he thinks of something, he will automatically look at me for a clue to how he should answer them. He likes me to be very close if we are out and about – I have tried moving away from him in a shop to let him look at what he is interested in, but he still moves away with me unless I instruct him to stay where he is, which he does – on the exact spot until I return.

School years 4-7

All hell broke loose when he started school. Perhaps in a different setting it might have taken longer to recognise his problems – but there were eighty-odd four year olds in one large room, being taught in separate areas and having to move round every half an hour or so. I am not actually sure it would be possible to design a worse scenario for a child on the autistic spectrum. He freaked – all day, every day. To other people this "freaking" manifested itself as a refusal to obey simple instructions and unprovoked aggression towards other children and adults – hitting and snatching with no sign of remorse.

He would shake, scream and cry uncontrollably and I would just have to hold him in my lap until it was time to leave or, once in a while, he would calm down enough to respond to what was going on around him. If he did engage in an activity he would then refuse to abandon it and move onto the next activity after twenty minutes as all the other children were expected to do and the cycle would begin again. For me the most frightening thing about his reaction to school was the way he seemed to "close down." He would chatter to me on the way to school and on the way home but as he walked into that room full of children it was as though a heavy metal shutter had come down in his mind, blocking out the busy, noisy little world of the classroom. He did not respond to me in the same way as he would at home but at least he still acknowledged my presence and seemed to gain some comfort from it. He was like someone in shock – he even looked pale and clammy. It was as though he was hearing my words but unable to grasp my meaning or what it was I wanted him to do. To me his fear was palpable but I do not know if the school staff realised how hard he was trying to "be good." From some of the staff I got the impression that they could see he was making an effort but from others I distinctly felt that they saw him as no more than a disruption and annoyance. He was so distressed he could not even speak to them.

At the first meeting I had with the school's SEN specialist, she insisted that he was completely non-verbal and had no speech at all. So that night I recorded him at home and played the tape for the Speech Therapist who had been called in, who told me that I was amazing with him and to carry on with what I was doing and she would try to get the school staff to adopt the same methods. What methods? I asked myself.

Luckily, the head teacher was very supportive and imaginative and made arrangements for my son to be taught in a smaller, out of his age group class, while he was being assessed and diagnosed. Of course, the Local Authority did not want to assess such a young child and, in spite of pressure from the school and myself, the statementing process took more than a year – a very valuable year when a lot of work could have been done with my son, when school became, even with the best efforts of the staff, little more than a containment facility. He only attended school in the mornings, arriving after the other children and leaving before the lunchtime rush (so, in effect, for two hours a day). The Head said that she had no concerns that his education would suffer from not being in school as she was sure that I would see to that. No pressure then.

I began to notice how nasty other parents can be. I do mean nasty. I wish I didn't. I'm not talking about people who don't know any better – we all have to deal with ignorance and stupidity. I mean smug, unsympathetic, unhelpful and just plain horrible. "There are *places* for children like that!" I was told by one mother in the playground as I struggled to persuade my son to stand in a line with the others. "I wish I knew where" I thought to myself. Her hair started falling out later, quite dramatically, and I actually found myself laughing – which is really not the sort of person I am, usually.

So we went from there to an assessment unit. Having been promised miracles, now that **professionals** had been given charge, I was full of optimism. There would be strategies and techniques and therapies, all geared to my son's specific needs and delivered by committed and competent **experts**. I'm sure you know what comes next. Within three weeks, they were at their wits end. It turned out that they liked the sort of child with learning difficulties who sits where they are put and does not answer back. My son got into terrible trouble one afternoon – he had been extremely rude to the Learning Support Assistant (LSA). He had told her that there was an "n" in autumn and refused to be told that there was not. In the end he had become so infuriated that he had started throwing things. He was six. When I said that there was actually an "n" the only response I got was that he should have accepted what the LSA had told him even if it was wrong. On another occasion he reported to me that he would not be going on the aeroplane (organised by the Variety Club as a Christmas treat for disabled children) because he was "evil". Apparently this had been said to him by one of the adults at the school, although no-one would admit to it, of course. On another occasion, he asked me what hell was like, because again someone (an adult) had said that that was where naughty children like him went. After a traumatic and turbulent year of such incidents – accompanied by deteriorating behaviour and violent outbursts by my son, more periods of part-time attendance, he was finally excluded, just before the school was due for an inspection. An emergency meeting was called with the Local Authority at which it was decided by everyone that he would be better off being educated at home until a place could be assigned to him at the local provision for autistic children.

The one place of refuge that my son found at that school was in the other special unit for "very naughty boys" which was run by a brilliant teacher,

Mr E, who was big on discipline, had a great sense of humour and lots of imagination. My son still talks about him and how kind he was to him. Children do remember. And so do parents. It was he who sounded a warning bell about the provision at the Special School for Autistic Children that we had fought so hard to get. "He's far too bright for that!" he said as we left the assessment unit for the last time.

I have been asked what, in my view, made Mr E a brilliant teacher or to be specific, brilliant with my son – from what I briefly observed he was also held in high esteem by the other children with challenging behaviour in his unit. The key characteristics would be –

- being alert to "triggers" or warning signs of stress/distress (these vary, of course, between individuals). Then take appropriate action to change the situation before an "incident" so that the entire day is not spent "fire-fighting" and the children actually have some time and energy left to learn;
- the ability to be able to give clear, precise instructions (not as easy as it sounds) so that everyone knows exactly what is expected of them and where the boundaries are;
- the kind of self-confidence that lets you laugh at yourself and invite others to join in – without losing authority;
- most importantly, a genuine interest in, and desire to get through to, that particular child

– and I don't think this can be taught, learned or faked.

We make such a lot of the inability of autistic children to read body language and faces, but my lad always seemed to be able to spot a fake – someone who espoused an interest in children with disabilities but had no interest in him as a person. Yes, he is an interesting academic study and yes, professional objectivity is a requirement of the job, but this can appear as indifference to the person with the condition. One of my pet hates is those with a little knowledge who talk about people with autism (or whatever) as "them" or "they" often accompanied by a list of clever tricks that "they" can do – as though they were talking about performing monkeys. When I am told what "they" can do and isn't it wonderful, I always say "well, what bloody use is it to them to have memorised the timetable, if they can't get on a bus by themselves or even find the right bus stop?" Let alone decide where it is they want to go today.

Like most people I grew up with the understanding that "special schools" were for freaks and failures or the products of dysfunctional families and this is in spite of having both parents working in the field of education – for they too would say the phrase "ESN"[1] (as it was then) in hushed and vaguely disapproving tones. So having had the bad taste to produce a child with "SEN"[2] my feelings of guilt and failure were enormous. I remember sitting with the

---

[1]   Educational special needs
[2]   Special educational needs

consultant psychiatrist in utter despair as he tried to convince me that just because my son couldn't get it right, it didn't mean that I wasn't getting it right. How can that be? In the end I just wanted someone to tell me it *was* my fault – because then I would be able to do something about it, change something, try *something*, that would make it all better – because that's what mothers are supposed to do, isn't it?

Some of the professionals (and they were legion) that we met were so upbeat and positive that I would come away from sessions feeling really energised and sometimes it would take several hours before I realised that nothing had actually been said or any action taken. Others would radiate that air of "what would you know, you're only a parent – *I'm* the expert" and I would come away from those sessions feeling pretty suicidal. Except that would only make the problem worse – because if I stop swimming, he drowns too. And imagine arriving in the afterlife with all *that* guilt and no chance to ever put it right. All this is going on against the background of the daily effort to manage the life of a child with autism. Day after day the same battles to do the simplest things – hair washing a nightmare of terrified screaming and thrashing. Toenail cutting was the worst thing for us and, once, I was so desperate after weeks and weeks of trying calm rational persuasion, bribes (first thing I tried), threats and tears that I came up with the brilliant (well, I was very tired) idea of cutting them while he was asleep. So my poor lad woke suddenly in the middle of the night to the sight of his mother standing over him with a pair of scissors. In the end I explained it to him in graphic and exaggerated detail what would happen to his feet if he did not let me cut his toenails – including surgery to remove the infected nail with the "magic cream" before the anaesthetic (knowing full well his absolute horror of the "magic cream" as he cannot bear the feel of it on his skin).

For behind every battle is the knowledge that if your disabled child is not clean, well-kempt, wearing clean clothes, properly fed, teeth cleaned, hair brushed, having their nails cut with timely visits to the dentist, hairdresser and doctor, the mighty machine of social services is waiting to grind your little family to fine powder – did I say "family"? Sorry, I meant "case". Because you stopped being a family long ago, didn't you notice? Now you are a schedule of appointments, reviews, referrals, reports and one false step along the path of the legislation can result in missing that place that you are convinced will change your child's life – and it will all be your fault. My strong advice at this stage – put everything in writing, trust no-one and take a witness with you to meetings, make notes and ask your witness to sign them as a true record of the meeting. There are lots of places that offer help and the Local Authority is supposed to tell you who they are in your area. Use them. No matter how used you are to meetings and decision making in your professional life – this is different.

The decision to send my son to a special school was surprisingly easy – as it was there, or nowhere.

He simply could not cope with mainstream and the social pressures of being with children who did not have problems of their own, and consequently more understanding parents (well, it does help when yours is not the only one). And staff specially trained in working with children with a range of problems would, of course, be experienced, supportive and committed, otherwise they would not be working with children with disabilities, would they? (As my son would say, "Are you being ironic there? You are, aren't you?")

Part of the problem, and I feel an undervalued part, of educating children like my son is getting them to school in the first place. Transport arrangements have been a great source of anxiety for our family right through my son's school career. The first obstacle being how I felt about sending my four year old off in a car with a complete stranger – after having instructed him never to go off in a car with a complete stranger. So for the first year we took him to school ourselves, during which time I got to know the driver (when he was picking up the other children) and so did my son. Eventually his teacher persuaded me that he would settle in class better if he came with the other children so we tried that for a while. It proved to be a traumatic experience for all concerned and often irate (and not exactly "trained to deal") drivers would demand that I "make my son behave properly" on the bus full of noisy other children. If he *could* behave on a bus full of noisy other children then he would not need you to take him to the special unit, would he? So if there wasn't a problem, there wouldn't be a problem, basically. My son has been excluded from school transport on three occasions until finally the Local Authority acknowledged that he needed to be a "sole passenger". Even now, when the taxi firm is pressed they feel perfectly justified in packing them all into a bus together – well, they are running a business after all and transporting children with disabilities is just another type of cargo.

My Local Authority has a protocol for transporting children to school – they allow five minutes waiting time (it takes longer than this some mornings for my son to put his coat on). They go into great detail on how wheelchair passengers and others with mobility/physical disabilities should be treated and that they should be handed over to staff the other end but my son can walk so it is, therefore, acceptable to leave him in the car park to find his own way. On one such occasion, he was missing for over an hour and a half. It seems the driver who was subcontracted by the firm who actually held the contract had not been told that my son was disabled or the nature of his difficulties and had just accepted him at face value as a polite, sensible, quiet boy – because he always behaved acceptably in the taxi. It did not occur to the driver to wonder why my son was being taken to a special school.

The word "autism" has no meaning for the average taxi driver and why should it? And should parents really be expected to stand in the street discussing their child's medical history with a complete stranger, every time a new driver turns up – how humiliating is that? On the whole we have been lucky with the drivers we have had – they are nice people, often parents or grandparents themselves and usually willing to help once they know how to.

School years 7 – 12

I know some parents agonise over allowing their children to be sent to a special school and others fight for the right for them to attend a special school. Is it better to be the odd one out in mainstream and at least have a chance of a "proper" education, or to concentrate on the social and life skills that someone with a significant disability is going to need. Dunno.

My situation, following my son's transfer to the local authority special school for children with autism, was something else again. Apparently he was the wrong sort of autist. He did not qualify as having a learning difficulty because some idiot had taught him to speak, read and write which meant that his conventional IQ could be tested. The teacher at his previous school declared her amazement at his natural ability to read at a meeting – I added loudly that I wished I had known about it sooner for then I would not have spent all those months at home teaching him to read. This was the same teacher who insisted that my son, aged 6, could not tell the time, while I insisted that he could. "Well, then, what time is it?" she asked him. He looked at the clock and looked at me. "The red hand is the big hand," I said. "Oh, then it's twenty-five past four!" he said.

My expectations were high at the new, special school. The head was a man of vision and energy. The school was small and quiet and had the flexibility of staffing arrangements to be able to give help when and where it was needed. For the first few weeks, when my son was settling into this new environment, everyone, including him, was optimistic. However, after the summer holidays and his return to a new teacher and a new class, the situation quickly deteriorated. Within a few weeks, I was attending meetings with the head to discuss ways of managing my son's behaviour. The home-school book began to be pages and pages of complaints from his teacher. To be honest I began to wonder when she found the time to write so much – usually four or five pages.

She included in one formal report to the local authority that my son believed that his banana was his friend (no, I'm not joking). When I raised this with my son, he could not stop laughing, "What an idiot!" was his response, "I was joking – isn't it obvious? How could my best friend be a banana?" But the complaints continued. On one occasion he was accused of sexual misconduct with another child – when I asked him what had happened, he told me exactly what had happened. The LSA had escorted him to the loo, he had pushed open one of the loo doors to discover that another child was already sitting on the loo and had said hello and had a conversation with him (he lacks the usual social inhibitions and has a little brother with whom he often converses in the bathroom at home). This was the extent of the sexual misconduct it turned out.

I realise, as well as anyone, how stressful it is to try to manage my son and others like him on a daily basis. However, I cannot say how stressful I found the daily torrent of complaints from the school. It became clear to me that this teacher was not able to cope with the situation and was unburdening herself on me. I tried talking to my son about the incidents in school but in his mind there was little connection between a "telling off" in the evening and something that had happened at nine o'clock in the morning – "what's the point in telling me off now for that?" he'd ask. He would return home distressed and aggressive – his little brother suffering the worst of his spleen. I would try to divert my son and put his little brother in a safe place, then return to try to deal with my son's anger and distress. Of course, in the meantime, my younger son was sitting all alone wondering what the hell he had done wrong to be taken out the room by his mother and left all alone. He began to show signs of emotional distress, both at home and at school, banging his head and scratching his face. His behaviour at school began to deteriorate – he hated to be praised, would tear up his work, would over-react to the teasing/bullying of other children, often lashing out at them.

How long should one tolerate a stream of complaints from school? It felt like being under constant bombardment – I did not doubt that my son was difficult to manage and that the lines of communication between home and school are critical. So at what point does such communication become part of the problem instead of part of the solution? I would say when it is done for the benefit of the adult and not for the benefit of the child. And that is quite another story. It did have a damaging effect on my family and increased my stress levels many fold. I felt as though I was expected to deal with these issues at long distance – when I had no control over the situation which had led to them in the first place. So my answer to the question – how long do you put up with it? is "Too long!"

These were very dark times for my family and I would sit alone in the dark, having listened to both my children cry themselves to sleep, wondering where the hell to turn. Even my poor husband seemed to be part of the problem and not part of the solution. He did not seem to get my son at times – even once saying that he should pull himself together, like he had a choice about being autistic. He did not get his inability to follow a complicated instruction, accusing him of being naughty or cheeky when my son did not deserve it. More than anything, my husband hated (and still hates) the way my son treats me – shouting, swearing, threatening and even hitting – I know his behaviour outrages my husband, even now. But returning the aggressive behaviour just makes things worse.

I was stopped in the street recently. There was some campaign about domestic violence – elder abuse etc. "Tut, tut!" I thought to myself, having filled in their questionnaire, "some families!" It was only when I got home that I realised, with horror, that I had ticked all the wrong boxes – it was as though I had just blanked out all the screaming, abusive language, the threats, the smashed furniture, broken doors, the aggression – because families like mine don't do things like that, do they? I cannot count how many mornings my son has reduced me to tears of despair, for trying to get him to get dressed and have his breakfast. I've laid the clothes out for him, I've run his bath, I give him his towels and all he does is shout and swear at me. Mornings are definitely the worst times. My youngest son has his breakfast in the dining room and my oldest in the sitting room, because otherwise he will (and has in the past) attacked his little brother for a) getting dressed by himself without being told; b) eating his breakfast without being nagged and c) being ready on time. We have just got into the routine of keeping them entirely separate in the mornings – getting them up at different times and just trying to avoid any kind of confrontation.

This is just normal for us. Evening meals are usually taken separately too. We do make the effort to sit together for Sunday lunch and I believe that the promise of a home-made pudding may be of significant value in managing behaviour (home-made bread and butter pudding is the current favourite). However, when eating out, the behaviour is exemplary and both my boys are utterly charming companions. They do know that I will (because I have) simply take them home otherwise. Let me make clear to the uninitiated that these treasured outings are not the result of my son simply deciding not to behave "autistically" today. These outings are meticulously planned and prepared for. The venue is discussed and visited beforehand to ensure that we go on a quiet night and at a quiet time. The date and venue are agreed days or weeks in advance with my son. The time that we will have to leave the house is, likewise, agreed in advance – literally to the minute. The route to the venue is agreed and the taxi booked well in advance. The children and I sit together in the back in the same order every time. Only certain subjects are allowed to be discussed in the taxi. At the venue we sit in the order that my son has chosen. We are now allowed to discuss a slightly broader but still restricted range of topics. For example, my son will ask us all in turn "what is your favourite horror film?" And we will have to take turns in answering. This is his "best behaviour". And believe me, it is greatly appreciated. For I can see how much of an effort he is making to keep everything under control – calm and quiet.

He is trying to limit the number of variables in the situation, with a lot of help and support from the rest of us, to a level that he is more comfortable with. Nevertheless, I would not expect him to maintain this for long – a couple of hours – the time it takes to eat a meal, is just about his limit even with the support and goodwill of three other people. And even then I know that the journey home will be a difficult one as his level of self-control diminishes and we will probably be treated to a door-slamming, hitting, screaming tantrum when we get home.

However, we will have achieved what we set out to do and, also, have spent a couple of hours appearing to the outside world to be a "normal" family. Unless, of course, something has not gone according to plan and my son has had a noisy, violent outburst in public, in which case no-one could possibly mistake us for a "normal" family and we probably will just not go there again.

I don't think I'm overbearing by nature (my husband might disagree with this, were he to be given the chance) but it helps to be seen to be in control. I have rules – some of them are written down – and I try to keep them simple and I try to stick to them. Our menus are prepared three weeks at a time and then put on the front of the fridge – my son finds this so much easier (and it's surprising how much money and time it saves). In all other respects my home bears no resemblance to the Von Trapp residence whatsoever.

While my son was at the Special School, my home was more like a battlefield. Every meal time was a strain, bath time, going out, staying in – anything and everything seemed to trigger a confrontation. Soiling became a big problem. Potty training my son was just a joke. He had no interest in it at all. I only realised just how bad the situation was, when potty training my younger son who was clean and dry, day and night by the time he was about two. It just was not an issue – one or two little accidents and there we were. My older boy just did not care, no, he really did not care. He would sit for ages encrusted in his own faeces and not think anything of it. Wetting the bed was a minor problem – we did get a referral to the clinic for this and they supplied us with an alarm which so terrified my son that he was too afraid to go to sleep – he quickly discovered how to disconnect it. He was also anxious about being electrocuted when he wet the bed. In the end I decided that wetting the bed was probably the least of our problems and just got on with the twenty odd loads of extra washing I had to do every week. The soiling was a much worse problem – a little goes such a long way in terms of being anti-social. My son just could not see why anyone else should mind if he smelled – he still doesn't understand it really but accepts that it is not polite.

I use that word "polite" a lot. To tell an autistic boy that it is not "nice" to play with himself, is clearly inaccurate – because he thinks it is nice. So I told him it is not "polite" to do it in public and he can accept this form of words. I am lucky in that he looks to me for explanation and guidance. In fact, he will often take something that I have said quite casually and apply it as though it were a "moral imperative" of Kantian proportions.

The soiling became such an issue that he started hiding his faeces in his bedroom to avoid a confrontation. I never expected to have to search my house for piles of human faeces – and there was no sign of the situation improving. School holidays gave me some respite from this – as this particular problem would disappear within a day or so of the holiday starting, only to start up again within the first week or so of the next school term. I don't suppose I managed the situation as well as I could – I found it hard to conceal my physical disgust and emotional disappointment. I think my relationship with my son was at its lowest ebb at this point. He was continually upsetting and hurting his little brother and I was so tired from the extra work as well as trying to care for everyone on a day to day basis – I just could not imagine how we could continue to live like that. Coping was so far beyond me – all I could think about was surviving the day.

I remember wailing to one of my oldest friends over the phone about the situation, just not knowing where to turn, if indeed there was anywhere to turn. As far as I was aware, the Special School was the end of the road. And they clearly were unable to cope with my son and his distress at school was bleeding into our life at home, which had become a nightmare – nobody was getting what they needed.

I remember one night, after I had gone to bed, noises from my son's room woke me (nothing unusual in that) and I went to sort him out to discover him sitting in his bed covered in urine and faeces, which he had obviously been sitting in for some time. He continued to shout and scream (about some game he had been playing and had gone wrong) while I tried to sort out the bedding and him. He obviously needed a bath and it really was the last thing I needed – I was exhausted already and the thought of another two or three hours cleaning and washing was just too much. I ran the bath, (cold first then hot as always to avoid the risk of scalding) and put him in, still screaming and shouting. By this point my husband had joined in and was shouting at him to stop shouting. I was trying to wash the dried on faeces off my son, it was everywhere – even in his hair – all the time he was shouting in my face and jumping up and down in the bath. I finished washing him and sent him back to the newly changed bed while I cleaned the faeces out of the bath and started on washing the stinking bedding – collapsing on the sofa and falling asleep some hours later – and getting up again just after 5am to start all over again. I could barely stand to look at my son, I was so tired and defeated. I think this was my lowest point. I would have been quite happy to go to sleep and never wake up.

I had tried to get some help out of Social Services - ask, plead, beg and they will happily ignore you. Give your child drugs or hit them and they are there in an instant – it seems they only like to manage crises not to avoid them. But eventually we did get some respite care – two hours a week, which I could spend with my other little boy. Also I found someone to talk to about the situation at home, as my son was referred to a child psychiatrist who has turned out to be such a lifeline for our family – I'm not sure exactly what he does but I'm very glad he does it. Puts things in perspective, I think. Reassures me that it is the situation that is "awful" and not me.

I see many families in my situation but where there

is a "natural" support system – grandparents, sisters, cousins, aunts, friends – willing to lend a hand. I am so envious. I know it's still hard to bear the responsibility of raising a disabled child but at least there is some respite, some support. With the disintegration and dispersal of families generally, I am sure I am not the only one left high and dry by family who are only too willing to call on one in times of need (theirs, that is) but disappear into the woodwork in times of trouble. When people ask if I have family, I reply that I have relatives, but no family – apart from my husband and my children. It's surprising how many people know exactly what I mean.

The respite carer that we ended up with, Paul, was lovely. We are still in touch with him – he sadly moved away from the area some years ago – but he brings his partner and his little girl to see us occasionally and we exchange cards still. All the professionals were amazed that none of the other professionals had got help for us before. The school were amazed because other parents with less challenging children were getting far more help. Social services were always amazed that the medical services had not done more to help us and the medical services were always amazed that social services had not done more to help us. Everyone, however, was always very pleased that they had records of me asking for some help – just shows that the system works.

Now, what made Paul lovely? Well, the same things that made Mr E stand out. Humour, intelligence, confidence and sincerity – oh, and they both had moustaches. Which may well account for the fact that my son, now 15 years old, refuses to shave his off?

Technically, because of my son's well-documented challenging behaviour, we are still entitled to respite care but after our long-time carer left, we were assigned a string of idiots, basically. Inept, untrained – they were simply people looking to make a few extra quid by doing a few hours for a care agency. Not one of them knew what my son's problems were or had been given any information or training by the agency. One girl's claim to be "very experienced" in dealing with "people like my son", was supported by the fact that she had a brother about his age! And it would be a different person nearly every time (I can't say I'm surprised if they were expecting an ordinary child) and the times would have to be re-arranged to suit them and often altered at the last minute, which would mean having to contact his school and re-arrange transport for him to come home straight from school.

In the end I told our contact at social services, having repeatedly complained about the behaviour of the agency and the carers (one even hinting that he wanted us to top up his money otherwise he wouldn't come any more), that managing the respite care was causing more stress than it was supposed to be alleviating so could we please not bother any more. There had been several incidents (for example, at the local leisure centre) when "experienced" carers had completely lost control of the situation and of my son putting both him and others at risk of injury. Apparently the risk assessment which had been prepared by social services and passed to the agency (I know because I signed for it) had not been passed to the carers.

But that small break did change things – I had a few hours to myself to think. To consider my priorities, which remained, as ever, to look after all my family to the best of my abilities. My husband seemed to come to his senses a bit too. He tried to do things in the house – he was brought up in a family where only the women cooked, cleaned or washed and, although not opposed in principle to housework, would rather avoid it if possible. But he does do more than he did. He also agreed to spend more time with our older boy – he is always quite nervous of taking him out in public in case he "goes off on one" without me there to put things back together. I started insisting on spending more time with my younger son – and he was much happier for having my attention to himself sometimes. Many small changes in the way we did things resulted in relieving some of the pressure on me. Oh yeah, and I had to admit that I was not Superwoman after all and couldn't do it all by myself – this was, without doubt, the biggest change.

It also gave me a chance to re-think my relationship with my older son. I explained to him how I felt about his behaviour and what it was that upset me. I explained that I was, also, very worried about his brother, who was harming himself at that time, and that I wanted to spend more time with him which meant that he, my older son, would have to spend more time with his step-father and behave for him. He said to me, "I know that I have had an unfair share of your love since I was born and I think it's only fair that I share it with my brother now." I was speechless. Did he really recognise that, all those mornings when he stood screaming in my face, the only thing that kept me going was how much I loved him? Probably too much to hope for – but it did make me realise how lucky I am that he is able to express his feelings verbally, for I would never have guessed that he knew he was loved, from the way he behaved.

Of course, nothing really changed that much – every morning was still a battle, school was still a nightmare for all of us. I felt like I could manage to keep swimming for just a bit longer, though. We struggled through a couple more years of Special School, the term time soiling continued – the school began to confine my son during the school day to a cupboard (quite a large cupboard, with a window) where they could lock him in, and did. They began to put pressure on me to have him medicated during the day – otherwise they could not see how they could cope with him. In the end, I agreed. I was fearful that a violent outburst could result in someone being seriously injured and these were occurring more and more frequently at school. So he slept on a pile of cushions in a cupboard when he went to school, put on weight, became lethargic and, I thought, sad. Then as he got used to the medication, his behaviour became uncontrollable at school once more. I was not happy about simply increasing dosages to keep him sedated at school. So the medication was changed to dear old Ritalin. As far as I could see this had little effect at all – apart from to keep the school happy. He did not have it at home or during the holidays – only for school and his behaviour there was reported to be as difficult as ever. He was sent home so often that I was unable to make any plans to go anywhere – we would get a call demanding that we come and collect him several times a week. I do not think that he completed a whole week of schooling. He would often be excluded for days, even weeks, at a time – not for his benefit, because obviously it was not going to cure his autism or address his behavioural issues at school – but it did give the staff a break. We kept being told what a wonderful job the school was doing – but they started excluding my son from school outings. From what I saw of the work he was doing at school and the work that he was doing for me at home, I think that boredom probably had a part to play in his challenging behaviour. The school was a one-size fits all set-up and, with respect, there is only so much painted pasta collage that one person can make!

Eventually, just before he was 12 (actually, it was on my birthday) he hit the deputy head-master over the head with a plastic sword. This was the final straw as far as the school were concerned and my son was excluded from that point. And I was once again responsible for his care, welfare and education all day, every day – as far as I was aware, for the rest of his life. To give the head-master his due – he kept my son "on his books", so that he could continue to have a hand in his educational placement. I believe that he felt my son had been failed by the system, which was too rigid to cope with special, special needs children. Certainly the attitude of some of the staff I encountered there, one speech therapist in particular, was that my son was somehow to blame for not fitting into the typical pattern of autistic "symptoms." There was once a cross-disciplinary meeting concerning my son – this sounds like a good idea but basically he was dragged into a room where about twelve adults all sat staring at him and interrogating him as to why he behaved the way he did. The adults were far more concerned with making a good impression on the presiding Professor, a man of great gravitas and experience, than they were concerned for the welfare of my son. This one speech therapist turned on my son and demanded that he "tell everyone what you threw this morning!" He looked puzzled, looked round at everyone and said "the only thing I remember throwing was a wobbly!" This utterly charmed the Professor and his entourage suddenly seemed to notice that his case was actually an interesting little boy.

The speech therapist, attached to the school at the time, used to delight in explaining to parents how dysfunctional they were, although she was the one turning up to meetings in torn and dirty clothing, smelling of alcohol and cigarettes. She tried it on with me, explaining how clever autistic people are and that my son would probably understand Wittgenstein, whereas of course, as a mere mummy, I could never hope to. I explained to her that as the core of Wittgenstein's work was based on semantics and generalised concepts of language I thought it likely that my son would find it quite hard actually, but that his mummy, with a degree in Philosophy, would probably be able to explain it to him when he was older. I do wish people would remember that it is the child with the learning difficulty. I may not understand all the jargon – but then that is rather the point of having jargon in the first place, isn't it?

*

At Home

I was glad to see the back of the place. My son's self-esteem was rock bottom and I was angry with myself for allowing the situation to continue when it was obviously not doing him any good either in terms of his education or his personal development. Here he was again, rejected by people that I had told him he could trust to look after him, feeling like a criminal and a failure. We had, when he was excluded from the assessment unit, been given six hours a week home tuition and a lovely lady came round to teach him maths and English. She also took the time to show me how the teaching of maths had changed since I was at school – which meant that I was able to teach him myself without either of us getting too confused.

My son was technically still on the roll of the Special School which meant that we did not get home tuition this time, but his class teacher, who seemed quite distressed at the situation, let me know what they had been doing and where they were going in class and I decided to get on with it myself. I knew that my son was capable of far more than had been expected of him at school so I was determined that, even though the system had failed him, I would not.

We sat down together and decided which subjects to tackle – my son has always been bright and keen to learn, which is a blessing. We decided on English, Maths, Science, Geography, History and French. He had done snippets of French at school and was delighted to discover that, armed with my rusty A-level, I could teach him some basic French. We analysed creative writing from different periods and in different styles. He once said that he could tell the difference between a man writing and a woman – so we spent many happy hours challenging this hypothesis – and I'm happy to say that he couldn't. We made our own litmus paper, with red cabbage and blotting paper and I do not think he will ever forget our experiments, which included him testing his own wee! I also assigned him part of my allotment and he was expected to grow, and care for, plants from seed, bulb and tuber. He was so chuffed when we made a family meal of the potatoes he had grown (with a considerable amount of surreptitious help from his step-father). We studied the Industrial Revolution – tied it in with history, geography, philosophy, art and literature. He sucked it all up like a sponge. I bought him a folding desk and would put it up in the sitting room so that he would know that it was time to study now. In the afternoons I would take him out somewhere – I felt that his social development was even more important than his education and that he needed to be able to relate to the local community and how it worked.

I would make sure that I walked my younger son to school, while my husband stayed in the house – so that I got to spend at least some time alone with him and be able to ask him about how his life was going every day. Then I would rush home, get my older son out of bed, washed, dressed and fed and then settle down with him to spend the morning "doing lessons" – spending a good three hours a day and making sure we did some maths and English every day. Reading has never been a problem for my son and we have a house full of books and after I had spent those early months teaching him the basics, he quickly became an accomplished and avid reader – once he realised that books are interesting and fun and have things you can memorise in them, which is something he has always enjoyed doing.

It is always nice to have something that you excel at. I have always thought that children learn best when it's fun and we have always played word games when travelling, adapted to the different levels of literacy, of course – I remember one long car journey having exhausted my imagination, my son (then about 7) came up with the brilliant suggestion of putting all the capital cities in the world in alphabetical order – I told him it was a brilliant idea but that the only drawback was that he was the only person I knew who could actually do that from memory. He is always surprised when my brain doesn't seem to be able to do the things that his can – and he finds it rather funny when I defer to his recollections because they are so much more reliable than mine. I tease him by asking questions about films (his passion) about which he has a truly encyclopaedic knowledge and often superior to some of the reference books which make the occasional error, to his disgust – and then I will ask him where his coat is, and he will just look at me and laugh, "give me a clue!"

Then after the morning session – with varying results, depending on his mood – and a spot of lunch, I would take him out somewhere to develop his social skills and to give both of us a bit of exercise and a break from the house. Then from 3.30pm onwards the usual round of managing a house with two small boys in it, preparing a meal and clearing up. I made a point of sitting and reading with both the boys every evening and we have happily worked our way through all the Harry Potters (I just love doing all the voices) as well as a few favourites of mine from when I was girl. After the boys went to bed, I would whiz round and do a bit of housework (never liked it anyway) and then, around 11 pm, I would sit down to prepare the lessons for the next day. I found it very satisfying to see the way his self-esteem improved as he began to produce some very good work and take a real interest in the things that we were doing together. To say it was a big undertaking would be an under-statement – there was simply no time for anything else in my life. No social life and I had to struggle to find time to spend with my younger son and as for my husband – he was so far down the food chain in terms of getting my attention, I'm surprised he stuck around. Although I am a very good cook!

This went on for months and I was quite in the rhythm of it – tired all the time of course, but resigned to the idea that this was the best option for my son, although not ideal for the rest of the family.
One afternoon I had a phone call from the Head at the Special School to say that he thought he had identified a suitable placement for my son at a fairly local school. I was not impressed. Having spent the previous months trying to put my son's shattered self-esteem back together, I was far from enthusiastic about going down that road again. "Leave it to us – We're the experts!" and then a couple of months later trying to explain to my lad why the people who claimed to like him and want to help him had turned their backs on him yet again. So I was fairly lukewarm about the idea but prepared to listen to what was on offer.

School Years 12+

A couple of gentlemen from the school (which was a private school run by a charity) came to visit us and I was quickly impressed by the fact that the head of the unit for autistic children was far more interested in talking to my son than to me and seemed to be keen to find out what he liked and what he felt he needed from a school. He then asked my son if he would like to go back to school – to which my son replied that that rather depended on what the school was like. And so he was invited to visit the school to see what it was like. The interview was focussed on what my son wanted to do and what he felt about things, I realise that a lot of young people with autism have a lot more difficulty in expressing themselves than my son but I was really impressed with the way in which his views were taken into account. I have found as a general rule in life that if you want someone to do something, the best way is to make them want to do it, if possible, so that the experience is a positive one, even if the thing in itself is not – probably watched "Mary Poppins" at an impressionable age, but it is true. And for my son who finds so many things frightening, bewildering and inexplicable, being able to cling to our little treats, routines and games has made life much more bearable for him – and even if I have to tell what my top ten favourite films are about a hundred times, does it really matter – if it makes a trip to the dentist possible?

We went to see the school – only 36 pupils and twice as many staff, fabulous grounds, fantastic equipment and I liked the way the staff dealt with "situations" – there were one or two while we were there – and it was clear to me that the staff were trained and experienced enough to deal with challenging behaviour, calmly and effectively. My son was invited to come to the school for a few weeks to see how he liked it and he jumped at the chance. So I spent the next few weeks sitting by the phone waiting for the calls to start coming – and they did come. My son found the prospect of going into assembly just too much so his key-worker, an exceptional young woman, Hannah, rang to ask how to approach him – I made a couple of suggestions as to how I would handle such a situation and they took my advice! They tried what I suggested and adapted it as they went along, and it worked – within a few weeks my son was going into assembly, in his own way and with support, but he was going.

On another occasion we had a call from the head of the unit – as soon as he said hello and who he was, my heart sank, I had had so many phone calls that started like that and ended with – "and please come and take him home". But he had rung to say what a good day my son had had and how pleased they were with his progress and the efforts that he was making to do what was wanted of him, which was clearly sometimes very difficult for him. It seemed like my son was finally in a place where they understood the difference between "won't" and "can't". It sounds so simple but try explaining it to someone who does not have any understanding or experience of autistic people. Like the Department of Works and Pensions.

At the end of the day, how well a school works is so much more to do with the people – we were so lucky to meet the head of the unit, David, and to have Hannah as my son's key worker. She was phenomenally good with him and brought out the very best in him – perceptive and committed and totally in control. He became more willing to try new experiences at school, to attempt new activities and his self-confidence continued to grow. And when he *was* having problems, which of course he did, she would tell me and we would discuss it and try to sort it out together so that we were always rowing in the same direction. She prompted and supported him to start an after-school film-making club for other young people at the school – which was very successful and gave my son a feeling of real achievement. The head of the unit would organise extra-mural trips, including several to the Assembly which have allowed my son to express his views and opinions on services and issues affecting young people with autism, directly to the Education Minister as well as to other committees and conferences.

The school is in two parts – as most of the pupils are residential. The pupils have a house where they have meals, go after school and live/sleep during the week. Although my son is a day pupil (we both agreed that we didn't want a residential placement), he still goes to his "house" first thing in the morning and from there to school. He takes his lunch in the house and sometimes stays on after school to socialise or take part in house meetings.

The school itself has very small classes and caters for children with challenging behaviour for a number of reasons – my son is in a class with other autistic boys who have had the same kinds of experiences that we have. Much of the school day is spent on non-academic activities and sporting activities in particular. My son has been encouraged to try many different things – including sailing, surfing, canoeing and climbing. He has been away on school trips on several occasions and these too have been successful. Although I have ensured that he had a brand new pair of socks for each day of the trip as he spends a huge amount of time matching his socks *exactly* every morning (even if one has been through the wash a couple of times more than the other, the pairing will be rejected). Of course, washing goes without saying. He has taken the same immaculate bar of soap on each of the four trips he has been on and returned it in the same state each time.

He has been following conventional GCSE courses in some subjects but I feel that he would be capable of more – the problem, as always, is persuading him to co-operate. Unfortunately, both his key worker, Hannah, and the head of the unit, David, have moved on to other jobs during the years that my son has been there and although the other staff have been good, my son does not seem to have built up that same bond of trust and rapport. He does find it difficult to establish new relationships and can (so I'm told) be quite quiet and withdrawn until he gets to know people very well, if he ever does.

When my son first went to the school he was very shocked at the fact that some of the other children smoked – it is a school where the children have challenging behaviour for many reasons and it is felt better to "pick their battles". Initially, he was picked on by the other boys for being autistic and he took his complaint to the teachers, who brought in the Ombudsman to investigate the matter. I was very impressed with this – before one had encountered the attitude of "well, of course he's going to get picked on for being autistic, what do you expect?" He, too, was satisfied that his complaints were being taken seriously and dealt with appropriately at that time.

I would love to be able to say that the present school has been the answer to all our problems. It has certainly helped. The quality of my life has improved exponentially – I am able to go out on my own occasionally. Which may not sound like much to most people but has been so difficult to plan and organise in the past that it has been, in practical terms, impossible. My son has only once been sent home early in the three years or so that he has been at the school and I was in complete agreement with the school's decision to do so. He still has very challenging behaviour at times and being in a group of like-minded young men can lead to intolerable behaviour. Also, with the removal from his school environment of the two key people that he relied on for support, he has found it difficult to establish such a close rapport with other members of staff as he had at the beginning. One is also aware that the school, like so many other charities, is under pressure to balance the books. Little treats that the young people had enjoyed – small amounts of pocket money and rewards for good behaviour, presents at Christmas – have disappeared.

This makes perfect sense to an adult accountant but to a fourteen year old autistic boy seems like an erosion of his human rights. It should be noted that even small changes, badly handled, e.g. re-organising the dining arrangements, can undermine an autistic person's view of the whole institution. The management of change is a crucial skill in the management of life for an autistic person and where possible managers should avoid making changes simply to "make their mark" and establish their authority because it will have the opposite effect. In my experience, my son and his friends regard people who change things "on a whim," when there is no sound explanation for doing so, as rather stupid and once this judgement has been made it often takes a lot of persuasion to convince them otherwise.

If I have to disrupt routines and do not know exactly what will be required of us, for example, if my son is going on a school journey or has to go into hospital for surgery and I am unable to tell him what will happen and when – I tell him so. I describe it as an "adventure" and reassure him that whatever does happen I will be there and we will deal with it together. So he now has a picture (indeed many pictures) of what an "adventure" may be, but knows that he won't be abandoned whatever. I have never told him that something won't hurt if I know that it might. Having his trust is very precious to me and I have seen how difficult it has been for other people to gain even a fraction of it.

I think that it's part of the reason I feel so guilty when things have gone badly wrong for him at schools he has attended in the past. I feel that I have encouraged him to place his trust in people who were not worthy of it – they were just doing their jobs, I know, and when my son became an inconvenience, a problem, an obstacle, he was simply removed. For the greater good, of course.

*

Now

I would love to be able to stand at the pinnacle of my experience of caring for my son, like a mountaineer reaching the summit of Everest, and be able to say "Oh yes, we've done it – this is my great achievement", but in reality life continues to be a really hard struggle most of the time, trying to balance the needs of both my children and my husband, look after a home and the dozen other things that seem to need doing every day. I know that every busy mother would say exactly the same thing but parents of challenging children will understand that I am talking about a *qualitative* as well as a quantitative difference. I find that my experience of motherhood is so far removed from those of my contemporaries that sometimes I do not even bother joining in the conversations because it always sounds so bizarre to the parents whose main concerns are whether their children get invited to the right number of birthday parties or have the wrong sort of party bags or shoes or whether their children should do French or Spanish at school. I do try to join in and offer bright and friendly observations but then someone will ask about my family and suddenly we're in another country completely and no-one else can think of anything to say.

At the moment my son has all the negative teenage behaviour that comes with being 15, magnified exponentially by his autism – because he really cannot understand why there is any need for him to modify his behaviour just to keep the peace at school or at home. At times he seems to have regressed to a much earlier stage in his development – his behaviour is more aggressive and physical, his judgement is poor - in terms of being able to apply "common sense" in that he seems to have less capacity to know when he needs to ask what is appropriate behaviour. Wanting to manage one's own life without parental interference is a natural part of growing-up but when you are starting from a damaged viewpoint – the outcomes can be very worrying. My son's attempts to deal with a bullying situation in school without referring his intentions to me, nearly ended in disaster. He decided to take a knife to school. When I asked him why he did not discuss the matter with me first, he admitted that one of the reasons was that he knew it was a bad idea but did it anyway because he wanted to be seen as someone capable of looking after himself. Which he isn't.

The natural rebellious tendencies of teenage life make him nearly impossible to reason with. He used to acknowledge the superior wisdom of his mother without (much) question but now, like other parents, I hear "Oh you just don't know what it's like". However, unlike other parents, in our case, this is perfectly true. His experience of being a teenager is so different to my own that I cannot draw real parallels from my own happy, mildly mischievous, educationally successful early years. I really do not know what life is like for him. I know what he is missing though and I grieve for that every day.

He talks to me about wanting a girlfriend and has quite specific requirements on the matter – he wants to have a sexual relationship when he is older (16, he says) but he wants to have a proper girlfriend who will be interested in doing the things that he enjoys. He is concerned that if he gets married his wife might be upset when he wets the bed so he thinks it is best if he doesn't get married. Also he still takes all his Action Men to bed with him and I think she might have some issues there as well.

I have tried to explain that relationships come in all shapes and sizes and it may well be that he will be lucky enough to find someone to share his life with. However, he should realize that the kind of relationships he sees on the television or in movies are not like real relationships and that he only has to look at the real lives of the actors and actresses to see that it can be disastrous to be unrealistic.

When I think about my son having a girlfriend, I feel

a bit like Groucho Marx when he declared that he would not want to join any club that would have him as a member. I try to listen to my own advice to him but I find it really hard to imagine what kind of girl could accept him and all his difficult behaviour. He's a nice looking lad and he's bright and funny but to be brutally honest, I dread the thought of having two people to look after instead of one, for the rest of my life. Does that make me horrible? If that is what it takes to make him happy?

Employment is another major concern when we are discussing the future. He wants to be a film maker. He has his own video camera but is reluctant to use it (when I say "reluctant", I mean he will not use it because he has decided not to but cannot really explain why). He was unable to have a "normal" work experience placement but was found a place on a supported course where he can do a bit of work with film editing programmes – which he has loved. But this is such a long way from being able to get on in what is an extremely competitive and unforgiving profession. I am, however, encouraging him to follow his dream – even if it leads nowhere – because that has to be much better than not trying at all and if he is prepared to make the effort, I say good luck to him. He does have an amazingly accurate eye and a great attention to detail, his memory and his knowledge of film are quite astounding – so perhaps somewhere the perfect spot is waiting for him.

But the daily battles continue as they always have – it still takes around two hours to get him up, washed, dressed and fed every morning. I could do it more quickly if I did everything for him myself but I am still convinced that he will one day learn to do the things he has to do without me standing over him. No sign yet though and I spend every morning prompting and reminding him of what he is supposed to be doing – I lay out his clothes where he can lay his hands on them because he won't get them out for himself, I run his bath for him – because he forgets to turn off the water and has it too hot. I have to make sure that he has something to eat and drink because he will pretend that he has eaten when he hasn't and then feels ill later and doesn't know why.

I persevere with trying to improve and extend his skills. At the moment I am teaching him to cook and encouraging him to make a family meal once a week. At the last attempt he only ran upstairs crying three times because when the water started bubbling in the pan he thought it would boil over and put the flame out and the gas would explode. So he just ran away. He is equally worried about water and the electric oven because of the danger of electrocution. He will not eat mushrooms in case they have somehow become accidentally mixed with toadstools (unless it's mushroom soup or sauce, which it seems, is OK). He will not use dirty crockery (I agree with him there) but minute flaws in the glaze have to be examined so closely that I feel like just chucking them on the floor (just to be on the safe side!) It can take him half an hour to find four plates to his satisfaction. As I have already mentioned, in trying to solve one problem, I seem to have created another.

I find it impossible to relate this dependant, unfocussed person with someone who will ever be able to care for themselves independently even at a basic self-care level, let alone make a home, find employment and form adult relationships. Again, I can hear a thousand other parents saying exactly the same thing – but as I have already said I am talking about a *qualitative* difference in how my son functions. It feels like he is not merely messy – he is incapable of being tidy. And he is not merely rude and aggressive – he really is incapable of caring how it makes me feel.

Sometimes he can appear "normal" and he can sound "normal". Some of our less astute friends think he is wonderful and cannot begin to grasp the enormity of the problem – unless they are treated to one of his outbursts, which leaves them open-mouthed and quivering. There's no question of "my Robert's just like that" then, I can tell you!

It is not all doom and gloom – one could simply not survive like that. But I suspect that it is easier to find the humour in situations with the perspective of time. Nevertheless, we are still a family and we mess around and have fun together. Once the front door is shut for the evening and the trials of the day dealt with, it is much easier to relax just a little. I avoid alcohol just in case I need to deal with a situation that requires me to have all my wits about me – so I tend to spend the evenings just doing things with the children. I am lucky that my boys seem to enjoy each other's company most of the time – so life could be a lot more difficult and I have a lot to thank my younger son for.

He is an absolute star with his brother and I sometimes think he has even more patience with him than I do. He has put up with so much already – not least being nearly always shoved into the background while everyone talks about, deals with and worries about his big brother. He just quietly gets on with his own stuff – he has washed and dressed himself in the mornings without a fuss, well, forever. This alone has probably saved what little remains of my sanity.

I wish that schools and other professionals who deal with children would recognise the pressure that the siblings of children with significant disabilities are under. When my younger son was much younger, he often used to copy behaviour or mannerisms from his older brother – because that's what little children do. Try to persuade an over-enthusiastic SEN specialist that copying an autistic behaviour does not actually make you autistic – well, you get the picture. I'm sure some people think it's catching.

I am not without blame myself either. Every little thing, with my younger son, sent me to the GP asking for a referral. He had problems saying his Gs and Ks and I was pushing for speech therapy. The SEN specialist at the school said he was behind in his reading when he was 5 and I was immediately pushing for an assessment from the

Ed Psych – it turned out he was five or six months ahead on his reading age, in fact. As soon as the school had been told that his brother was autistic, my younger son was marked out as a "potential problem" and every little hiccup regarded as the possible onset of something more sinister. But, as I say, I am not entirely innocent on that score, either. I felt guilty that I had failed to pick up on my older son's problems straight away and I was determined to make sure I did not do this with my younger son. But who wants to grow up under a microscope?

The Future?

Having meandered my way into the more or less present, I wonder what I can say that I have learned along the way. That trying to solve one problem often causes others to appear. That choosing one's battles is an essential survival skill. That being positive does work but be prepared to be brought back to earth with a bump if you want to get any help at all because you will have to go through every horrible, degrading, embarrassing detail of your family's life before anyone will even listen. I hate encountering "new" professionals because I know that I will have to drag out all the horrible experiences I have had for the past 15 years and parade them in front of yet another stranger.

I put so much emphasis on the positive aspects of my son's condition – in order for us to survive as a loving family – that I find it extremely harrowing to have to go into "negative" mode. I have built up walls and barriers that would shame the Thames barrage to protect myself from dwelling on the negative aspects of having an autistic child. When people ask me what my life is like I find myself telling them about all the wonderful things my son is capable of. I tell them all the funny, clever things he has said and how loving and imaginative he is. And this is genuinely how I feel, but it is how I *have to feel* in order to keep going. When I have to sit down and fill in forms which require me to justify the fact that my son needs someone with him all the time, that he can't cross the road by himself, or dress himself, or wash himself, without supervision. That he can't nip to the shops or the library without being taken. That he is liable to wander off, can't remember what he is supposed to be doing, gets frightened among people and is liable to lash out or run into the road – I feel like I am being torn in half. I feel like I am betraying him – because, although I know living with him places a heavy burden on me and the rest of the family – that is not how I feel about him, most of the time. I find it a difficult and harrowing experience and I consider myself to be a confident, well-educated and articulate person.

I know that I will never know peace of mind again in my lifetime. I know that my dying thoughts will almost certainly be about what will happen to my poor lad when I'm gone (assuming I am not being eaten by a lion or wondering where that lorry came from). I think of my younger son and worry about the burden that I have placed on him because I do expect him to look out for his older brother, if I am honest, and hate the thought that his life, too, will be defined and constrained by my other son's disability. After the age of 16, when "society" no longer has a legal obligation to provide some social and academic activity for my son, I know that his future is uncertain to say the least (I am avoiding the word "bleak" because it is too obviously the word needed here). He may be able to start a college course, but without adequate support, the chances of him being able to finish it are slim. As for employment – I am told that there are sympathetic employers out there somewhere. But how would my son actually get to his place of work, even assuming work was available? The professionals I ask about this say "oh, there are schemes, oh, don't worry, there are places" which, of course, translates as "why should I care, he'll be off *my* books by then." I may be wrong. I would quite like to be wrong.

Jane and James' Story

It is good to tell our story, because the pressure of keeping silent becomes just another thing that we have to learn to cope with. On the other hand, we are stepping out of the shadows and into the light. We are revealing our wounds, our scars, and we do this tentatively. We write the words and then we gaze warily about us as if anticipating punishment or loss. We would really prefer to keep all this to ourselves, smiling relentlessly and telling everyone that things are fine when in fact we are struggling just to get through each day.

"Louise building tower. Louise building tower"
(From my diary- August 29th 1993)
"Very, very happy"- (diary January 29th 1994)

Birth- Four Years

"I never thought I'd see myself looking like this!"
I remember saying these words after catching a glimpse of myself in a shop window a few days before our daughter's birth. I was nearly 38 and was vastly pregnant due to the growth of an enormous fibroid alongside my unborn child. This same fibroid had threatened to prevent me from even getting pregnant but was now only significant because its presence meant that I'd be having Louise by elective C-section.

It was a beautiful birth and we were ecstatically happy with our new baby. Friends and family rejoiced too having never expected this from us, a couple who met and married in our thirties. We were an adventurous couple, living and working in

Tanzania and then Japan in International Schools.

It was to Tanzania that we took Louise at 6 weeks old to return to our previous jobs and to give Louise the chance to experience a largely natural life, away from the influences of T.V., consumerism and the "I want" culture. James had travelled on ahead of me to start the new term. I arrived with Louise a few weeks later suddenly cut off from my own family support network and dependent on friends in the community undergoing a sort of baby-boom at the time, Penelope Leach's book and, hopefully, common sense. I also carried with me vials of vaccine for the first triple vaccinations and some clean syringes. In a country rife with AIDS it was advisable to trust one of the local missionary doctors to administer these rather than the local hospital.

Then I found I had to try and get Louise into the routine everyone had told me about. This was not easy. Louise liked to feed for enormous lengths of time before she would sleep. She did not sleep for very long and then would like more feeding. She would invariably wake in the night at least four or five times, requiring a long feed before she would go back to sleep. James was working and I was on maternity leave. We were both exhausted. Louise didn't like to be left alone, to be put down, to be away from being held. I could not do anything without having her attached to me in some way.

My return to work was hard and traumatic on account of lack of sleep and the normal rigours of dealing with a young baby. I have a photo of myself holding Louise at 4 months old, tears streaming down my face as I prepared for work one morning after another night of maybe four hours sleep.

However, during those first few years Louise thrived and grew. She reached all the usual milestones at the correct time and walked at eleven months. Prior to that, she had never really crawled but performed a strange sort of knee shuffle. Just another of our quirky little baby's quirky little ways, we thought. She started talking and spoke with the local accent that the ex-pat children developed, mixing her English with Swahili words for common events and objects. I described her as "relentlessly cheerful". Always on the go, hugely energetic with a huge personality seemingly developing.

There were signs, though. Signs that gave us a little cloud of anxiety from time to time but which could have been part of "normal" development. "Playing" with the other children in the playgroup involved lots of physical interaction which they, and their mothers, didn't always appreciate. A good shove. Or a quick bash on the head. She was a runner, too. Take your eyes off her and she'd be racing off, oblivious to where she was going, oblivious to danger. Running with a curious splayed-legs gait that a physiotherapist friend commented on. Seemingly very slow at developing the drawing skills that her peers were already displaying during their toddler-hood. Still waking through the night every few hours. Watching the same video over and over again until we knew it off by heart as well and could quote from it verbatim.

When Louise was almost three, we left Tanzania and moved to new teaching jobs and new lives in Taiwan. We were looking forward to introducing our daughter to some of the ways of the more modern world. Such as continual water and electricity. In England that year we had our usual health-visitor check. No concerns were raised. No alarms sounded.

Taiwan was hot, crowded and polluted and we had to live on the sixth floor of a block of flats. A far cry from the space and light of Tanzania. We tried to introduce her to the children of colleagues of a similar age. However, play dates were invariably disastrous as Louise just did not seem to know how to play. Social occasions with other families started to be a bit isolating, a bit of a disaster. Other children would play together happily their parents relaxing and socialising, while one of us would have to trail Louise to make sure she wasn't creating havoc.

She was enrolled at a local Chinese nursery as were many of the ex-pat children. Louise, tall for her age with blonde curls and an angelic face, was particularly prized and fussed over at the nursery. But we began to hear the same story again and again. Can't settle. Needs lots of attention. Can't do, developmentally, what the other children can do in terms of fine and gross motor skills. Can't pedal a little bike. Can't draw anything representational. We just wished everyone would leave our daughter alone and see her for what she was – a unique and sparky individual who was just not fitting the mould. Her language skills were great. She was beginning to read. She was very funny and exuberant. She just loved to swim and was obviously very comfortable in water. But she just wasn't the same as everyone else's child. Louise was starting to be different...

People were beginning to tell us how to be firmer with our own child, how to be better at parenting, how to stop her running around and being noisy and how to sleep properly and how to play properly and how to be like everyone else. With Louise all social situations were potentially stressful, which meant that since her birth, what was once for us a lively and happy social life, was dead. When we were with other people there was more or less constant stress as we tried to watch and monitor her behaviour, which was frequently inappropriate. To be with other people meant putting ourselves through the strain of being hypervigilant and it was exhausting, very upsetting and often ultimately unsuccessful. People were usually bewildered and exasperated by Louise or what they perceived as her parents' lack of control or interest. We no longer had anything which resembled a normal social life. We were starting to feel like we were fighting for Louise's right to be who she was and defending our competency to parent.

*

"She's SO ready for school"- Health Visitor
"I love you in the whole world" (diary- August 27th 1995)
"Am I shiverin' with life? I'm shiverin' with life" (diary- May 31st 1996)
"You know, in England Louise would be in a special school"- Louise's first teacher, Reception Class Taipei British School. October 1995

Starting School(s) 1995-98

At the end of our first year in Taiwan we returned to England for the summer holidays to see family and friends. As usual we saw our local Health Visitor who commented on Louise's readiness for school. She was now four and, although very young, was ready to start school in Taiwan under the British system in the British school where I taught.

We thought that now that Louise was going to be in school under her native system, everything would be all right. In fact, everything was starting to be all wrong. The Reception Class teacher, who 13 years later I would still like to inflict great pain upon, seemed to take an instant dislike to Louise. Apparently, Louise couldn't wait in a line, would scribble on other children's' work, couldn't sit still for long, was constantly disruptive etc. etc. We were continually getting negative feedback about our much loved daughter and we couldn't understand it. It's almost impossible to perceive how this lonely and anxious girl could be perceived as a trouble-maker, but her teacher was convinced exactly of that. It's another area of almost inexpressible pain for us, that Louise's first experience of school was to be constantly bullied and shouted at; to have no encouragement but only persistent punishment; to have all her sad and brittle hopes scorned and destroyed. We still have copies of the letters we wrote complaining of the vicious cruelty of her first teacher; who knows how much irreparable damage was done to Louise's self-confidence by the sadistic bitch? Why were we getting it so wrong? Why couldn't people appreciate her for who she was? Was it a question of conformity?

When this teacher told me out of the blue one afternoon that she thought that Louise would be in a special school were we in England, I unravelled. I remember sobbing over the Head of School, a personal friend. I was supposed to be at work and was being told this in the middle of my working day.

It was decided to let Louise be "observed" by the Educational Psychologist equivalent at the local Counselling Centre. I still have his report which remarks that "Asperger's Syndrome can be ruled out". He suggested that Louise may have ADHD and thus we embarked on the long journey of different diagnoses and different "experts" giving different opinions of our daughter's differences.

Of course, James and I had never even heard of Asperger's Syndrome and only vaguely of ADHD which seemed to be a purely American affliction. We instantly read up on these and were horrified to think that our daughter could possibly be SO different.

We took Louise out of my school at the end of that year. She was now eligible to start in the Kindergarten class at the American School where James taught and we thought a fresh new start where Louise's cleverness would be recognised and celebrated would make all the difference. She was reading very well, seemingly practically self taught, although writing was very difficult for her and numbers seemed to make very little sense to her. Well, writing is always hard for left handers and maths was never my strong subject. Things you tell yourself to make everything all right.

To our horror, Louise's place at the American School wasn't guaranteed. Colleagues there already knew of her through social interactions and she had to be seemingly *tested* to make sure she could attend. She was given a place but right from the start expressions like Red Flag were used, inattention, spatial awareness, proprioception[1], social skills, developmental delays…. We were summoned to meetings with teachers, Principals, counsellors. We couldn't understand why her extraordinary reading skills couldn't be appreciated more and why people kept telling us that things were wrong, wrong, wrong…as if it was our fault… as if we were inadequate parents. Louise kept getting it wrong at all social occasions as well. Any party she was invited to I had to go along too, as

---

[1] Proprioception – sensory information which travels electrically via neurons to the brain giving us a sense of our body in space.

her minder. To make sure she didn't do too many inappropriate things. Finally, it was suggested that she be monitored at school for ADHD. Attention Deficit Hyperactivity Disorder.

This was duly done with the appropriate Connors Scale paperwork and an appointment was made for Louise to see the (American trained) Paediatric Psychiatrist at Taipei Children's Hospital. Yet another expert, yet another session of tests. A diagnosis of ADHD resulted. A prescription for Ritalin. For God's sake, for an exuberant 5year old, who couldn't be exactly the same as everyone else's 5 year olds! Recommendations for star charts, behaviour charts, charts for good, charts for bad.

So we started to drug our daughter. Friends told us we would start to see miracles happen before our very eyes. Our problems would all be solved. Louise would begin to conform, she would write with incredibly neat handwriting, she would listen attentively to her teachers, all her motor problems would be over.

Louise became what her teacher wanted her to be. A very quiet, very still child. She didn't roll off her chair any more. She didn't shout out. She also lost her appetite during the day. She also became very angry later on in the afternoon when the medication wore off. She threw colossal tantrums in the street. I joined various emerging internet parent groups of children diagnosed with ADHD. I began to be an expert on ADHD, the brain, Ritalin, stimulants etc.

etc. Louise started to attend weekly sensory integration sessions after another battery of tests. Her system became used to the drug. She needed more to keep up the appearances of being an everyday child. We became advocates of Ritalin, believing what the experts told us.

But the miracles didn't happen.

Toward the beginning of Louise's second year at the American School when she was in First Grade[1] we were called in to see the Elementary School Principal. He told us that we would have to make other arrangements for Louise at the end of the school year. They couldn't help her any more, they didn't have the facilities. We should go and live somewhere near a big teaching hospital where we could get Louise properly diagnosed. We might never know what it was she has. But she couldn't stay there. And neither could we, in that case. James was the Head of the Art Department at the biggest and best International School in the Far East. His job was huge and prestigious and he was magnificent at it. I was scrabbling around at supply teaching work, hating schools, hating teachers, hating myself for being one, hating everyone. Louise was being rejected. Again. Our relationship was starting to suffer.

*

---

[1]   First grade – children are usually between six and seven years old.

Anna Van Der Post et al

Wrong Diagnoses and their repercussions especially on our relationship 1998- 2002

We moved to The Netherlands in 1998, our relationship tattered and torn, ready to start work in another International School. We felt battered and bruised. Telling ourselves that we would get a better understanding of Louise's condition in Europe, that the liberal Dutch would surely be much more helpful and understanding of educational differences. The school was already prepared for Louise's ADHD and declared it could cope well and that Louise was very welcome. Hope at last.

In England, that summer, I took Louise to a private Educational Psychologist for an assessment to take to her new school. We had a new diagnosis to take with us. Severe Dyspraxia. A new syndrome, a new set of rules to look up, to become familiar with. A new report which, again, didn't tell the world that really our daughter was just a misunderstood genius and that it didn't matter.

That summer I also took Louise to a Cranio Sacral Therapist. I took Louise to a Behavioural and Dietary Therapist. She declared Louise was allergic to potatoes and tomatoes and dairy produce. She prescribed Louise homeopathic remedies and sound therapy with special CDs and headphones. We did everything suggested but they made not the slightest bit of difference to Louise apart from depriving her of her favourite foods. We are such easy targets. All someone has to say is that they can help Louise, and of course we will pay all if not more than we can afford.

It was that summer that she started her curious garden jogs. Running up and down the garden, clapping her hands above her head, waving them wildly, mouthing something to herself. "Telling stories" she said she was doing when asked. (She still does this, ten years later)

We moved to Holland taking Louise's Ritalin prescription with us. Taking all the baggage of rejection, inadequacy, fear of the future and helplessness with us. Our own relationship imploded spectacularly for a while amidst all this.

We stayed in Holland for four years. During that time Louise was possibly happier at school than she has been before or since. She was certainly different from the rest of her peers with her social inadequacies and her educational differences. But she was more accepted although very much on the fringes of social interaction. She made her first (and only, so far) good friend who lived next door and was "different" too. (But not SO different...) We talked to Louise's class about Dyspraxia and what it meant and about her differences. It was at that time that she started pulling out her eyelashes. Adding this habit to her already bitten down nails and regular hand flapping gave her a markedly strange appearance. Her teacher at the time did a bit of research and declared that she thought Louise might be autistic.

We were terrified of this new word and again

researched all we could find of this new condition. We comforted ourselves with the reassurance that this could not be so because, apparently, children with autism were not emotional. Louise was emotional and loving, just didn't get things quite right. We always had to rehearse and role play social situations with her and encourage her to make eye contact because that's what people do.

At this time, Louise was attending more Sensory Integration sessions arranged through the local Health Service. She was still taking Ritalin prescribed by the local GP although we had secretly started to phase it out as it didn't seem to be making any difference whether Louise took it or not. She had grown to such an extent that the dose was probably totally inadequate but the Dutch attitude to medication of this sort was rather disapproving so we felt all right to take our own decisions. It was also arranged that Louise be tested at the local Children's Hospital to see what diagnosis they could come up with.

After another battery of tests we were given the experts' opinions in a cheerless hospital office while Louise played outside. They told us that, in their opinion, Louise had Asperger's Syndrome, that she would never function normally in society, that she would be better off going into a home where she could be trained and taught necessary social skills. And this was the so-called liberal Dutch telling us this! They were suggesting that we put our daughter into residential care!!!

We both cried in each other's arms that night, out of Louise's earshot. A very bleak future picture had been painted but we could never accept that. We rejected their diagnosis putting it down to cultural testing differences and never went back there again. In fact we told no-one about this diagnosis and kept the horrible secret to ourselves. Bizarre in the extreme.

We also saw another private Educational Psychologist during that year who again didn't wave a magic wand. I really was expecting this one to say that everyone else had made a really serious mistake about Louise and that everything would be all right. But she didn't.

*

"Maybe you should start looking for another school for Louise" - Special Needs Teacher.
"It's heartbreaking seeing friends play together"
"I hate this autism" Louise- March 2008

Returning to England- The Diagnosis
Living with a teenager (2002-2008)

In 2002, we left Holland and came back "home" to England after 18 years overseas. It was to be the first time that Louise had lived in England for any extended period. James and I both had new jobs at an International School just outside London and Louise was entitled to a free place there as the child of teachers. We had explained about her

ADHD and about her Dyspraxia diagnoses but not her Asperger's because that didn't exist as far as we were concerned. We knew that this was a big gamble accepting a place at this school for Louise but it was to be a short term measure while we found out what else to do. We were foreigners in a way, returning to live in our home country, and didn't know what else to do. Besides the school had said that they had a very good Special Needs department and that they knew all about ADHD and Dyspraxia. So we forged a bit of Louise's last school report that the admissions department wanted to see and everything was set.

"New" country, new school, new home, my father died and "they" were on to Louise's case more or less straight away. It is a very academic school and it very quickly became apparent that Louise was struggling both socially and academically. She was teased and bullied despite James and me going in and giving our "Dyspraxia" talk to her class. It was heartbreaking to see her walking alone across the campus or to be approached by yet another teacher who wanted "a quick word about Louise" in the middle of the working day.

Just after Christmas we were told at yet another meeting about Louise that perhaps this school wasn't the best place for her after all. What did we want for her? They only wanted what was best for her (as if we didn't) and that she could only stay until the end of the year. More tears, more fears, more changes, more rejection all round. While keeping this news from Louise and keeping everything on an even keel.

It was suggested that approaches be made to the local authority to have Louise assessed with a view to eventually getting a Statement of Educational Needs. And there we were yet again the bad, uncaring parents who didn't do everything quite right. We had to go to our local GP first to start the ball rolling. I think she was the first person in all those years who treated us like intelligent beings. We told her our long story. She listened. She cared. She got us an appointment quite soon after with the paediatric consultant at the local Hospital. He was the second person in all those years who treated us like intelligent beings (so you see, it can be done). After an afternoon with him, he declared he thought Louise had Asperger's Syndrome. But he told us to go away and read Tony Atwood's book and see if we agreed with him. Meanwhile he gave us the name and number of the Outreach Teacher from the school for Autistic Children which was very nearby (but which we had never heard of). He gave us information. He gave us hope. He was lovely with Louise.

Anyway, Louise was visited by the Local Authority's assessment person who decided that she didn't even need to do that, despite the latest diagnosis, and that Louise wouldn't get a statement. So we are in free fall again, and wondering what to do next. The good thing – maybe – is that whatever Louise's problems are they do not appear to be sufficiently serious or complex to warrant County Council getting her Statemented. Or maybe they just don't want another child on their books. Maybe their books are full and their quota has already been reached. As time went on we reconsidered the initial relief that we felt when we were informed that Louise would not be statemented. Perhaps we were a bit too quick to see it as proof that Louise was not so disabled after all – we were fooling ourselves and being foolishly optimistic.

Fact is – she was refused only because the council is breaking its own rules, trying to avoid having to pay for another statemented child. Thanks Local Authority. The local Secondary school refused outright to even consider Louise as they said that they certainly didn't have the facilities for her needs. Thank God.

We applied to go to Tribunal and had the date set and prepared the necessary paperwork. It had taken at least ten meetings with various professionals to reach this point. The outreach teacher from the autistic school came and observed Louise in our school and agreed with the diagnosis. My sister had rung the school and talked to them because James and I were almost at the end. Almost couldn't tell the story any more. We had been fighting on her behalf for years. Told it so many times through the years. We were just so tired of the whole f...ing business. This is the tiredness that makes lying down and curling up into a foetal position such a tempting idea. So desperate were we that we actually discussed group suicide. All of us in the car with the engine running and exhaust pipe through a window. That is how desperate it can get.

The Deputy Head of the autistic school came to our house and observed Louise. "Do you think she's one of yours?" we asked. "Oh, yes," she replied. She wanted to give Louise a place in the school but couldn't without a statement. It was a Catch 22 situation. We wrote to our MP and told him the whole story. He said he would look into our case.

We were invited to meet with the Local Authority Head of Special Needs at the Council Offices. She told us that our own school had written to her telling her that we were unable to accept their recommendations and that we were in a state of denial - did we know about this? Of course we didn't. They had recommended that Louise be enrolled in a local primary school to repeat the final year. We were apparently in denial that Louise had problems and that we were unable to see that the school could not meet her needs. Well of course we knew and accepted that Louise had problems but we didn't know what else to do or where to go. No assessment – no statement – no school to go to. The Head of Special Needs met Louise and told us, there and then, that she would be recommending that Louise be statemented if we were to withdraw our tribunal application. We are all at the mercy of bureaucracy, a lack of transparency and officialdom.

Louise started at the autistic school in September of that year. It's hard to compress the agony of those first months in England into a few paragraphs. The despair and the guilt and the fear and the utter loneliness. But for the very first time in Louise's lifetime we encountered people who did want to help us, who treated us like good, caring parents and who most importantly, wanted to help Louise, too. Because our lives have so little fun or positive things, the tiniest kindness, that to others would hardly be noticed, take on huge proportions and this is worth mentioning because those involved in our children's care can easily make a big difference.

It took a long, long time and many "experts" and many diagnoses and many tests and many waiting rooms and many moments of sadness and despair. Our experiences with experts have been consistently negative throughout the years of our dealings with them, and we have little faith either in their judgement or their humanity. They have seemed disinterested, aloof, unfriendly, imperious, unfeeling, insensitive and unkind: experts in China, experts in Holland and experts in England. We are left in corridors or hallways or waiting rooms with our arms around each other while the experts shuffle away or look on somewhat surprised by our emotion and our despair, perhaps embarrassed that we don't wait to get home before weeping.

Over the years, between them, they have devised a list of things that they think Louise should focus on. All the ideas, goals and objectives on the list are completely familiar to us, of course; it's a list we could just as easily have given them....We go through the list with them and are very polite – at the end of the meetings we actually thank them for compiling the list. We could have compiled it in ten minutes, and its taken them six months, but no matter.

Louise has now been at the school for 5 years. It's taken a hell of a long time to repair the damage of the years. I often wonder what happened to the sparky little girl who seemed to be "so ready for school" at the age of four. She's now 17 and the future beckons. For the first time in her life she has ambition and wants to go to college when she's finished at school in 18 months time. I don't know how realistic this is as she still can't even cross the road by herself but we've started the process with meetings with the various agencies concerned.

She is such a mixture of little girl and moody teenager. Loud techno music will blast out from her room but at the same time she is still obsessively collecting plastic figures from her favourite TV series. She is tall and statuesque and just starting to lose weight and take shape yet still wants to wear nothing but tracksuit pants, t-shirts and trainers. She blushes at boys she likes the look of out in the "real" world, yet imagines herself in love with her favourite cartoon character.

I find myself grinding my teeth in sheer frustration and utter boredom as we trail through Woolworths looking at the toys as we have for so many years. Yet I have to tell myself this is not about me but about giving her the reassurance of routine that she still so desperately craves and needs.

The same routines. The same words spoken. The same, the same - but so different.

Right Here, Right Now

Here we are at home, the three of us, coming up for Christmas again

We haven't been on holiday this year. We haven't had a holiday for years. I tell myself it's because I hate flying or that after years of travelling I prefer to be at home. When James and I have the "Why don't we go on holiday?" discussion though, it invariably comes down to the same thing. Because Louise's ROUTINE would be completely disrupted, completely up the spout. Without her familiar surroundings, animals, possessions she becomes distressed and edgy. She needs vast amounts of comfort, reassurance and love. She will sometimes erupt into a distressing "meltdown" of tears and bereft sadness. And it is the saddest thing in the world to see the mouth of this beautiful teenager turn down like a little girl and to see the tears stream down her cheeks. It breaks my heart.

Then there is the explaining to do. Telling complete strangers that the reason why your child might seem to be spectacularly rude or particularly impolite is because she has a developmental disorder which means that she cannot perform those everyday social interactions which are practically instinctive for the neurotypicals. (However much you tell them, though, they are probably secretly thinking that with a bit of discipline and perseverance those good manners and social graces could surely be taught.)

Haunting me down the years are those accusations of "bad parenting" from those whose paths we have crossed. from family, to friends to colleagues who thought perhaps we were "spoiling " our little girl.

So, if we were on this mythical holiday, then what would we DO all day? James and I have had years of Theme Parks and Disneylands and swimming pools. It can be tiring and boring for us, her parents, doing the things we've done for simply years as the three of us grow older. There, again, we are the only people who can listen to her special language and limited topics of conversation.
"What colour is the cat?" might mean "I'm hungry and tired and I need to go home now"
"How many cats have we got?" could mean "I really need to go and be alone now".
"What colour are Daisy's whiskers?" might mean "Just give me a bit of reassurance that I'm doing this right".

And so on.

As for social occasions….
I think Asperger's Syndrome is infectious. We like to stay close to home where all is safe and familiar. The opportunities are a bit limited anyway as any kind of "respite" is simply not available. It's OK. It's what we've grown accustomed to. Anyway, a family member asked us to her son's 21st birthday party

last year but asked us not to bring Louise as it would be "inappropriate". Ok, so if that's how you all feel then let it be. They certainly miss out on the "other" side of Asperger's by not even trying to get close to our daughter. For she has a remarkable insight into people and will come out with some cracking observations that leave you wondering at her perspicacity. There is a spiritual side to her which reveals itself in an intense remark or strange conversation. An ability to get right down to the bare bones of an issue which can pass other people by. A fine lavatorial sense of humour and a sense of the ridiculous which can leave her helpless with mirth. That's the side people miss out on when they just observe her as Jane and James' rather awkward family member and miss out on getting to know her.

On the other hand, we are fiercely protective of our daughter. We love her so completely, we understand her, we support her and we think we have done a pretty good job. We are a solid trio bound to each other by love. As she transitions into adulthood she is changing, she is beginning to want her voice to be heard and to be listened to.

We've come a long way.

*

Rachel's Story

Just William

Introduction

I've been fighting on William's behalf now for the best part of the past decade. It comes and goes in waves - my attempts to rally the education department, the social services and the medical professionals into action. I usually come away feeling that the situation is hopeless. No-one knows anything, no-one has any idea on how to deal with the situation, certainly no-one has any answers, the buck is passed, and I'm left with feelings of isolation, anger, frustration and resentment, finishing off with resignation and a naïve hope that everything will sort itself out in the end.

We've visited numerous medical professionals over the years who have carried out both cursory investigations and in depth analyses. But it seems no matter what the results of the tests are, William's situation remains the same. He's been given IQ tests by an educational psychologist, and the results were that William had a high IQ. One doctor found that he is left handed, legged, eyed and eared. We've been encouraged to complete the Connor's questionnaire for diagnosis of ADHD several times, which is always fairly inconclusive with responses between school and home differing widely. Regular visits to the child and family clinic render William monosyllabic and bored. At family therapy, which we attended after a suggestion by his current paediatric consultant, he refused to participate after the first session and went to sit in the car.

We've also been visited at home by numerous people. Social workers (or the social police who, it seems, only appear when something goes wrong, except at weekends) have provided no actual, practical service to us whatsoever, even though they have often mentioned a mentoring service in which I have expressed an interest. Educational psychologists, whose sole function in my experience, is to act as the LEA's go-between, liaising with the Youth Offending Team, amongst others. They all ask me the same endless personal questions, and I feel drained having to go through my, and William's, life history again and again to complete strangers. It's all the more draining, knowing it will make no difference to our situation. It's just another instance of lack of knowledge sharing in my mind. And the individuals are not concerned about our situation; it's just their job. One social worker came to visit us at home and spent the afternoon asking me very personal questions. I met her subsequently at a review meeting at William's school and she couldn't even deign to acknowledge me. Their priorities appeared bureaucratic: complete assessment number 53; attend the latest multi-disciplinary meeting, but do not suggest or provide anything that would create a difference or effect outcomes. It was quite obvious William and I were just a case for her, our lives contained in her buff folder.

*

Ages 0 – 5 years

Life at Home

My pregnancy with William was extremely uneventful. He was born slightly over term and was delivered by forceps, but apart from that everything was normal. He was a beautiful baby and young boy and a lovely companion most of the time. He was a pleasure and delight to me and his grandparents. He passed all his milestones early and impressed the health visitor with his skills. He was very quick to start talking and his insatiable curiosity led him to ask "why?" about everything that was said or that he saw:
"How wide is the Severn Bridge?"
"How big is the sea?"
"Do dead people have Christmas?"
"Are sparrows nice birds?"

Pushing him along in his buggy he'd be constantly chatting away and when queuing in a shop once, the lady in front turned round and was aghast to be told he was only just two, exclaiming that he was far too small to be talking like that. He loved being read to and, once at primary school, learnt to read at a remarkable speed. In fact at that age he seemed able to absorb any information he was given.
'William is rather a live wire. Can I cope with questions from 7 in the morning to 7 at night?'
May 1995

As a young boy I remember him having an innocent

obsession with pipes. Pipes of any kind – drain pipes, exhaust pipes, also cables, which lead onto an obsession with electrics. He wired a plug when he was two years old – correctly as well. I can remember him constantly plugging and unplugging items – radios etc., and me trying to tell him that he was not to do this. In retrospect this was perhaps the first instance of any problems with him. I couldn't get him to accept that when I said "No", it meant that he was not to do something. He was intent on fiddling with plugs. No, was not an option, so I just had to compromise and explain to him that he had to ensure the socket was switched off before he plugged anything in - and this worked.

'I'm not sure whether he's ignoring me or genuinely can't hear me when I ask him to do something'.
March 1997

On one occasion around the same age, he wired a plug on to one end of a piece of cable and plugged it into a socket, then wired a plug on to the other end, went into another room and also plugged that end into a socket. When he turned the socket on there was a loud pop. Luckily the electrics were still intact, it was just the cable that had burnt out. He didn't do this again, so I think he learnt that it was not a particularly good idea.

I would buy him toys as normal, but William always took them apart with a screwdriver. I'm not sure if he was finding out how they worked, or whether it was just for the pleasure of unscrewing all the little screws he could find, or if he just got bored with them. I had a box full of toy parts, which I thought he might make one day into another super-toy. I ended up just throwing them all away realising that the dismantling was more fun that the assembling, or re-assembling. I suppose another parent might wonder why I let him do this: it wasn't a question of "letting" him. I tried to explain that if he took it apart then it would no longer work, but that wasn't important to him. He still takes things apart to this day, but now it's on a bigger scale. He's probably carried out his forensic examination on 4 or 5 computers now. Luckily I used to work with computers and there were always old ones looking for sanctuary. I have still not got to the bottom of why he takes everything apart.

His favourite and enduring toy up until he was about 14 was Lego. He could build things and take them apart to his heart's content and nothing was broken.

He may have been difficult but, in retrospect, to me it was just normal – I had nothing to compare him with and I loved him dearly. He was bright, clever, quick, eager to learn about everything and I felt very proud of him.

*

Ages 5 – 12 years

Things started to go wrong pretty quickly once he started school . Even in reception his teacher often called me in after class to have 'a word.' It never seemed very important then. After all, I knew he was a very bright little boy and had no problems academically. What if he did talk too much? He was four! Full of life and curiosity. He was even then accused by his teacher of being disruptive and silly, of not joining in with the songs, or doing what he was supposed to do.

'William's teacher called me in after school this afternoon: "William does get very silly at times and I sometimes wonder what's going on in his head"'
Jan 1998

As he progressed through primary school it became more and more obvious that William was not quite like the other children. He was on another wavelength. I'm not sure what the rest of his class thought of him, but he was certainly never invited to parties, and usually when it was someone's birthday the whole class would be invited. He was never bullied, though. In fact he was always totally confident and unselfconscious, just more wrapped up in his own agendas where other children did not figure.

'William's teacher says she finds it very difficult to get through to him. He's quite isolated as he doesn't communicate with the other children.'
June 1998

I don't believe there were any specific triggers for William's behavioural problems at school. He was so keen to start school and had such an insatiable curiosity about everything. He wanted to write stories, do maths problems, listen to stories and make Lego models, but the actuality of life in the classroom did not match his expectations. I think he got bored with the repetitive nature of lessons and was never that much into colouring-in. He knew that $2 + 2 = 4$, and wanted to move on but was held back. He'd started writing me basic stories at an early age at home, but repetitive handwriting and maths exercises made him stop completely. A note from his teacher when he was 4 ½: - "William loves writing, knows his sounds and forms his letters correctly".

I found him one morning before school, when he was about six years old, with 20 or 30 sheets of plain paper. On each he drew a large circle in the middle and at the bottom he wrote "Name: _____". He was setting work for the other children in his class. He wanted them each to draw a road sign.

When he was seven I have a note in my diary:
He said *"I'm going to take a chalk to school and write everywhere – Stop the war in Kosovo"*,
"Why?" I asked.
"So the military action doesn't blow up all of Kosovo".
He was very aware of the world around him, liked watching the news and took a keen interest in current affairs.

By the age of eight he refused to write at all.

His problems attracted the attention of the educational psychologist who carried out various IQ tests on William, confirming that he was in the top 4% of the population. Nothing changed at school, however, as a result of these tests. I don't think they knew what to do.

Towards the end of his time at this school, I was called in one afternoon after an incident in which he'd "completely trashed" the classroom. The school reported: "Our concerns were heightened by his continued behaviour – he used to bark, jump around like a kangaroo and was very difficult to contain within the confines of the classroom. One afternoon he tipped a box of coins onto his head, kept the box on his head and began swimming amongst the coins... He jumped from one table to another and was becoming a danger to himself and others. At this point he trashed the classroom and the children were removed for their safety..." On arriving, I saw William looking washed out, pale and drawn as if he'd had some kind of fit, a rage. I took him in my arms and he calmed immediately. There seemed to be no trigger for this outburst and once started, no one at the school was able to stop him, let alone calm him, and as a result William was excluded for five days. Since that time, these episodes increased in their frequency and ferocity with the object of his aggression frequently being members of staff. It's almost as if he's possessed by a demon. Later on I'd get phone calls from the school and I wondered if they were talking about someone else. Perhaps they were phoning the wrong mother.

A major characteristic of William's behaviour, especially when he was younger, and up until very recently, seems to have been his 'idées fixes'. Once he gets an idea in his head, it is very difficult to re-direct his energy and focus. Indeed a major characteristic of Asperger's syndrome is the inability to switch easily between tasks. This does seem to contradict his ADHD diagnosis in that, if he is involved and absorbed in his chosen task, he can continue at it completely focussed for several hours – or longer, hence the ambiguous answers to the Connors questionnaire. This could often be an advantage – he would occupy himself for whole afternoons, days even, constructing various Lego machines – which was fine as long as nothing else needed doing. Scheduled events were more likely to be successful if he was continuously reminded that at such and such a time we needed to be doing something else, but if something came up, an impromptu visit to the shops for example, there would be trouble.

At home I could obviously minimise these crisis situations, if necessary by just not going out. I do remember getting very cross on occasions just wanting to go five minutes to the corner shop to pick up some milk for example and William refusing to budge. I felt trapped – a prisoner in my own home.
It's easier now. As he's older I can just leave him behind, but when he was younger it was the cause

of many arguments. Not only did I feel completely frustrated that a small boy was holding me hostage, but that I had become isolated from the outside world because of him. I'd moved away from my friends at the end of my pregnancy and was finding it very difficult to build a new social network. I was missing out on getting to know the other mums waiting at the school gates and whenever we did go out together to the park, for example, William's behaviour would be so strange that we were generally avoided – well, there was perhaps a touch of paranoia there as well on my part - and with my blinkers on I wouldn't have noticed any friendly approaches either, but would have scurried away to be free of judgment. He would sometimes monopolise the slide and refuse to let anyone else go on it, getting quite aggressive in the process. He never quite got the idea of 'playing' with other children.

At school, however, it was a different matter. He would have been forced to stop and start tasks all day, with teachers not necessarily having the time, resources or energy to take William aside, explain to him what was going to happen and divert his attention calmly to the next task.

There is no way that he can be forced to do something against his will. Threats, bribery, rewards, verbal or even physical threats – all have no effect. He never seemed to respond to the idea of star charts either, nor has he ever been interested in gaining my praise. The idea of him doing something just to please me is anathema to him.

One afternoon I went to collect him from school as usual and found him lying on the floor, the teacher squeezing hold of his arm. His classmates were all there as well waiting to be collected. I heard another girl say something – I think she was trying to explain to the teacher what William had just been trying to say. The teacher shouted at her to be quiet, and continued to shout at William. She was obviously losing control very quickly. I was horrified and made the decision shortly after this incident to take him out of school and for him to be home educated. I don't think I ever got to the bottom of this incident, but he'd only recently started a new academic year, and this new teacher was not equipped to deal with someone like William. His previous teachers had been very accommodating and flexible in their approach. This one was of a different generation, quite strict and unforgiving. William and her were never going to find their peace.

I felt his behaviour was not going to improve and was now too late to be ignored. If he was left to continue at that school the situation was just going to escalate and not only that but his behaviour was having a negative impact on the other children in his class.

I found it very difficult when other children in his class would come up to me on my way to pick him up and say – "William's been naughty again today". I hope I didn't tell them to shut up and mind their own business. I know I certainly felt like it. It was that word 'naughty'. He wasn't naughty. His behaviour wasn't malicious, just different, Just William.

I don't want to pass blame on to the teachers at William's school. They didn't know how to deal with him either and had no support themselves from anyone who did. The national curriculum didn't help. There seems to be no spontaneity in schools any more, with lesson plans and timetables being followed rigidly, and an evidence based education with focus on league tables and performing well in inspections of paramount importance. With 30 + children in a class and no flexibility, it's a wonder any child survives.

After four years at home bringing up William as a full-time single mum, I had only just returned to work since he'd started at school, so my mother (a retired teacher) and I decided that we would educate him at home and I would continue to work. I also decided to move back home, since William would be spending most of his time there. William had his usual room in the house and I moved into the granny flat. We were there for 18 months.

It wasn't a decision made lightly, but we could think of no alternative. We could move him to another school, but things would have been exactly the same. What else could we do? Wait for him to be excluded after another incident? Or anticipate this and remove him from the system? The latter seemed to be our only choice.

Home Education (Aged 6 years)

Home educating was taking its toll on my mother. It was very difficult getting William to do anything he had no interest in and I would often delay my return from work rather than face up to the trials of the day. This was obviously not a permanent solution to the predicament. I couldn't expect my mother to teach William full time, especially as I'd often come home and she'd be close to tears, and neither could I see myself leaving work and doing it myself.

I felt very guilty, but could see no alternative. I didn't want to be living, at 38, back home with my mother and stepfather in the back of beyond – they were probably thinking the same thing. If I left work, I would have had no income and no chance of ever leaving again, nor could I imagine ever getting any social life of my own. On the occasions when I was at home with him, I would carry on with his education and realised that even if he seemed not to be taking any notice of what I was trying to teach him, miraculously the information would sink in anyway. Together, my mother, step-father and I did many things with him during the time he was out of school, most probably more than if he had remained at school. It was obvious he benefited from being at home – preferring the company of adults anyway.

He was far better able to cope in the calmer home environment and, more importantly, in the absence of other children. But, nevertheless, we decided that after six months, the best course of action was to re-introduce him to school.

Back At School

We decided to try and get him back into the local village school. I mean he wasn't that bad: Just William, really. After a lot of preparation and liaison between school, the LEA, educational psychologist and ourselves, a package was drawn up which seemed perfect in theory. It was a small village school and we were all very confident that it would be a great success. In fact, it was the complete opposite – an unmitigated disaster. William lasted one whole day and two half days. I heard that parents had written in to the school, complaining that their children had been traumatised!

It was a fairly relaxed open plan school which in hindsight is probably not ideal for an AS[1] child although at the time I thought it might be homely and relaxing and a similar environment to what he was now used to, and of course at this point we had yet to have any kind of diagnosis. At one point William had climbed up the ropes on the climbing frame in the gym and refused to come down. He had also jumped on to a table in front of the teacher, waving his arms and shouting. On another occasion he'd caused panic as they thought he'd run out of the school gates after a tractor. As we were living in a mainly farming community, tractors and other various farm machinery had become one of his passions. He was also obsessed with lorries, large vans, and construction vehicles. He would

---

[1] AS – Asperger's Syndrome

keep lists of them on a database, and his favourite magazine was Farmers Weekly from which he would cut out pictures of various vehicles and stick them in a notebook. He also loved to explain to the unfortunate how all these farm machines worked!

On a small positive note, in the short time that William was at this school, he did find a friend in the Rector who on occasions visited the school and spoke to him about spectra and the refraction of light. William was very keen to show him his electrical kit and together he was hoping they could perform some experiment.

The class teacher and headmaster both said that they had never experienced such behaviour before and I was sent a form to sign saying that I give consent for a request to be made for a placement at a pupil referral unit[1]. I signed, thinking this the only option left.

Just to finish off this rather unpleasant episode, William was shortly afterwards involved in a serious accident. When he was eight, for some reason he took it upon himself to clean the outside windowsills of the upstairs windows. I tried to stop him doing this, but once again was unable to persuade him to change his plan of action, his idée fixe. I had jobs to do, so had to leave him, assuming, I suppose, that at eight years old he would be safe enough, and realising that it was just not feasible for me to watch

---

[1]   Pupil referral units are a type of school, set up and run by local authorities to provide education for children who cannot attend school.

him 24 hours a day. I was outside opening the greenhouses when I heard a terrible noise, exactly like a bag of bones landing on the path around the side of the house. I ran and found William unconscious. He had fallen about ten to twelve feet, landing head first from what I could make out, onto a concrete step. I probably shouldn't have, but my first reaction was just to pick him up.

I ran inside and as I lay him on the carpet he regained consciousness and started screaming. I phoned the emergency services, but the noise in the house – William screaming, the dog barking – was overwhelming, making it impossible for me to hear what the person on the other end of the phone was saying –and I was panicking. I realised I was going to have to override my feelings of horror that my little boy was close to death and take control. From then on I became rather clinical. I was aware he had broken his arm but had no idea as to the extent of the damage to his head apart from a rectangular swelling appearing dramatically on his forehead. At one point his lips started turning blue, so I cleared his airways. I checked his legs and made sure that he still had feeling and therefore had not injured his back or neck and then sat and waited for what seemed hours, trying to soothe a confused, semi-conscious young boy in great pain. Because we were so remote he had to be airlifted to hospital by helicopter where he was in intensive care over night. Five days later I returned home with a very skinny little boy with panda eyes, a bandage round his head and his arm in plaster. He had fractured his skull from ear to ear and from forehead to back of neck, as well of the base of his skull and broken his wrist.

I knew his brain had not been affected when the next day, while still in hospital, I continued reading his Enid Blyton book to him and mispronounced a name. He was very quick to correct me, which was a huge relief!

This incident was indicative of William's total inability to judge risk and danger.

The neurosurgeon that saw him at the hospital said it was rare for a child of his age to fall; usually they are much younger children who are understandably not able to assess the risk. It was a miracle there was no permanent damage.

Following this accident and the disastrous episode at the local primary school, the LEA[1] arranged for him to attend a day unit located at the Child and Family Clinic, which offered education for pupils with, or being assessed for, mental health problems in partnership with the National Health Trust. Staff there included teachers, nurses, occupational and family therapists, psychotherapist, social workers, clinical psychologists, and a consultant child Psychiatrist. It was usual for children to remain in the unit for up to 10 weeks in order for an assessment to be made – William was there for almost 6 months in order for them to reach their diagnosis. He was now eight years old when we finally received a label for his eccentricities –

[1] Local Education Authority.

Asperger's Syndrome. I'm not sure that having a label helped, but it did mean we could look for a specialist educational establishment for him. I was optimistic – everything would now be sorted and no one would have to worry about him again – we now knew what his problems were, there would therefore be solutions. Wouldn't there?

Still on the hunt for his next school, I visited a local Pupil referral Unit following a recommendation from the LEA but realised, on talking to the woman who ran it, that it would have been totally unsuitable and inappropriate. Other than that, according to the LEA, William's only choice in county – there was no provision for children with AS – was an STF[1] for children with social and learning difficulties. The unit was just being opened, attached to a primary school not too far away. William was the first pupil there and although the capacity was for 7 children, while he was there, there were only a maximum of 4 at any one time. This was not a long-term answer for him as it was designed for children with emotional/behavioural difficulties to be sort of re-programmed and then returned to their original school. But although it was not an institution specifically geared towards dealing with children with Aspergers, the staff there were excellent and did a lot of constructive work with William.

I think William may have been slightly calmer at this school because, when he started, there was only him and one other pupil together with several staff

---

[1]   Specialist Teaching Facility

and LSAs[1].The head of the STF unit was also very competent and I think William had a lot of respect for her. It's difficult to quantify this respect William carries for certain people but it is very obvious: some people have it and others don't. His teacher here was very firm and consistent and never got angry with William. She presented a slight detachment towards William and that coupled with her obvious affection for him was something that worked very well, and that he could respond and react to positively.

When William was unsettled he would usually calm by sitting with a book in the reading corner, although, if he ever arrived at school with a book, he would need to go there straight away as he would not settle until he had finished the whole book.

He remained here for about three years. Immediate disaster was being avoided. Although his individual problem was not being dealt with, we were at least able to find some sort of stability. I was able to combine full-time work with school hours, by working extra time at home in the evenings and while he was at this school. It was at this time that we moved into our first house. Things seemed to be moving forward.

The LEA seemed unable to come up with any alternative to the STF so I realised it was up to me to find somewhere for William to go to school.

---

[1]   Learning Support Assistant

I searched on the internet and came across an independent residential school in Somerset that specialised in dealing with boys with Asperger's Syndrome. I also managed to speak to another mother whose son went to this school, so was able to find out more about it. It seemed to be highly recommended and the LEA actually agreed to fund William's placement there. I felt very excited. He was about to attend a school that had experience in Asperger's Syndrome. There would be other boys there with similar problems, so he wouldn't be the only one. I was confident these people would be able to cope, if anybody could.

In fact the true extent of William's problems seemed to come to a head during his time there. A combination of his age, being with other children all day and away from home, led to extremely violent outbursts and aggression towards staff members, rarely to the other children, and never to this extent when he was at home. He was also on a cocktail of medication – he was prescribed a very high dose, I've since discovered, of Risperidone, together with Concerta – which clearly did nothing to alleviate his violent episodes. It was also not monitored closely enough, and meetings with the consultant were very unforthcoming. This consultant actually told William on one occasion that if he didn't change his behaviour he would be locked up. Which was helpful!

Concern about William's situation led to a referral to a specialist consultant who performed an in depth consultation with William, my mother and myself.

Over the course of the day his diagnosis of Asperger's Syndrome was confirmed together with Hyperkinetic Conduct Disorder[1]. It was also recommended that he continue with his medication.

Getting his education sorted (although that's a bit of an over-statement) had so far been a constant struggle. I was writing letters, phoning and meeting with the educational psychologist, his paediatric consultant and SEN manager at the LEA on a weekly basis. On one meeting with the SEN Director at the council offices I was explaining how William would refuse to do any homework (I think in William's head, school was for school work, home was for play and there was no way he was going to mix them up) to which the Director replied – "no offence, but my children don't like doing their homework either".

I always got the feeling I was banging my head against a brick wall. They were aware of William's history, his behavioural problems and resultant exclusions. Did they think it would make me feel better saying that? Or were they just implying that I was making a fuss?

*

---

[1] Hyperkinetic Conduct Disorder - a disorder characterized by excessive activity, emotional instability, impulse control difficulties, significantly reduced attention span, and an absence of shyness and fear.

Miscellaneous Incidents

For many years, especially when William was younger, whenever we went out together for example to the shops, I would have my blinkers on. I had learnt that other people were so quick to judge my child's behaviour. So many times I've had people – and it's usually other women – shaking their heads, rolling their eyes, tutting with disgust at William's behaviour. They look at him and then their eyes slide over to look at me. At supermarkets he'd quite often go behind the checkout and try to take money out of the till. On a train journey once when William was spending most of his time examining the automatic doors, one person commented, "Do you not teach your child how to behave properly?" Quite frankly a lot of people out there are horrible. I wondered if I ought to carry around a card to flash – "MY CHILD IS NOT NAUGHTY HE'S GOT ASPERGER'S SYNDROME". I also used to wish he had some physical, some visible disability instead. The instant implication that I was a bad mother would not have been the overriding judgment then, no doubt.

There have also been some rather humorous incidents, for example when a pair of be-suited Jehovah's Witnesses were doing house to house calls on our road William appeared from the back garden with the hose pipe and started spraying at them. I was saved.

There have also been some very heart warming and touching moments. I took William when he was about nine years old to the National Botanic Gardens of Wales. He was always very interested in visiting places. He'd not necessarily be interested in the things you were supposed to be interested in, but he enjoyed himself none the less. There was a short film being shown in the gardens, which we watched. Afterwards he was examining all the cables in the room. I managed to shimmy him along and got out, without any problem. We were walking back to the car when I heard someone running behind us. Thinking someone was going to go into a tirade about how awfully my son had behaved during the film, we continued walking briskly. This woman stopped us – she had recognised her now grown up son in William. She had pursued us to talk about her William and how difficult and wonderful they can sometimes be and she was evangelically empathetic. While we were talking, William was happily throwing stones into a channel of water. Another woman went past and told him to stop. My new friend walked over to this woman and had a stern word with her – I'm not sure what she said, but it did the trick. That felt great! Someone was sticking up for us at last.

Another occasion, this time when visiting Kew Gardens, some elderly ladies were being pushed through the hot houses in their wheel-chairs. William went up to one of them and gave her a kiss. She was delighted luckily, although her reaction could have been so different. The others saw and they all wanted one too!

Ages 13 - Present

Things came to a head at his school in Somerset with him thumping the headmaster in the face. Following this, they drew up a plan for his continuing education there which would have cost the LEA a small fortune, £225k a year. It would basically have involved him being segregated from the rest of the school, with his residential and academic needs being met on a one-to-one, or even a two-to-one, basis. On one level I felt the school were pandering to him, but also that they had no alternative. Over the space of three years, William was excluded at least seven times, usually for a minimum of three days, and the last exclusion being a final exclusion after which he was off school for another five months. And this, a school specifically for Aspergers!

These were very harrowing times. I was working full-time and often had to leave work in the middle of the day and rush down to Somerset from South Wales to collect him. Luckily I had a sympathetic employer and my line of work enabled me to work some of the time at home but my unscheduled absences also meant that I was not able to climb up the career ladder to the dizzying heights of 'manager' and get the corresponding salary. Perhaps that was a good thing. It seemed to be everyone's career plan to become a manager of something-or-other. I relied heavily on my mother and stepfather to help with William and without them I don't know what I'd have done. I wouldn't have been able to hold down a job (for what it was worth) and would have had to go back on benefits. I could never understand why colleagues at work got so stressed about things. To me, going to work was totally stress-free. It was my sanctuary from William.

Again, it was never clear at his school in Somerset what the triggers were for his violent behaviour. It may be that he became over-stimulated in the presence of other children. School meetings I attended were always very frustrating. It seemed in theory that plans drawn up could not possibly fail and we (teachers and carers included) all left feeling optimistic, but invariably William fell through the cracks and soon became a cause for concern again. At the end there were no options left.

Shortly after his final exclusion the school in Somerset decided that his teacher should come down to South Wales and tutor him at the house for a week. This was just to get some idea of his behaviour in the home and some ideas of how to move forward in the event that his continuing at this school was still an option. It was concluded that his behaviour at school was definitely exacerbated when in contact with other pupils such that, at times, he could become unmanageable. It was evident that one-to-one teaching with a teacher, completely separate from all external distractions and away from contact with other pupils, was an essential ingredient to his support package. In order to provide this at a residential school, together with the waking night support he would need and staffing levels of two-to-one (both academically and residentially) was going to cost a small fortune.

So I left it with the LEA to find a new educational placement for him. Following a period of five months or so at home, with no formal education, William started at his current school[1] and seems to have found a niche for himself there. It's not ideal in my mind, but he is still there, and I now cannot remember the last time he was excluded. So, he may be smoking, and talking like a yob – up until about a year ago, despite being brought up in South Wales, he has never adopted the accent, but spoke instead in an almost home counties' twang. He's now developed this new accent which perhaps more reflects that of his peers (and I suppose this is the first time he has ever had peers) being that most of them, except for the small Aspergers contingent, are there for predominantly other varied emotional and behavioural problems (perhaps not the best mix). He now looks forward to going into school, speaks with his "mates" when home at the weekend and generally problems are few and far between. I don't think, despite his intelligence, that he will get many qualifications. But that doesn't matter any more. He's started doing some work experience at a garage close to the school, which he really enjoys. Social Services (Yes! Social Services!) even arranged for him to go there twice during one half term as he enjoys it so much. He arrived back home with oil-smeared hands and oil-

---

[1] National Children's Home School – this is a charitable school that specialises in Aspergers and children with emotional and behavioural difficulties.

smeared but smiling face, telling us that he'd been helping, doing various MOTs[1] and changing the shocks on a Fiesta... Or something. On one of the occasions I'd forgotten to give him any money for his lunch so drove in with it. Another young lad in the office called over to him – "William, your Mum's here. You're in trouble now". He came in, dressed in his overalls and big steel toe-capped boots, a cup of tea in one hand and a fag in the other, black streaks over his face. I asked the boss how he was doing and he was full of praise for him. He even said he would give William a job when he'd finished school.

So, William is employable after all! That was such a good thing to hear – someone is actually going to pay him for his time. And he's very happy doing that kind of thing. I imagine he's in his element. It also means there is light at the end of the tunnel. In the past, I've always stopped myself from looking into the future as it seemed far too bleak. With this suggestion of employment, I can now afford to take a peek at tomorrow.

*

---

[1]   MOTs – Ministry of Transport Test which is a mandatory test in the UK to ensure a vehicle meets the minimum safety levels required by law.

Life Today

William's In Trouble

Not so long ago there was a distinct possibility that William would end up in a Youth Offending Institute. He is already deemed to be a Persistent Young Offender[1] by the police and is quite likely to be remanded in custody following any further transgressions. He's already spent one night in a police cell for breaking the conditions of his bail. I don't think it bothered him that much though. Certainly not as much as it bothered me. I'd left him with a copy of The Guardian and his Maplin[2] catalogue and his only comment in the morning when he was released was that he hadn't slept that well because there was a strip light on in his cell all night. He also proceeded straight away once we were in the car to show me his Maplin shopping list and that's the last I heard about his ordeal. I know it may sound rather awful but I actually said to the custody sergeant after he'd been phoning around to find out if it was possible for William to return to school, or home, that it suited me fine, him staying in custody, as my husband and I were going out to the theatre that evening! At least I knew I wouldn't have to worry about getting another phone call from

---

[1]   A young person aged 10-17 years who has been sentenced by any criminal court in the UK on three or more occasions for one or more recordable offences and within three years of the last sentencing occasion is subsequently arrested or has any information laid against him for further recordable offence.

[2]   Maplin – a company that specialises in computer and electronic equipment.

the school telling me that he'd absconded or punched a member of staff in the head or whatever. I felt terrible leaving him in a cell: to sleep on a thin blue plastic covered mattress, with a thin blue blanket, and a microwave dinner. Another occasion when I could have just burst into tears over the inadequacies of any system to cope with my young boy, whose only crime was to have been born with a miswired brain. They would have been wasted tears though, and for that I felt anger as well towards William for getting himself in this position in the first place, and anger at myself for being powerless to stop it.

When William was arrested for the first time, I was horrified. I felt shame, guilt, anger, frustration, pity and helplessness – I couldn't get him out of this one. But after the nth time, I think I became a bit blasé about being called to the custody suite; listening to William being interviewed; having his rights read to him; finger-prints, photo and DNA taken. It was a world I'd only seen on the television really. I never thought I'd end up being a part of it. We had acquired a very competent and sympathetic solicitor, who was also present at any interviews and court appearances, and although I don't believe he had any experience with Asperger's Syndrome, he certainly does now.

They were not the friendliest bunch of people, the police, and despite my efforts to smile at them all and just be pleasant (I refused to see this as a negative experience) they usually refused to reciprocate. But worse, they seemed to make no allowances due to the fact that William was a minor, nor that he had Asperger's Syndrome. I even started an argument once with the custody officer. I found myself in a very difficult position – I felt as William's mother that it was my duty to be on his side (as no-one else seemed to be) - the school insisted on pressing charges after any transgression and the police were treating him as if he was just a run-of-the-mill criminal. Who was on William's side? I asked the Custody officer if he even knew what Asperger's syndrome was. He asked me to step into an interview room, and proceeded to tell me that I was insulting his intelligence.

I've thought hard about the prospect of my son being charged and imprisoned and it makes me very sad and very angry. If it does happen then I will be obliged to transfer my fight from the education authority to the prison service. Which should be interesting. I once heard that more than 80% of the inmates in Swansea prison suffered from some sort of mental disability – either ADHD or autistic spectrum disorder. How can this be, that we are obliged to lock so many youths away with obvious, yet probably undiagnosed, problems?[1]

I wonder what effect it would have on him if he were to be locked up. On the one hand I think that he would probably get on quite well when inside:

---

[1]   A recent report by the Office for National Statistics, Psychiatric Morbidity Among Young Offenders, found that 9 in 10 young offenders aged between 16-20 years old showed evidence of mental illness.

there would be strict boundaries and routines, a regimented environment, everything would be unambiguously black and white. I certainly don't think he'd spend time dwelling on his predicament and wishing he were elsewhere — he has never outwardly expressed any kind of homesickness, he is where he is and that is what matters. It's just something that doesn't seem to enter his head. So, what's the point of locking him up, it won't stop the re-offending. He would not emerge from prison a reformed individual; it won't cure his Asperger's. Instead, I imagine his behaviour would deteriorate once released as he would have been overly influenced by other inmates and he would be outside in a non-regimented environment as a potentially rather lost soul. The same problems would still be there when he was released, and he'd be back to square one in the outside world.

This is all hypothetical speculation obviously and one positive step since then has been that William has told us that from now on he is going to try as hard as possible to stay out of trouble with the police. He even asked me if I would get him a reward if, by the time the summer holidays arrived he'd remained out of trouble, which is a first. Usually it's me trying to bribe him and now he is showing some element of self-control – a great step forward.

William has now remained out of trouble for the past seven months. He has really made an effort and that effort is in part due to his maturing. In a way I am inclined now to believe that the school did the right thing by pressing charges. Although William has learnt the hard way, I think he has learnt a valuable lesson. He has had experience of police, solicitors, courts and the youth offending service; has realised he does not want to get involved any more with that and as a minor he will not have a criminal record carried forward to later life. I suppose it's better to have gone through it as a minor rather than be sheltered from it, then have to face up to the same things but with more serious implications as an adult.

*

Weekends

Since William's been away at school during the week, I don't think I've ever looked forward to a Friday afternoon and his imminent return. I need to prepare myself mentally for the weekend and to prepare a smile and some kind greeting for when he arrives, and hide anything away that could possibly attract his attention – e.g. the whisky, my purse. Then of course I start to feel guilty – why don't I look forward to seeing him again? I imagine other people excited at seeing their children after a week away at school; all the things they'd have to talk about together; excitement about activities, trips, visits to family/friends over the weekend. The heart-warming feeling of having their offspring with them, the admiration and pride they will feel at their achievements at school, the pleasure of listening to their amusing anecdotes.

Instead I have William thumping on the front door then demanding a cup of tea and disappearing to his room for the duration of the weekend. Me shouting after him "take your shoes off before you go upstairs please" as always. Sometimes I even get a smile, which is a good start to the weekend, very occasionally I get a hug – well, I hug him, and if I'm very lucky he will reciprocate.

But after that, getting William to do anything is extremely difficult if not impossible. He spends most of his weekends at home not even bothering to get up. If we go anywhere he prefers to stay at home with his computer. So I only see him at dinnertime. I've stopped knocking on his door periodically during the weekend to see if he's OK.

He has also started smoking as most of the other children at his current school seem to smoke as well. It's quite horrible seeing him with a fag in his mouth, but it made me realise why so many mental patients are smokers: turn them into addicts, be in control of their tobacco and then they become extremely biddable and controllable. It makes me cringe to see him smoking and listen to him coughing constantly as a result; I also feel pity that he feels the need. He is so impressionable; he probably thinks he fits in better with his peers. But, on the other hand, the violent outbursts seem to have abated recently, so I can't really complain, and try desperately to keep my nagging to a minimum.

Relationships

I generally find life very difficult with William and rarely feel love towards him. When he was younger we sometimes used to have awful fights – not physical, just shouting – which came about usually over his stubbornness and refusal to carry out the simplest, or what I considered to be simple, requests. I suppose in hindsight I should just have left him alone, but I kept thinking, especially after his diagnosis, that he should still be able to carry out simple tasks. Even now I have difficulty getting him to do anything, including making himself something to eat, even a cheese sandwich. I can't work out why he won't do it. It's not that he can't. Is it just laziness? But then if I don't do it for him he just wouldn't eat and he's skinny as it is.

I would often say horrible things to him in the heat of the moment. For example I used to read him fairy tales, some of which even I found quite disturbing. One was called "the New Mother", which told the story of two young girls who were very naughty and whose mother left them to be replaced by a new mother with glass eyes and a wooden tail. I would tell him if he was really naughty that I'd have to do that. I'd be left with no choice, and when I was extremely angry with him I've told him I didn't want him to live in my house any more and he could find somewhere else to live. And many other things - enough to make me cringe.

We don't communicate much, except on his terms, which usually involves talking about computers or cars. I often say I don't understand what he's talking about and to his credit he does try to explain to me, often quite patiently. I try to talk to him, and often just think aloud in order for him to hear and try and react to normal, mundane day-to-day stuff that goes on at home. Sometimes he just tells me to shut up, or that he's really not interested, but other times he will respond in a very mature way. The pattern now seems to be that on a Friday afternoon when he comes back from school, he's in a very good mood, so I try and talk to him then as much as possible before he retires to his lair.

When he comes home from school I ask him how his week's been and his usual response is just a grunt. Have you done anything interesting? "Not much?" Been to the cinema. "Er, yeah". Does he really not remember anything he's done, or is he just being a teenager?

When he's home from school he spends most of the weekend up in his room on his computer. I feel guilty that I'm not doing stuff with him – I did used to when he was younger and it was just him and me together. We'd have days, especially when it was wet outside, when we'd just play Lego all day, lying on the carpet. Now, I can't get him to spend any time with me at all. But then he is 15, what teenage boy does spend much time hanging out with his mother?

I worry about him. But I've realised that worrying is such a negative, time-wasting emotion and communicating my worries to William does not help. I just need to concentrate on the positive and be up-beat and confident with him – which is difficult as most of the time that's the opposite of what I actually feel.

I get very frustrated with him, and I'm sure that's mostly a manifestation of my guilty feelings – because I don't spend time with him, talk to him, know what's going on in his life. But at least it's calm at home now, and if I do want to go out, then I can just leave him. As long as it's just for a couple hours. But if he is left, we do make sure that everything private is locked away, as he has a tendency to appropriate things that he "finds" like a magpie. One morning not so long ago, after he'd got in the taxi to go to school, we realised that he'd been up and around during the night. A bottle of whisky had been drained – there wasn't much left anyway, which I suppose was lucky, and at the shops later that day I realised that my purse was completely empty. I confronted him with this on his return, and he did eventually admit to taking it, his reason being because I never lend him any money. I explained that he shouldn't need any more as he did have pocket money and that he should perhaps log what he spent his money on during the month and then we should perhaps review the situation. He didn't say anything more after this.

We've found the answer to an easy life, well at home anyway – he is not asked to do anything, except clear up after meals, bring cups down from his bedroom, put rubbish in the bin, take shoes off before going upstairs, and to put dirty clothes in the linen basket. But even this seems too much and rarely gets done. I no longer ask him to tidy his room – I just go in once he's gone back to school and sort it out myself – even if it does sometimes take the whole day to tidy and clean it, especially after the holidays. If I do ask him to do anything like shower or brush his teeth, he has been known to say, well, as you've asked me, no I'm not going to. And at the end of the day, not showering is not the worst crime.

I know people will be thinking, why don't you just insist. Put your foot down and make him tidy his room. Well I did once, and he ended up being escorted off the premises in handcuffs into a waiting police car. I'd been kicked in the groin and my husband was left with a black eye. We learnt at great cost what happens when we retaliate. There are also simmering arguments within our extended family as to who is at fault with regard to William. Some say all he needs is a bit of discipline, which suggests I have given him none. A recent forensic assessment spoke of a lack of boundary setting at home, which I found very upsetting. Everyone seems to have an answer. Well, they're welcome to try!

I always have to be one step ahead of him. I have to anticipate his response to what I'm going to say, and work backwards from that. Perhaps rephrasing my question in order to get the required answer. I feel I can never be myself with him. I have to act a part. It's very draining watching your words all the time.

He is not affectionate towards me at all, in fact usually recoils from any physical contact from me. The exception to this is once a year on my birthday. Birthdays are very clear events – it's my day, everyone is nice to me, people give me gifts and I am allowed to give him a hug and a kiss upon receipt of his offering.

As regards William's relationships, he has recently begun to form firm friendships at his school, and this also seems to be very important to him. Apart from his cousin who is three weeks younger than him, and with whom he has always had a very close relationship, I think this is the first time that William has ever spoken of "mates". He also now has a girlfriend of sorts. Well, she's a friend and she's a girl. They meet up on Saturdays quite regularly now. William walks to the station by himself and catches the train to town, and texts me when he's on his way back. Just like any other teenager. And I don't spend the time when he's away worrying about him – he does seem to be getting quite independent and, dare I say, responsible.

*

Concluding Thoughts

Unfortunately I can't be sure whether any of my strategies in dealing with William have been successful or not. We have a relatively calm home life now with few if no battles with him, but his school life, although relatively stable now, is still prone to extreme, unpredictable volatility.

During the process of writing this, I have discovered how very important it is having people on our side. It would have been really traumatic being interviewed by the police and having to attend court had it not been for our friendly and competent solicitor. William's resultant reparation orders[1] would have been extremely difficult to handle if not for the sympathetic YOT[2] workers. We also had the benefit of committed, and very kind teachers and carers at William's schools. They have always felt genuine affection towards William and given him (and the wider family) their unstinting, invaluable support, which was reciprocated – even if he did sometimes send them to hospital!

I can't say that over these fifteen years I have any hints as to what has made things work or not work. The only thing needed I suppose is super-human patience, unrelenting self-confidence, constant un-shifting boundary setting, a certain affectionate detachment, a quirky sense of humour; a totally

---

[1] Reparation Orders - are designed to help young offenders understand the consequences of their offending and take responsibility for their behaviour.
[2] Youth Offending Team

stress free life and a laissez faire attitude!

I have found throughout his life that everyone is intent on forcing him to conform to a "normal" pattern of behaviour. Eccentricities are frowned upon. The National Curriculum is a straitjacket. I can't help wondering what's going to become of society if differences are not applauded and encouraged. I believe a healthy society needs all different kinds of people – how boring if everyone was the same. I also can't help feeling that there must be other children in the UK or further afield with similar problems to William's, but there seems to be no knowledge sharing amongst the professionals. I suppose though, a major problem with Asperger's Syndrome is that the manifestations of the syndrome differ so widely between each of them. Each child has his/her own little syndrome.

If it weren't for society (and I'm not condoning Margaret Thatcher here)[1], there would be no problem with William. I remember at primary school, their main problem with him was that his social skills weren't as they should be. But not everyone's going to be a team player, an extrovert, a gregarious live wire, a social butterfly. And surely that's a good thing?

I hope deep down that William knows I love him. We can sometimes laugh together. He sometimes lets me kiss him – although those moments are

---

[1] Margaret Thatcher famously said that there was no such thing as society.

getting more and more rare – even though he does say "if you do that again I'll kill you", well, he has to save face somehow doesn't he? I think, somewhere in there, in the murkiness and strange goings on in that boy, he does have a smidgen of love for his old mum.

My metaphor for his teenage years, but perhaps it's applicable to all teenagers, is that he is in a state of metamorphosis, like a chrysalis. As he pupates, his insides are churned up. Everything is topsy-turvy, with hormones rampaging around causing confusion. He's a child but also a young man. When he emerges from the other side of his pupation he will be a perfectly formed young man. My butterfly. Well, I can only hope.

Writing this has reminded me of the good times. No matter how hard it's got, I remember my young lad and know he's still in there somewhere.

As the days/weeks go by, I'm sure he's that little bit stronger: with more confidence and self-esteem. Or perhaps my confidence has increased in him as I've begun to see what's important in all this, and it's rubbing off on him, and that I can make a positive difference to my son's life. And if all it takes is writing our experience down – in my own words, warts and all - taking stock of his (and my) life, then maybe we can learn to relax and see our children on their terms. It can only be a good thing. We need not get ground down by the system, but just carry on our personal fights. It's what all parents have been doing for their children for millennia. It's just ours are a little more special. To us, if not to anyone else.

~

Martha's Story

Luke

My son is 18 now, although you wouldn't know it to talk to him, or even to watch him. He graduated from high school yesterday with friends he's had all through school, some even from preschool. He went to the prom, just like his friends. He was on the varsity bowling team this year, with some of his friends. He may be going on a "double date" this summer, just like his friends do now. Some of his friends will move away to college, some will stay home and go to the community college, including him. The only difference, is that he will be in the continuing education department, while the others are working on their degrees.

He will be in a special program, Transitional Skills, which teaches life skills to special needs students. Each student is expected to come up with a goal and mission statement and a plan of action for their career and their future. I think it should be a required class for all students! The class subjects may be a little different, but the program is treated like a campus organization: they elect officers, plan group events, and even have to do a community service project. **My son is going to college,** despite the odds against him, which oftentimes included the school district and many "professionals" we have seen over the years.

There is light at the other end of the tunnel. Some tunnels are just longer than others.

*

In the Beginning

When Luke was a baby, around three or four months, before he could sit up, he loved to sit for hours in his soft, bouncy seat and play with the toys that were suspended across it. He would grasp the wire that held all the toys, and then use his thumb to spin the center ball, around and around and around. We thought "Oh, how cute! His fingers are going to be flexible enough to play the piano!" Looking back, it was the first time we remember his fixation on spinning. As he grew and we put him on a pallet in floor to encourage him to roll over and scoot along, he preferred lying on his back watching the ceiling fan. As he grew, we started buying the "boy" stuff – cars, trucks, building blocks of all shapes and sizes. And yet, they were all treated the same; the cars and trucks were always lined up, either like a parking lot or a procession. The blocks were always stacked straight up – he never built buildings.

We always thought that was funny – just his way of playing. He was our first child, of course he was perfect and physically healthy. He was small, but following an appropriate growth pattern, so why would we think there was a problem? He reached all the first year milestones within the range expected; granted they were all at the end of the range or a day or two later, but they were there.

*

Preschool

It wasn't until he started going to a Mother's Day Out program that we really realized that he was a little different[1]. *But most of those kids had older siblings to learn from*, we rationalized. But going into the 4 year old class was really telling. Those kids could get dressed by themselves, some of them could tie their shoes, they were writing letters appropriately – *what is with these kids? Don't their parents ever let them play? Do they sit around with flashcards and have them practice everything all day? I'm glad my kid knows how to play. I thought kindergarten was for learning all of that stuff!*

It was during this time that we started going down the alphabet list – all the different diagnoses that fit part of the problem, but not the whole thing. But first we had to try play therapy with a psychologist before the insurance company would authorize a psychiatrist visit. So he went to play therapy. And while the therapist tried to find out why he was worried about so many things, why he was obsessed about time, why he didn't like change, Luke lined up the army people, or the clocks, or the animals, or whatever toy that therapist brought out. He was no more engaged with the therapist than those toys were! After three or four sessions like that, he recommended we see a psychiatrist to consider a pharmaceutical approach.

---

[1] During this time our second son, Simon, was born. He was so easy compared to our first one, but of course at that time, we had no idea what was headed our way with the third one!

Severe GAD (Generalized Anxiety Disorder) was the first set of initials we ever received. We went on to several more, including OCD, ODD, ADD, and ADHD[1], but each time it just didn't feel right. I didn't have the feeling in the pit of my stomach that I thought I should have. Then I would think that I was crazy and we had an answer and some medicine that would make Luke fine. Each new set of initials brought out some other symptom that had been hiding. It was like the Whac-a-Mole game at the arcade. Just as you hit one mole, another pops up, and the longer you play, the faster they pop up, and then they're popping up more than one at a time. At least that game ends. Our game wasn't ending or slowing down.

When it came time to get ready for kindergarten, his teachers in the Pre-K class were hesitant about his readiness for kindergarten. I still remember their words 13 years later. They weren't sure that he was ready for kindergarten, but they didn't think he needed another year at preschool either. He started kindergarten and was definitely behind his peers, but it just seemed to be a lack of maturity. After all, he was our first child, and wasn't "streetwise" like the kids with older siblings. We also added to our family; his youngest brother Daniel was born on the second day of kindergarten. And all the books say it is normal for older siblings to regress a bit when the new baby is brought home. Again, we thought everything was fine, that he was just a little behind

---

[1]   OCD – Obsessive Compulsive Disorder. ODD –
Oppositional Defiant Disorder. ADD – Attention Deficit
Disorder. ADHD – Attention Deficit Hyperactivity Disorder.

and would catch up by 5th or 6th grade. He had articulation problems and began speech services at school[1], but it was strictly for articulation. There was never any discussion of any help other than that. He could read fairly well, but was having some difficulty with comprehension. I had no idea that speech services could have helped with that. So at the end of kindergarten, they wanted to put him in the "Bridge" program, basically an extra year bridging kindergarten and first grade. We said no, because we didn't see a big problem…yet.

Ages 6 - 9

He went to first grade[2] and with the help of a wonderful teacher, we got him into Content Mastery, where he did better with certain things, but the abstract concepts were still difficult. We began having conferences every six weeks to try to find out why this sweet little boy was having so many problems keeping up with his peers. He never exhibited behavior issues at school; he always saved them for home. And this was still a part of the "alphabet years" and we kept playing the Whac-a-mole game with symptoms and new medications. I saw a counselor, as I was increasingly frustrated at what to do to parent this kid.

In second grade[3], another wonderful teacher tried to help us find an answer to all our questions. She

---

[1] Speech services – this can offer more than articulation, it is also about semantics and pragmatics and reading social cues.
[2] First grade covers ages 6-7 in America
[3] Second grade covers ages 7-8 in America

consulted textbooks, we had a conference with her almost every three weeks, she even called her college professor to see what he could suggest. Unfortunately, in 1997, there was no autism awareness. At that time, the diagnosis du jour was ADHD, so that's the way his education was being approached, as a student with ADHD. But he wasn't responding to that approach. He still needed something else, something we couldn't quite put our finger on. I described like we were working on a puzzle. We had all the outside edges, the easier parts so to speak, but what we didn't have was a giant puzzle piece in the middle that would connect it all together. That was before I knew about autism and the puzzle piece symbols.

Pizza Parlour

I haven't mentioned the embarrassing moments yet. When he was younger, probably between 5 and 8, we went to a pizza buffet on a warm evening. Most of the specific details of that evening are forgotten, but I know he was wearing sandals, and I think we were celebrating the end of a sporting season. At some point in the evening, I saw him chewing his toenails, right there at the table where we were eating, and in front of his friends and peers. I don't know how many people saw him, but he had his foot up to his mouth, with the sandal still on his foot, trying to get rid of a bothersome toenail. We were mortified! *How do you gracefully and calmly leave a restaurant without freaking out every one else there*? And we had no idea what was still to come in junior high just a few years later.

*

Trying to write about the pain and pang and knife stab feeling in my heart as I watched his class on the playground, still gets to me. Tears still well up and it is hard to breathe and think about the teasing and bullying that went on. Watching another kid make fun of your own kid just makes you want to stop living sometimes. Luke was always blissfully unaware of the teasing – he was just having fun. On the other hand, I'm caught between a rock and a hard spot. If I charge out to the playground and tell these "friends" where to get off and go, I feel better because I have done something about it. Unfortunately, as soon as I leave, it will only get worse for him. But if I stand by and do nothing, it won't be so bad for him, but I lose all ability to function from the inside out. Breathing, controlling the tears, and maintaining a tiny bit of composure are impossible.

I continued seeing my counselor and she suggested having testing and evaluations done outside of the school district. (At that time, I had no idea about IDEA[1] and having the school district do the evaluations.) We hesitated because of the expense involved, but finally realized that we had to do something, and we would find a way to pay for the portion the insurance didn't cover. In the meantime, I also continued to research – using that new World Wide Web. Our neighbors had a

---

[1]   The Individuals with Disabilities Education Act.

computer with a modem, and I ran across a website for the South Carolina Autism Society of America Bookstore. I ordered their information package on autism and Aspergers Syndrome. We looked at all the signs and checked off all but one or two. We asked his teacher, and she agreed that she saw all those signs in class, too. At Luke's next psychiatrist appointment, I asked her about autism, and could it be possible that Luke had it. Her reply, "Oh, no! He always speaks to me and looks at me when he replies to my questions." Little did I know that teaching him manners would hinder our search for an answer! So we moved on, relieved that it wasn't autism.

My counsellor got us connected with a psychologist whom she trusted and respected. He gave us his report and at the end, he stated, "I highly suggest a neurological evaluation". I called our family doctor, who did some research for us and found a local pediatric neurologist. We made an appointment, and probably within the first five minutes of meeting Luke, the doctor said, "Folks, I believe he has Aspergers Syndrome" and explained a little bit about it. By the end of summer, we had finished the process, had the bloodwork done to rule out Fragile X syndrome, and had a written report for the school that confirmed her suspicion of Aspergers Syndrome. We headed to third grade thrilled to death that we had an answer and now we knew what he needed to get his education!

*

Third grade[1] begins and he has a wonderful teacher, Mrs M. who tells her class that they spend so much of their waking hours together that they should consider themselves family, and treat each other like it. They may have differences but they will always look out for each other. Today, nine years later, I am still grateful to that teacher. The students, now high school graduates, who were in that third grade class respected Luke and always had a smile and hello for him.

Third grade was also our first experience with an ARD[2] meeting. We felt totally blindsided. We were so excited to go to this meeting and tell the school personnel what we discovered, now we knew what to do to teach Luke! *Hooray! We have an* answer! *The teachers will be able to get through to him and everything will be fine!* Our life completely turned upside down that day, and remains that way still. I can still remember that feeling of being sucker punched in the gut as if it were yesterday. No one tells you (certainly not the school district) how the process works. Oh yes, you are given the state required handout, about 10 pages of tiny print, outlining your rights, but reading it and interpreting and understanding it are vastly different things. After the meeting I wrote the Principal a letter about the way things were handled, and sent copies to a

---

[1] Third grade covers ages 8 – 9 in America.

[2] Admission, Review and dismissal Committee meeting is where the student's IEP (Individualized Education Plan) is created by school district staff and parents. It may be done as a team with both parties working together, but oftentimes it becomes a contentiaous conference over who is right, the parents or the school district.

lot of people, but I never received a response.

One part of the evaluation was an interview with the parents. It was done by phone, and the person doing it let it slip that from what she read, Luke wouldn't qualify as autistic, so we wouldn't be doing an exhaustive interview, just the basics. So when it came time to meet again to go over their assessments, the person scheduling the meeting called to see if a particular date and time would work for us. My reply was that if they were going to agree with our evaluation and diagnosis of autism, then that date would be fine; otherwise, we would need to schedule around my attorney's and paediatric neurologist's schedules. There was a pause, and she said she would get back to me on that. About 30 minutes later she called to say that the first date would work – we didn't need to schedule the other people. I still wonder if they would have agreed with us if I hadn't done so much reading and threatened the use of a lawyer. I also wonder how many students didn't get the services they need because the parents didn't know to do that, and the school district could get away with doing as little as possible.

That meeting was also the first time a Speech Therapist made an impact on Luke's education. The state were claiming that Luke didn't exhibit one of the key traits of autism but she refuted their assumption citing many examples where Luke had displayed that particular characteristic in her presence. So the state could no longer deny the existence of that trait and they stopped arguing and gave in to the autism diagnosis. Third grade was a pretty good year for Luke, mostly due to the wonderful teacher he had.

It was during fourth grade[1] that we contacted the local Autism Society and got as much information as was available. One of the articles recommended calling the state department of mental health and mental retardation services and get on the interest list for services. They verified that he was eligible to receive "services" and put our name on the waiting list. They estimated the waiting list to be around 13-15 years long at that point. The more money that was appropriated by the state legislature to fund this department, the shorter the waiting list became. That was the spring of 1998.

Ages 9 – 12

Fourth grade was a rude awakening for us. Not every teacher is as compassionate, caring and genuine as Mrs. M was. His teacher this year definitely preferred to work with girls, and didn't want to do anything extra or out of the ordinary. It didn't matter that we had an IEP[2] that said those things should be done; she just never got around to it, no matter how often I asked. And the spineless jellyfish we had for a Principal was not helpful – he wouldn't demand it. He asked her to try to get these things done. BFD[3]. Again, that was before I learned all about the right way to approach these issues; in

---

[1] Fourth grade cover the ages 9 - 10 in America
[2] IEP – Individualised Education Plan
[3] BFD - Big F....ing Deal!

hindsight, I should have documented everything in writing and filed a complaint with our state education agency, the organization that supposedly oversees public education in our state.

But it really makes me mad that here we are trying to teach our children right from wrong, that anything worth doing is worth doing well, two wrongs don't make a right, the right thing is usually the hardest thing to do, etc. etc. etc. All those "clichés" that we believe our children (whether special needs or not) should learn as they grow up in order to be good citizens. Yet, I go to the school, the place I have entrusted with my precious children's education, and they do the bare minimum to get by. They say they will do it and don't follow through. Essentially, if you are a parent of a special needs child, you will have to parent the entire school district. You wind up treating them as your children. To the child: "If you don't clean your room, I'm taking away your TV time." To the school: "If you don't follow the IEP, I'm filing a complaint." And you now have doubled your workload. Not only do you have to monitor your children, you now have to monitor the teachers, the aides, the administration, sometimes even the state agencies to see that your child is getting an education. We survived, and that in itself is an accomplishment.

The Pencil

I don't think they (the school staff and administrators) really believed that there was anything "wrong" with Luke until they witnessed it after school one afternoon. Luke was the child that wouldn't break the rules - EVER – so they never saw the behavior we dealt with at home. One day he earned a pencil in his class, and when he got home, he couldn't find it. A typical fourth grader would be able to use another pencil or at least wait until the next day to see if it was at school. But that's not the way we live it. He was certain he left it in his desk in the classroom. I knew that if that were true, we would probably have to go back to the school to look for it.

That would mean putting all three boys in the van: Luke, his first grade brother, and his four year old brother, and going back to the school, all the while praying that someone would still be there and we could get in to the classroom to get the pencil out of the desk. I wanted to avoid that, so we completely cleaned out the backpack, looked in every nook and cranny in the minivan, and couldn't find it. I tried to calmly talk to him about looking in his desk the next day, but that seemed to make it worse. Someone would surely steal it or throw it away before he could get back to it. He wanted to look— NEEDED to look in his desk and get that pencil. So we all got in the van and went back to the school. Luckily, the Principal and Assistant Principal were still there and we explained what was happening, and they let us go back to the classroom. All four of us head to the back of the building. We get there and the door is locked, so we all four trudge back to the front of the building and ask them to come open the door. They seemed very annoyed that I was giving in to this "whim" but opened it anyway, and left us there to look. We looked in his desk, the desks right around his and eventually all the desks, the trash can, the teacher's desk, the entire floor, the cabinets and counters where they turned in their work, and there was no pencil. Well, there were actually plenty of pencils, but not *his*. He had held it together up to this point without completely melting down, until I had to say the dreaded words, "It's not here." I suggested asking his teacher for a new one the next day, but he wanted *his* pencil. And then he became determined to find it in that room, and refused to leave until he found it. At this point, there was nothing left to do but to pick him up and carry him out of the room.

Here I go down the hall carrying my 9 year old son who is kicking and screaming "Let me go! I want my pencil! You can't do this!" while keeping an eye on the first grader and especially the four year old. Both the Assistant Principal and the Principal come running out of the office to see what the commotion was, and stood dumbfounded as we walked by. The Principal held the two sets of doors to make sure we could get out. The Assistant Principal went in the office and then came out with a "special" pencil and offered it to Luke; he wouldn't even take it in his hand. He wanted *his* pencil. The two administrators started asking what I wanted them to do to help. I told them *It's okay, I've done this before*. But don't you need help getting him in the van? *No, I've done this many times before.* Are you sure? You've got your hands full here. *No, I've done this before and I'm really too tired to talk about it.* They stood there and watched as I forced him into the van and fastened the seat belt tight enough that he couldn't squirm. The first grader had already buckled himself in and I helped the four year old and then we finally got to go home. As we drive away, I can see the two administrators standing on the sidewalk watching, as if they didn't believe what they just saw. We went home and sat in the rocking chair with his special quilt and we rocked and he cried his little heart out. He sobbed, and both of our tears mixed together to completely soak the left shoulder of my shirt. We probably sat and rocked for 30-45 minutes and then he was able to go about what was left of the day. He was fine, but it would take me a day or so to get over it. I have no idea how long it took his brothers to get over it. The next day at school, everyone in the office was so concerned about me, asking if I was okay after yesterday, and how in the world did I handle it. I explained to them AGAIN that it wasn't the first time he had done that, it was just the first time they had seen it. I swear that from that point on, they really did try to help. They just didn't know what to do.

*

Fifth grade[1] taught me a lot, as well as Luke. Between 4th and 5th grade, the kids all seemed to mature, some both physically and emotionally. Everyone but Luke, that is. There has always been a small gap between Luke's developmental age and that of his chronological peers. Each year when school starts, you can see how much his NT

---

[1] Fifth grade covers ages 10-11 in America

(Neuro-typical) peers have grown, and the gap widens slightly. But this year, the gap went from a stream to the Nile. Being home with him all the time, you just get used to how he is. You learn that everyday he's going to ask the same questions. And you learn to give the same answers every day because he will continue to ask until you give the right answer. And when you're already emotionally and mentally and physically drained, you just give the right answer the first time. It's not about teaching moments, it's about survival moments. And then you see his peers. They are starting to notice that he's not "keeping up" with them as they mature. So, this became the year of the explanation. I decided it was time to explain Aspergers to his classmates, and after getting approval from the counsellor and Principal, we set it up. The homeroom teacher was all for it, so we scheduled an afternoon to talk to his classmates, first just those in his homeroom, then the entire grade in the cafeteria for a general talk. I think this was one of the smartest things I ever did.

I sat in the teacher's rocking chair and the class sat on the floor at my feet. Luke was "helping" another teacher with the reasoning that the kids wouldn't be afraid to ask questions if he weren't there. I started off by telling them he had Asperger's Syndrome, but because the names was so long, we just called it AS. The ulterior motive in that was that some of the students would have taken the pronunciation of Aspergers as an invitation to tease. I told them a lot of people have challenges because some part of their body doesn't work the way it is supposed to.

For instance, wearing glasses isn't a big deal these days, but in reality, it is because the eyes aren't working properly. Hearing aids, wheel chairs, casts on broken bones, etc. Some are permanent and some are temporary, but you can see those.

But Luke's was inside his brain, where the cells that are supposed to talk to each other can't always connect. Just like a busy signal on the phone, or it rings and no one answers. (Remember this was before everyone had cell phones and answering machines.) I told them about stimming[1], that *it makes him feel better, like when they are feeling sick and they want Mom's special quilt or the raggedy stuffed animal or something like that. He is having the same feelings, but is dealing with them in a different way. The biggest difference is that having a special quilt or stuffed animal doesn't annoy everyone! And yes, he drives me crazy too! I'm his mother, I would give up my life for him, but I get frustrated and annoyed and downright mad sometimes, and I understand y'all do too. The difference is in the way we deal with our feelings.* That afternoon, I could literally see the light bulbs turning on over each of their heads. They got to ask questions, and as I answered them, the light bulbs got brighter. It was the same thing when the rest of the 5th grade (about 100 students in all) asked questions and got real life answers. The rest of the year was relatively uneventful.

---

[1] Stimming - to describe the self-stimulatory behavior seen in individuals with autism (e.g. hand flapping, finger wiggling, rocking etc.

In our school district, elementary school is Kindergarten through 6th grade, junior high is 7th–9th grades, and high school is 10th-12th grades. The biggest issue in 6th grade was getting ready to go to junior high and cope with seven classes a day.

*

Ages 12 – 15

Seventh grade[1] passed without too many incidents. He had a study hall period that he used for doing his homework everyday. I gave each teacher he encountered during the day a small notebook with sections on General Asperger's Info, All About Luke, Contact Information, Resources, and Teaching Tips. He ate lunch by himself almost everyday at the beginning, but after bringing it to the attention of the counsellors and others, they began to arrange lunches so that he had someone to sit with. It was still hard for me to be on the campus as a volunteer and see him sitting alone with his lunch box and same lunch every single day. And again, years later, it still makes my heart hurt.

*

Eighth grade[2] was a test of everything for us; the hormones went wild. It was like giving 18 year hormones to an 8 year old. His body was ready to grow up, but his mind just couldn't handle it. And

---

[1] Seventh grade covers ages 12 – 13 in America
[2] Eighth grade covers ages 13 – 14 in America

there was no way he could comprehend the gravity of his questions or actions. Thankfully, there were never touching incidents that I'm aware of; he would always ask for kisses. He asked me, his brothers, friends, relatives, neighbours, and yes, teachers. Some teachers understood and reacted appropriately, telling him that it was inappropriate and not something he should be doing. Others were appalled and complained to the vice principal. It would have been much more productive if all the teachers responded in the same way – by handling it directly with him. So he quit asking for kisses and started asking for sex. All the minute details of this incident have thankfully been forgotten. Essentially, Luke asked one of his teachers if they wanted to go have sex at lunch and when she said no, he said something to the equivalent of, "Oh come on, my mom does!" I had no idea this was going on at school until I got a call from the Vice-Principal saying she was required by law to make a report to Child Protective Services about that statement.

They visited his brothers at their school and called and talked to us, and then went to interview him. Within a few minutes of talking to him, she realized he had no concept of what he was saying or asking, and closed the report. We found a therapist who counselled patients like Luke, and he even arranged a trip to the juvenile "jail" to try the "Scared Straight" strategy. That didn't work. At the end of the year, he still didn't understand, and even wrote in one girl's yearbook, "Let's get together this summer and have some sex. Have a good summer." And signed his name. Mercifully, the girl and the mom understood what was going on and her yearbook was fixed. Then a friend from the Autism Society gave me the name of a book that might help, and it really did. The book[1] was very straightforward and we sat down together on many separate occasions and talked a lot about the text and the pictures. Then came the computer porn. He printed the stories and the pictures. All the attempts at stopping it were useless, and I finally decided to stop fighting it. I didn't want his siblings seeing any of it, but when he had it to look at, he didn't seem to bother others as much. So we happened to have an old briefcase in the house, and I put everything in there: the book, the stories, and the pictures. And I told him I never wanted to see it again, because that stuff was private, and not for anyone else. And as long as he kept everything in the briefcase and I never saw it, he could keep it in his room. Years later, I still haven't seen the contents of the briefcase, but I know it's in his room. There are only a few people who know about the briefcase, and it's not something I'm proud of, but it fixed the problem. That was a very long year.

It seemed to be that we alternated good years and bad years. We didn't suffer two bad years in a row, but we couldn't build up two good years in a row either, until the 10th grade, and the rest of high school.

Age 16 Upwards

God works in mysterious ways, and has done so

---

[1] See Suggested Reading section.

many times in our lives. One of our biggest blessings was Luke's bus driver on the regular bus route to high school. Most high school kids would do anything to avoid riding the bus, but the bus ride was the highlight of Luke's day. He always talked to the driver, who just happened to be the head of a Special Olympics delegation, and she invited him to come play basketball with them. It was life-changing for our whole family, and Luke's own personal miracle. He found something he could excel in (he's not the best, and not the worst), and he has made some very close friends. I dare anyone to attend a Special Olympics competition, and not come away with a smile. Even practice is uplifting when I get to chat with the athletes.

Through Special Olympics we learned of a social group that is for young adults, and he joined that immediately. He has a busier social schedule than the rest of us! Supper club, bowling, the movie group, and his Special Olympics sports keep him very busy outside of high school. But he stays busy with high school also. We were lucky that his high school offers bowling as a Physical Education Credit. The only caveat is that they have to provide their own transportation from the bowling alley to school. The school district personnel didn't want to let him take it, because of that reason. I had to explain that I am a stay at home mom and that the kids are my job. If I have to pick him up from the bowling alley and take him to school everyday, then that's what I would do because it would make Luke's days in high school MUCH less stressful. He got so good at bowling that he made the junior varsity bowling team as a junior, and the varsity as a senior.

Then in December of 2007, we got a letter from the state government saying that his name had reached the top of the list. Ahhh....how wonderful... it was early!!! In 1998, we were told it would be 13-15 years. Wow! Only 9 years instead of 13! And how truly typical for us....just when Luke's ship was sailing in, Daniel's (our third son) was sinking. So we meet with our case manager and find out that he needs a re-evaluation because of the amount of time between our first application and now. *Whose fault is that? And guess what? His autism hasn't gone away. Imagine that!* And we also have to apply for SSI and Medicaid[1], and be denied. We know we will be denied because we always have been, because even for a family of five, we make too much money. In other words, living paycheck to paycheck means you don't qualify for any type of assistance. This is the end of December and Luke will turn 18 before the end of January and qualify by himself because of his age; but we can't wait until then because of the state deadlines and so, we have to wait for the denial letter, which actually came after his 18th birthday, and then reapply for him as an adult, and get okayed. It was June before he got his first Social Security check.

So for now, my son is in college, and I have seen

---

[1]   SSI – is the equivalent of the British Disability Living Allowance and Medicaid is an American program for eligible individuals and families with low incomes and resources.

big changes. With the help of the habilitator, he has cleaned his room up (a MAJOR project) and keeps it clean. He does his own laundry and can clean the bathroom. During the next school break, I think we are going to work on cooking. He already buys some groceries for himself and sometimes for me too. For his college classes, he always does his homework without prompting and participates in their club. He was even nominated to run for club president.

The Future

In the immediate future, Luke will continue his college class until he can no longer benefit. We want to find him a job for now so he has a specific reason and motivation for getting up every day, and to gain some experience for a future, more permanent job. Eventually, I think he would like to live on his own, meaning away from us. It might be in a group home, with a roommate, assisted living or some other circumstance, but I know we want that to happen. He's still pretty immature and hasn't quite grasped the concept of what it would mean to live independent from his family. I would also like for him to have a job that he really enjoys and is meaningful to him. And someday, I would like to see him have a girlfriend, maybe even get married. I'm guessing that's what most parents want for all their children, regardless of abilities or inabilities.

Simon

Simon is my second born son and even from a very early age, I knew I could depend on him. One of his blessings is that he has always been independent, and never worried about what others were doing or what they thought. I tried to walk in the classroom with him on his first day of preschool as a three-year old. He stopped me at the door and said, "You can go now." I'm not sure he's ever really needed me since then. And that breaks my heart, because I have been thankful for that on so many occasions. And then my heart breaks all over again. I still cry as I write about this 12 years later. He learned at the age of four how to deal with his big brother and all of his "quirks," and that sometimes you just have to tune him out. I know a lot of adults that still have trouble with that.

He has always been a little ahead for his age. He started walking at 10 months, and always amazed his teachers with his ability to learn anything quickly. He enjoyed math and science very early on; I would make up math problems to keep him happy and quiet during church – before he even went to kindergarten. He came home from the first day of kindergarten very upset with school, because he didn't get to do any math, and he didn't learn to read. I didn't know whether Luke was really far behind, or Simon was really far ahead. I finally asked his first grade teacher, whom I trusted to tell me the truth, if he was average or really bright. Her response was that he was really bright and far ahead of average kids.

One time I took Simon to a Sibshop[1] workshop and he didn't particularly enjoy it, and had no desire to return. So we didn't. He seems to deal better with everything by himself, rather than with others in the same situation.

To my knowledge, Simon has never been embarrassed by Luke in public, but I'm pretty sure Daniel (my third son) has embarrassed him on a few occasions. I don't know what the difference is. At home, Simon has had friends over and Luke has asked them to kiss him, or he forgets to put on pants before he leaves his room and has on nothing but tightey whiteys. Daniel isn't so much embarrassing at home, rather he is more annoying. These days, Simon asks Luke to come watch him play basketball or whatever the current sport is. And Simon in turn watches his brother play Special Olympics basketball games, and even went to one of the bowling matches.

As he has grown older, he has almost taken on the role of the third parent in the house. He offers to help both brothers with various things, and will often jump in to explain something when he can tell I'm exasperated or just plain exhausted. He is very mature for his age in certain areas, and he will be an amazing husband and father one day. Even though we have always told him (and meant it) that he was not responsible for his brothers once we are dead and gone, he has always planned for it. When he was much younger, he talked about playing a

---

[1] Sibshop -workshops for siblings of children with special needs.

professional sport and having a house big enough for Luke to have his own apartment inside the house. We have tried to do the appropriate financial planning so that if he is able to and chooses to, he can be as involved as he wants with their lives.

His chapter here is much shorter than the others, and I believe that he accepts that fact. And although I'm aware of it and acknowledge it, I don't have to like it. We've always tried to make sure he got the same attention as the others, and I have to point out *quality* versus *quantity* here. The quality of an hour at the batting cage versus two hours at a therapy session or meeting is sometimes hard to grasp, much in the same way Luke would prefer three $1 bills over one $5 bill.

Though he wouldn't like the sound of it now, I think he would be a very effective teacher and coach. He has the innate ability to see the big picture and understand it all at once. And his experiences growing up give him a tremendous amount of compassion. But all I really want for him is to be a good person, find a job/career that he enjoys and finds rewarding, and hopefully marry and have children one day. That's what I want for all three of my sons.

*

Daniel

Birth - Age Five

Daniel was born on Luke's second day of kindergarten. He was a happy and easy baby. Anyone could take care of him. And he was so flexible with his schedule! Some days he spent as much time in his car seat as he did out of it! His birth was not complicated, and he met all the developmental milestones. As he grew, we began to notice similarities between him and Luke. At a time when ADHD was the diagnosis du jour, and parents everywhere were devastated to hear that their child was indeed ADHD, we were hoping that it would be the **only** diagnosis we would face. Throughout preschool, temper tantrums and meltdowns were regular occurrences. Because of his late summer birthday and immaturity, everyone encouraged us to keep him home an extra year before sending him to kindergarten. But as the youngest of three, he was familiar with the elementary school his whole life. By the time enrolment for kindergarten started, he knew which teacher he wanted, which room he wanted her in, and even which days he wanted to bring lunch from home rather than buying the school lunch. He also knew that five year olds go to kindergarten; so, how do you say no to all that forethought and expectation?

The first few days of kindergarten were great and Daniel's behavior wasn't even an issue. He had been to preschool and was perfectly fine with me leaving him there for the day. Like I said, he had it all planned out. Then the "honeymoon" was over. While Luke had always held his temper tantrums until he got out of school and then would meltdown at home, Daniel had no problem melting down absolutely anywhere, any time, and for seemingly any reason. He often spent lunches and recesses in the Principal's office for things like throwing a chair when asked to clean up his art project, stomping on his classmates' hands, spitting on them, pushing them, shoving them, etc. The one thing that I wanted to happen during that year was to have Daniel's brothers meet him at his kindergarten classroom at the end of the day, and walk down the street to where I was parked. I was going to be free of school traffic! Instead, more often than not, I was called to come in and pick him up because he was tearing up the room, or he was in the Principal's office.

Even though I had already survived the toenail incident at the pizza parlour with his older brother, I could still feel the other mothers looking around to see who the mom of the bad little boy was. And then there was the knowing head-nod, as if to say, Ohhhhh, it's her? And she volunteers with the PTA! She ought to know better! Of course, what they didn't know, was that at home he wasn't any different than at school, and that parenting can't cure Asperger's. This was also during the time Luke was going through his aggressive stage, my father-in-law had just passed away the year before and I was still helping my mother-in-law a lot and on a regular basis.

I spent a lot of time that year sitting next to the bathtub and crying after the kids went to sleep. Getting out of bed was the hardest thing to do everyday. Many times I would meet my husband in the driveway and tell him, **I... have... to... go... for... a... walk!** before he could even get out of the car. I would cry all the way around the neighborhood, and then come back home and be able to deal with it again for a while. Luckily, I found a psychiatrist who immediately put me on anti-depressants, and I haven't been off of them since!

It became apparent that we needed professional help other than what was already available at the school. We (the teacher and us) had tried several interventions and they were only working about 50% of the time. So we took him to see the same pediatric neurologist who had diagnosed Luke. At the meeting, to go over the results of all the evaluations, the first thing she said was, "How does it feel to be the parents of a genius?" *Ok, so he's bright, but what about Aspergers? There is a fine line between "genius" and very high functioning Aspergers.* She wouldn't diagnose Aspergers at his age, but did say that it was a possibility. ADHD was obvious, and we began giving him Ritalin. When he left preschool in May, he didn't know the alphabet, and could barely write his name, but he could do math. By Christmas he was reading and doing math well above his grade level. The Ritalin helped, but only for a couple of years.

*

Ages Six - 10

In first grade, things were going along fairly smoothly. Every now and then, I would get a call from Daniel's teacher saying she didn't know who was in her class, because it wasn't the Daniel she knew. I would find the Ritalin (that had not been taken for one reason or another) and take it to him at school. Within about 30 minutes, he was back to what the school viewed as "normal." That was about the biggest problem we had at school, but I think I knew somewhere deep down that it wasn't going to be that easy. At home, I was miserable. Luke and Daniel fought all the time. The only approach that worked was "divide and conquer." We kept them separated as much as possible. It didn't fix the problem, but it gave us a break from the bickering.

By second grade there were a few issues with a couple of teachers at the school who were very controlling and didn't understand different learning styles at all. Those were the teachers that had answers like, 'Because I said so'. The first rule of parenting and teaching these kids is that you never, ever enter into a power struggle with them. And those teachers who felt the need to control everything had to have the last word. And that continued into third grade, and there were more and more incidents. During all this time, he was in speech therapy for articulation, so we were already having meetings with diagnostic personnel, teachers, and administrators. At the second grade meeting, I told them that I was sure we would have to go ahead with the Autism Evaluation because the gap between him and his peers was starting to widen. They agreed that it was there, but not really detrimental to him at that point.

At the third grade meeting, I told them I wanted to go ahead and get the evaluation started, because I knew how long the process was. We started before Christmas and had our meeting about the results in early spring. Collectively, the brilliant autism team of one psychologist, one speech therapist, one occupational therapist, and one diagnostician, determined that he wasn't autistic, just ADHD. *I was stupid. I told them I didn't care what label they used, as long as his needs were being met; but I also told them that I knew he was Aspergers. I lived with one Aspergers kid already; believe me, I know when I'm living with another one!!!!!!!!!!! Yeah, the first one was so much fun, I decided to make this one autistic too. I don't get enough grief from the world by having one, I should really have two. Oh, and this will really mess up the middle son's world. Heh, heh, my secret evil plan was working! By creating this through bad parenting, I was giving them a challenge at their jobs. Wow, I'm brilliant!*

Fourth grade however was the beginning of the end of his time in public school[1]. It started when I requested the two teachers who I KNEW would be able to reach Daniel and who he would respect. Instead, they put him with two others, because one of the teachers I wanted him to have did not want him in her class. These two teachers were fine for

---

[1] Public school is state funded education in America.

most kids, but they connected with their students on an emotional level. For Daniel, that was a foreign language. And one teacher was just not that smart or that quick. Bad news for our "little professors." *Okay, sure, there is a whole school of thought that I used to subscribe to myself, that says the teacher is right, and you must respect him/her. Now, I believe that the teacher must earn a student's respect, even if one is an adult and another is a child. Those are fighting words to some people, but I stand my ground on that. His teacher made mistakes, and he pointed them out to her. I'm sure he wasn't polite, but the school's big concern was that he was correcting a teacher, not that the teacher was wrong, and that he needed to be taught some social skills. My parenting skills are blamed for his Aspergers qualities, and then he doesn't get the help he needs.* I cry when I think about everything that has happened, everything I have allowed to happen. I cry because I wasn't strong enough to take a stand back then and force the school to educate him and not be annoyed by him.

And then I cry harder because of what I put my middle son through.

One day, during recess, Daniel was "rebelling" and running away from the teacher who was yelling at him. First of all, I told the teacher that if they would not chase him, he wouldn't run away from them. He would stop running if they stopped. *But what do I know? I'm a bad parent! I don't discipline my child so he acts like a spoiled brat. I don't support the teachers because I questioned the school's reactions when he corrected the teacher (and he was right). So anything I say can't possibly help; if I won't discipline him at home, then they must do it at school.* But when they continued to chase him, I went to the cafeteria and asked Simon to help us "catch" him and calm him down. That must have been the most embarrassing moment of his life up till then. I can't apologize enough to him for doing that. I should never have involved him at all. Lucky for me, he has turned into quite an extraordinary young man, in spite of my parenting skills!

We did manage to get him switched to the teachers I had requested, and surprise! They were much better suited to Daniel. One of them was "the meanest teacher in the school" according to the rest of the students, but Daniel defended her and tried to protect her every chance he got. *When will professionals learn to listen to us!*

Before we changed teachers, I also rescinded my agreement to the Autism Team Evaluation from third grade, and pointed out several areas where I felt they were lacking and where they had misinterpreted the data. I had charts and graphs, and it was a very professional looking document. I'm still proud of the fact that I approached them with data, not emotions. That was a big step for me. They offered an evaluation of the information by a different Team of Autism Specialists within the school district. And once again, I stupidly agreed with something they said. But when this team said he didn't have Aspergers, I requested an Independent Educational Evaluation, and they granted the request. The IEE found that Daniel did meet the qualifications for a student with an autism spectrum disorder, and a plan was made for the next year.

And once we finally had the appropriate plans in place, why in the world did I think they would actually refer to them and follow them?

Ages 10 - 12

During fifth grade, Daniel's aggression began to increase to the point that we turned to medicine for help. While it helped level his mood and calm his anger, it increased his appetite and he gained a lot of weight, around 40 pounds. I try to block a lot of this out of my mind because it is so painful to think about. I feel such guilt about that whole time in his life. *I wonder now what I could have done to avoid the medication; should I have been stronger emotionally and mentally? What if I had more patience with him, or what if I tried homeschooling him? There are so many things I didn't try, and I wonder why I didn't. And if I was too depressed to try all those things, why didn't I call my doctor and change my medication? What was I thinking? I know I thought about how hard it would be to homeschool or change schools. I liked working in the PTA at the school and knowing what was going on. In a way, it kept me sane, because I could think about something else. But I think I was too selfish to drop everything I enjoyed, and thought I needed.* Even though he was on medication, the school still called me to come pick him up quite a few times that year. And I cried every single time they called.

A Nightmare of a Year - Sixth Grade

The beginning of sixth grade was quite busy: Daniel's dwarf hamster died on the first day of school, we started remodelling the bathroom on the second day of school, Daniel had his 11th birthday on the third day of school, and he wouldn't go to school on the fourth day. And on the fifth day, he went to school like nothing had ever happened. From my journal: 'On the way to school, I told him we could just consider yesterday as a "mental health day" because even adults get overwhelmed and need a break. Monday, Sally died; Tuesday, construction started; Wednesday was his birthday. Not to mention the first three days of school. We talked about having one of these "mental health" days once a month but after discussion about the number of months in the school year and the number of absences allowed, he suggested one every six weeks. My thoughts are that now he has some control over it he may not need it anymore'. Boy was I wrong!'

There was another incident on Wednesday the following week. Teachers said one thing at the beginning of the day, changed it at lunch without any warning whatsoever, and it went downhill from there. It ended with the Principal taking away something of Daniel's and Daniel wanting to call the police to report him for stealing. People with Aspergers tend to have a very rigid understanding of right and wrong and taking something that belongs to someone else, without their consent, is definitely 'wrong'. They are frequently very highly principled. In this instance the Principal punished Daniel for something which Daniel did not understand. In Daniel's mind confiscating was stealing.

Tuesday, Wednesday and Thursday of the next week was the beginning of the end. I don't think there was enough medicine in the city to keep me from getting depressed. From my journal again: 'It was the book: The terrible, horrible, no good, very bad day. Only I actually lived this one. So did Daniel. I don't even remember how it started, I just know that somewhere along the way, something isn't working. Mrs. T had the nerve to call the HJH SRO[1] Officer S. Luckily for us, she knows Luke and the rest of the family so he didn't end up in jail or even handcuffs. By the time I got there, they (Principal, Vice-Principal, Officer S, the Counselor) were holding him to keep him from leaving to go to recess. He had had a bad morning apparently and things got worse. A small incident, badly handled, had been allowed to escalate into a major event. He was in such a state that I told them that we needed to go to a room to calm down. We managed to get him to the counselor's office. I told them to let Daniel and me be alone in there, yet everyone came in with us. I asked them to leave and sat down on the floor with Daniel and braced myself against the door so he couldn't get to it and

---

[1]   HJH was the junior high school across the street. The SRO was the police officer assigned to that campus and who stays there all the time.

we just sat there until the cycle finished. After a while (20-30 minutes?) he was getting calmer and I started distracting him and eventually we came home.

Mrs T suspended him from school (out of school)[1] for the rest of the day and Wednesday also. The rest of the day was fine. Mrs. T called and tried to talk to Daniel but he did not respond to her at all. Wednesday, Aug. 30 Daniel didn't remember Mrs. T telling him he was suspended for the day. Thursday, Aug. 31 I asked Daniel on the way to school if he understood why he wasn't at school yesterday. This was our conversation:

Mom: *Do you know why you didn't go to school yesterday?*
Daniel: *Yes.*
Mom: *Why*
Daniel: *Because Mrs. T suspended me.*
Mom: *Do you know why Mrs. T suspended you?*
Daniel: *Because they had to call Officer S.*
Mom: *Okay, do you know why they called Officer S?*
Daniel: *No*
Mom: *Well it was because you weren't following the rules.*
Daniel: *YES, I DID!*

I dropped it after that. I also asked Mrs. T to talk to Daniel and explain why and what things were done.' What is the point of punishing a child who does not understand what they have done wrong?

---

[1]   Out of school suspension requires the student to be kept at home.

Another Incident!

A couple of weeks later, there was another incident that ended up outside at recess where according to classmates, it looked like the Principal tripped him and took him down like they do on the TV show Cops. It all began when he had failed to complete some homework because he had left the book at school. On the way to school I pre-warned him that he may be required to stay after school to do the homework, I did not mention that he might have to miss his recess (so he was not prepared for this eventuality). At recess time the school tried to make him stay inside to complete his homework. Daniel knew that he was not supposed to miss recess because he needed the physical movement. Daniel was planning to complete his homework after school. So they either didn't know about it or just ignored that and tried to make him stay inside to do the homework. They called me, and by the time I got there, it was almost time to go. They told me he had ISS[1] the next day and I told them fine, but don't call me because I just can't talk about it anymore. I did send a written request for an ARD meeting ASAP. I just didn't know there was so much more to come.

The next day, Daniel refused to do ISS. He went to his classroom and wouldn't leave. The school called me again, and I asked enough questions

---

[1]   ISS is an alternative setting that removes students from the classroom for a period of time, while still allowing students to attend school and complete their work.

(why weren't they asking questions?) to figure out he didn't want to miss his school pictures, and he didn't think he did anything wrong. He was supposed to go to recess, and that was what he did. The Assistant Principal assigned him to the alternative school where they must earn points to come back to their regular campus. This environment would work and make an impact on my middle son; however, for Asperger's kids, it is totally inappropriate! I tried to talk to the Vice-Principal and "Behavior Specialist" and explain that I wasn't against consequences for him, but they needed to be meaningful to him, not us. Punishment for punishment's sake is just not acceptable to me; however they were fine with it. I gave them an article about this exact same thing, and they glanced at it, and went back to arguing with me.

I left without signing the papers and told them I wouldn't be taking him to the other school. The Vice-Principal made it clear that Daniel was not welcome back or allowed on school property until he spent his two days at the other campus. This was on September 13 - we had only been in school for one month and these were the major incidents that had happened. I quit counting all the minor ones. And they all happened because the teachers weren't trained like they were supposed to be, and didn't handle anything involving Daniel in an appropriate manner. It seemed to me that they were unable to adjust their approach, I was never clear whether they actually understood Daniel's condition and why he behaved as he did. Many of the professionals who we encounter have a rather disconcerting tendency to interpret the causes of any undesired behaviour as stemming from one of three possibilities:- Manipulation, Attention seeking and Lack of boundaries. These explanations for the reasons behind our children's bad behaviour are, more often than not, wrong. It shows a dangerous lack of understanding of why our children behave the way they do. If suggested reasons for behaving badly are flawed, then what is offered will also be flawed and the problems will not be resolved. When this happens and our children continue to have problems, we ultimately are blamed. When the environment is appropriate these children rarely kick off. I tried to appeal the decision with the Principal, but in less than 13 minutes I had gone from my vehicle to his office, tried to appeal, asked for papers to withdraw him, and went back to my vehicle. The bad thing about this is that due to all of this, Daniel couldn't go on the field trip that the sixth grade takes every year. It's all about team building and cooperating with others; yet, Daniel couldn't go. He was sitting in the front passenger seat of my minivan when I told him he couldn't go. He actually kicked the windshield from the inside of the van and broke it, like if a boulder had hit it. That was just about the breaking point! I really understood the meaning of the phrase, going postal.[1] Here I am hanging on by the skin of my teeth, trying to help my son, and here is this other group (the school)

---

[1]   There was a period of time in the US where there were more than a few postal workers who lost their minds and went back to the offices where they had worked and shot all of their co-workers. It's not funny, but the phrase has become part of slang here in the US.

that I should be able to depend on for help, and for whatever reasons, they have made it ten times as bad as I ever remember living through.

At an appointment with my therapist, I cried and ranted and raved and still didn't feel better, but she suggested that we take him to the other campus. It wasn't going to help him, we knew; but it also wasn't going to harm him. We could use it to help prove that the district can't provide an education for him, and would have to do something different. So after talking it over for a long time, John and I decided that we would try it. When I called the coordinator to let her know that we would be bringing Daniel to that campus, I asked if the teachers were familiar with Aspergers and had ever worked with children on the spectrum. Oh, yes, they are totally aware of the situation. Silly me, I interpreted that to mean that they knew what they were dealing with. When I couldn't get Daniel out of bed and called to let the teacher know he wouldn't be in, she said, "This is ridiculous! He's in 6th grade for goodness sakes! He needs to get over it and do the consequences already!" That's a direct quote. Daniel finished his two days and nothing changed. I was probably the only one not surprised by that.

At this point, the district convinced us that a "brainstorming" session would serve a better purpose than calling a formal ARD. A "brainstorming" session was conducted and an action plan was put into place to help the teachers with Daniel. All of Daniel's teachers, the Principal, the district's autism liaison, the so-called autism specialist (also a psychologist) participated in this session. The Assistant Principal was not present for any part of it.

*

Don't Make a Mountain out of a Mole Hill!

In October a relatively small incident was allowed to escalate out of control. A small disagreement in Daniel's class was not defused by the teacher, a teacher that was part of the "brainstorming" session. The incident spilled over to the lunch room. The two school personnel that were involved in the lunch room were not part of the "brainstorming" session. Also, they ignored directions from the autism liaison, who was part of the "brainstorming" session, who was in the lunch room at the time. The trainer tried to get the other personnel to leave Daniel alone to allow him time to cool down. She specifically told them to stop talking to him.

This recommendation was not followed and the incident escalated into a full crisis including another restraint. For this incident, the school (actually the Assistant Principal who wasn't in the brainstorming meeting) decided that the only recourse to the above incident was 10 days of AEP[1]. We said we would not take him, we had requested an ARD, they talked us out of that, and now we needed to

---

[1]   AEP – Alternative Educational Placement is a place where children with disciplinary problems are sent. It is a strict, rigid environment and is inappropriate for children on the spectrum.

schedule the ARD with our attorney. I think they thought I was bluffing about the attorney. At the ARD there was discussion of placing Daniel into the PACES (a behavior based program) at a different location. We finally agreed upon the placement because we thought that it was either that or 10 days of AEP. The program's brochure states that the program "Creates opportunities for individuals to build new skills and return to the group strengthened." Maybe for neuro-typical kids, but not for mine. My kid needed structure, it was the unstructured time that caused every single incident we have had at school. But I can't convince them that structured is not rigid and inflexible.

That turned into yet one more disaster for this poor kid. It became a battle every morning to get him to go to school. And there were many mornings that I just didn't push it when I probably should have, but it was all I could do to get myself out of bed. I couldn't deal with him too. I looked into homeschooling, even though I had always said I would probably have to kill them if I tried to homeschool them. I also looked around at a couple of private schools, but they were either too far away, or they required uniforms, and with the sensory issues Daniel has, that would have been inviting a brand new battle for every morning. He wears shorts even in winter; I created the rule that if it's below 40, you have to wear long pants just to protect your skin. That was the other thing with this group of teachers – they had some serious control issues going on. Yes, teachers need to be in control, but to truly be in control, you don't have to announce to the world and prove it all day every day. Being in control of these kids is all about not creating power struggles. Instead of saying, "I want you to finish this worksheet before you can go to recess," just say, "This worksheet needs to be finished in time for you to go to recess." No emotions, no trying to control his actions. Just stating a fact and leaving the emotions out gave them control – if only they would have used it! One time, I actually walked up to the classroom and found Daniel and his teacher in the hallway outside the classroom and she was telling Daniel, "Look me in the eye when I talk to you. "He can't! He has to look somewhere else while you're talking, and then he can look at you and respond. Did I need to tattoo this on his forehead?

His behavior in class continued to deteriorate; I maintain it's because they were giving this Gifted and Talented kid worksheets to do everyday and they were not addressing those academic needs. If you have to sit at a desk everyday and be bored, I seriously doubt that your behavior is going to improve. He destroyed bulletin boards, knocked over desks, and tore up books and papers. Oh yeah, he's learning a lot in here!

By the end of the spring semester, we had requested a change in placement and had been in a three-day marathon ARD meeting planning for the next year, which would be at the junior high school and require a lot more independence and maturity. The district wanted to continue placement in the same program at a different school; I wanted him in his home school with an aide. I spent several days preparing a transition plan, addressing everything I could possibly think of after searching the web. My plan was completely ignored, never even referenced.

And the icing on the cake was when two, not one, but TWO, junior high school Principals PROMISED that he would be handcuffed and taken to juvenile services if he exhibited any of the recent behaviors like destruction of property. My attorney was appalled to say the least. After three days of meetings, I couldn't think straight, John was stressed to his limit after missing so much work, and I was totally out of touch with the other kids. The house looked like those people's houses on the TV show 'How Clean is Your House?'. And I didn't care. I really didn't care how it looked, whether it was clean or not, whether we had food in the house, or clean clothes to wear. My self esteem was not just low, it was non-existent. Every day when I finally got out of bed, there was some new problem/crisis to confront and hopefully solve. I have a few comfort foods that I fix when I am down and feeling utterly desperate about a situation. I made those foods every day for a little over a month, in true depression or eating-disorder mode. I preferred to have the food by myself, not even telling anyone else that I had actually made it. That was the one little piece of my world that I could control.

To make a long story short, essentially due to his academic abilities, Daniel had a lot of trouble in public school because of their cookie cutter approach. It was impossible for them to educate him as Gifted and Talented (GT) and Aspergers. He needed the GT academics, but the behavior was from the Aspergers. And their (incorrect) logic was that if he's that smart, he can learn to behave. His behavior was more often a *re*action rather than an action. When we disagreed about the proper placement and supports, we eventually hired a lawyer, filed due process papers,[1] and ended the process at mediation after we withdrew him from school rather than have him be placed in the wrong environment. I say we *ended* the process at mediation because I do not feel it was settled. There was an agreement by both parties as to what would take place in order to withdraw the complaint, and of course a confidentiality agreement along with that; but in my mind, it is most definitely not settled, because they can do the same thing again to someone else, who maybe isn't as stubborn as we are, and that student will be stuck. That was all during his sixth grade year, and as I said before, it could be a separate book entirely, although it is in reality a study in futility.

---

[1]   It is essentially suing the school district for not providing a free, appropriate education (FAPE) as guaranteed in the IDEA (Individuals with Disabilities Education Act).The problem is that the State Agency that oversees the process also hires the "independent" hearing officers, and school districts are allowed unlimited use of funds for attorneys to fight the parents. Oftentimes, the attorney fees are 10 times more than the actual cost of implementing the appropriate placement or support.

Ages 12 – The Present

Over the summer, I continued looking at private schools in the area by searching the internet. I found one that I hadn't heard of before, but sounded really interesting. They claimed to be a full inclusion school, and accepted students of all abilities, including Dyslexia, Down Syndrome, Autism, Bi-polar, etc. The founder had a doctorate in special education and she believed in a classical education with the Charlotte Mason philosophy and style. Without going into too much detail, Charlotte Mason was an educator in the Victorian era, and she used just good common sense (in my opinion). I read all I could find on her and her philosophies and classical education and while it wasn't the reason for finding out more about the school, it wasn't a reason not to, either. I talked to the Founder/Principal several times on the phone, and she answered all my questions.

I took a tour, and then took Daniel and John back for a tour, and really liked what I saw. She doesn't have students grouped by traditional grades, more by ages and abilities. There is the grammar school, pre-k through about 6th grade, and upper school, which is about 6th grade through 12th. There are no more than 12 students in one classroom and each teacher has a full time aide. The hours are from 9:30 – 3:30, Monday through Thursday. Fridays should be family time. There is no homework assigned and, for the most part, the students work at their own pace. For example, they all participate in the same history lesson, but to varying degrees.

It sounded really interesting, except that it was a 30 minute drive from our house. But after we learned that a nearby private school was closing, we paid our registration fees, and notified the school district (as we were required to do) that we were withdrawing Daniel and then filed the due process papers to ask the district to pay for the tuition. That was one of the most painful experiences/processes I have ever been through. But it was well worth it.!

It had taken us three years, two Autism Evaluation teams from the school district, one Independent Educational Evaluation, and the continual threat of lawyers to convince the school district that he was indeed Asperger's. Three years of all our lives.

Today, he is in the eighth grade of this private Christian school[1] which accepts students of all abilities, including autism, bipolar, Down Syndrome, and the list goes on. It is his second year – there are no special education classes, resource kids[2], short buses[3], etc. Here we have a school full of students learning and being successful in their education. He now plays on the basketball team, and is learning not only to identify his feelings (anger, sadness, frustration), he is also learning to control them.

---

[1]   This academy practices the concept of full inclusion.
[2]   Resource kids – is the name given to those in special education and usually used in a derogatory way.
[3]   A short bus as the name implies, is shorter than a normal sized school bus. Short buses are commonly used to transport children with learning difficulties like ADHD or Autism to "special schools" for education.

The biggest difference I have seen between the private school and the public school (state school in the UK) is the level of dedication. There are some public school teachers who are dedicated, and they do the best with what they are given as support. But for the majority of them, it is just a job. The teachers at this school are there 100% and more. Instead of calling the parents to come pick up their kid having a meltdown, they stick with it and finish it. The meltdown doesn't have to end when the bell rings at the end of the day. Being sent home (which is an escape) is not an option here. His teacher stayed with him one night until 6:30 pm and has stayed later with others to prove their point. There was only one instance of restraint, but as soon as he calmed down, he was talking about it with the behavior specialist and working on ways to handle the situation better if it happened again. And the other difference is the way the teachers engage with their students. At public school, the teachers pull up a chair and sit and chat with each other during recess, and "supervise" from afar. Daniel's teachers are on the playground watching and listening, because as they put it, that's where a lot of learning opportunities occur.

This is my favorite story, and my worst, about pulling him out of public school: On Christmas morning of his seventh grade year, we were trying to be humorous and hid their presents. Daniel looked around and said, "That's okay Simon, we already got our Christmas present this year. You know – the academy!" That a 12 year old boy would consider a different school from public school as a

Christmas present amazed me; then it truly saddened me. What had I done to them all these years? How miserable could they have been? But I've also learned over time that I have to be thankful that we found the school when we did, and we have to move forward from here.

We finally finished our dealings with the school district in May of 2008; it has only been since then that I have slowly started to come back to life. During the fiasco that was Daniel's sixth grade year, I had requested a copy of all records that pertained to Daniel. I found a few things that made me mad, but one of the things that embarrassed me was a note written by the psychologist, "mom cries a lot." I learned early on to detach the emotional side at Luke's meetings; I have yet to learn how to do that with Daniel. Is it because he is the youngest, my baby? Or do I still feel guilty about everything that I let happen to him, when so much of it didn't have to happen. It's almost one in the morning again, as that seems to be the only time I have to write. And after reliving that nightmare, I want to make my comfort food and have it all to myself. But I'm so tired, and I really don't have the energy to fix it for myself, and if I ask someone else to fix it, it just doesn't work. So, I guess I'll sleep for now, and maybe tomorrow I won't want it as badly. I sure hope so.

Miscellaneous

Luke and Daniel's Key Problems

The biggest issues for both of them are transition/change and taking everything literally. I've often said if I could run 10 minutes ahead of them into the future, and tell them what was coming, life would have been a lot easier. And if you say you're going to run to the store, you should be putting on running shoes to actually **run** to the store. Because of Daniel's intellectual skills, I've often teased him that he could be a great lawyer one day, because if there was a loophole to be found, he could find it! And the simplest of changes can be a problem. I remember that pledge week on PBS[1] was a nightmare, because the schedule was interrupted. We would see the entire program, but with a lot of interruptions, and that was too much for them to handle at the time.

Friends and Family

I sometimes describe my life as a cross between the movies *Groundhog Day* and *Rainman*. Every day is the same, regardless of what happened yesterday or what was learned yesterday or the week before. No one knows how different it is raising these kids, yet they all think they understand. I can't decide which is worse, hearing "Well, it could be worse" or "You poor thing! You really have your hands full!" Yes, it could always be worse, but in most instances, it is the wrong time to

---

[1]   PBS – Public Broadcasting Service

remind us of that or to point it out. I consider myself quite the optimist, but every now and then you just have to acknowledge that some things in your life suck. Period. And while I do appreciate the good intentions that come with that statement, it is not always an immediate reaction.

And I don't want your pity. Yes, I have my hands full, but so does every other parent of a special needs child, regardless of what that need is. What I personally would like is for someone to say, "Wow! Really? Tell me about it. How did you know? Is there research going on" etc. Don't pretend it's not there, and try to shove it under the rug.

It's hard to be my friend, because my world is dominated with autism, but the truest friends I have, acknowledge that our kids are different, but that it's okay. If they invite us to something, they will ask, "How will the kids handle this? Is there something we need to do differently?" And I appreciate them more than I can ever tell them.

*

Me

What is there left of me? I'm not sure who I am. I'm the bitch who believes my children deserve a free, appropriate public education, even if it might be harder because of their differences. I'm the volunteer who wants to make a change for all children, not just mine. I'm a sports mom who sees the value of learning to be a part of a team. I'm the wife that doesn't have a formal job, yet never has the time for housekeeping, yardwork, cooking, sewing, or little home improvement projects around the house. I'm a daughter that worries about her mother and grandmother being alone. I'm a woman who would like to spend more quality time with her husband. Even if there was time left for me to be just me, I'm not sure I would have the physical or mental resources.

~

The Best of The Rest

Sarah and David's Story

My sixteen year old daughter is beautiful, clever and funny. How I would have loved to have been like her when I was sixteen. But this is how she is on a 'good' day. Good days can quickly turn bad, and become one of the days when she is angry, unable to communicate, exhausted - disabled by Asperger's. I wish I could make it all better, make it go away, wave a magic wand so she would be 'normal'. Don't tell me to celebrate what she does achieve, or tell me that it could be worse. I know this and it doesn't help. We are still adjusting to her diagnosis, and are angry at ourselves and consumed with guilt.

From the time she was about two, we knew that things weren't quite right. Kate's behaviour often gets the comment from family and teachers that they are 'walking on eggshells' as so many things can trigger her temper. We believed that as she grew up, she would be able to tell us what was wrong, or explain her behaviour. I wish I'd shouted, made a huge fuss, and not been fobbed off by reassurances from professionals that she would 'grow out of' her volatility and lack of co-operation. So many years have been wasted, when no-one believed there was anything wrong. We asked for help time and again but the conclusion was always that her problems could be resolved by us managing her better. Bad parenting and weak discipline were implied. I think the possibility of sexual abuse was hinted at on one occasion. What she needed, we were told, were anger management techniques and parenting courses for us. She was not a priority for anyone's attention. Like so many girls, she remained below the radar because she wasn't self-harming, and her academic results were good.

It was clear, as time passed, that her emotional and social development was patchy, as if she had become stuck in the mind of her much younger self. Whilst happy to listen to boy bands and try out make-up, she was just as happy playing with toys. Even last year, boys were still 'smelly, boring and only interested in football'.

Probably one of the worst things you could think of doing to a child with Asperger's would be to take them away from everything and everyone they know, to start a new life in another part of the world. A fresh start for Kate, then thirteen, was one of the reasons we decided in 2006 to do just this, being ignorant of the underlying reasons for her behaviour.

The small town we've moved to has a new secondary school, trying new approaches to teaching, and smaller classes. It also has to be said that the standards of behaviour expected here are well above what now has to pass as acceptable in many schools in the UK. Where fewer children had 'behavioural issues' Kate stood out like a sore thumb. After a generous settling in period, it became clear that again, all was not well. Kate's form teacher requested that I take her to the family doctor as she could not cope with her in the classroom. Kate was having violent outbursts and storming out of classes.

Things moved quickly after seeing the doctor. There was no problem in being referred to a psychiatrist, although Kate doesn't like him, and doesn't see the point: 'I'm not mad'. After this came referrals to a psychologist and a speech pathologist, for more tests. Finally, after thirteen years, we were able to put a name to Kate's demons. At the same time, a support group was set up here for parents with children on the Autistic spectrum. The relief was enormous, to know at last that we weren't just useless parents. She did have a real problem.

Relief didn't last long, because knowing why doesn't change anything. Day to day we still deal with the same problems, although now we can anticipate and manage some of them a bit better. We still have questions, but ones that no-one can answer. We aren't sure what effective help and support we can give, what is 'out there' and how to access it. There is so much we all need to learn for Kate to stand any chance of leading an independent and productive adult life.

It would be easy to blame Kate's late diagnosis on inefficient or incompetent professionals, teachers or medics, in the UK. I resent the UK secondary school that added Kate to the special needs register, simply on her behaviour record. They benefitted from extra funding, promising help which never happened. We wonder how different things might be if we'd had the right help years ago, but it's only in the last two years that the extent of her disabilities have become apparent. So many 'if onlys'. Being angry at the past, which we cannot change, seems like a waste of energy now. Our doctor cannot believe Asperger's was never picked up, but I'd done research on the internet, years before, and didn't think it 'fitted'. Kate's main problem did seem to be an inability to control her temper. At one time it seemed more like Oppositional Defiant Disorder. I mentioned this to the psychologist we saw when Kate was eleven. She asked 'Was that on an American website? They have a syndrome for everything over there.' An examination by the school nurse at this time also notes 'no evidence of any ADHD/ASD type disorder was observed'. We doubt anyone we sought help from knew enough about Asperger's to consider it a possibility. No-one saw Kate at her worst. She could behave impeccably, and we must have looked like frauds. Asperger's supposedly affects more boys than girls, or is possibly under-diagnosed in girls. I assume that diagnostic criteria and research is based on boys. So, if professionals lack knowledge, and Aspergers presents differently in girls, an accurate and timely diagnosis is unlikely.

School has always been a nightmare. Just getting Kate there is a real achievement. She rarely manages a full week's attendance. As term goes on she needs more late passes, and more days off. Thankfully, bullying hasn't been a major issue yet, although the other kids notice she is different, and complain that it's unfair that she gets away without working. She's been called 'freak' and 'retard' both here and in the UK. Her form teacher has been very supportive since the diagnosis, and has a good understanding of Aspergers. The same cannot be said for all her teachers. To see comments on her report such as 'needs to ask for help' are so frustrating. Kate cannot ask. Every missed lesson or homework task mounts up, as does my annoyance at the time spent trying to contact an ever-changing list of teachers. I feel like a broken record, explaining over and over, trying to gain their understanding and co-operation. They expect me to have a magic solution, to be able to control this thing. I feel inadequate and inarticulate in trying to advocate for Kate. I'm failing her, because I lack these vital skills.

I can't imagine a future where she will be able to hold down any kind of job, pursue further education or live independently. An IQ of 120 is little benefit when she cannot, or won't complete the simplest of tasks, and seems unlikely to achieve much academically. Why is it assumed that all those with Aspergers have some fantastic and redeeming talent for maths, computers or science? If she did, it might compensate a little for everything else that is missing. Kate's ideal life would probably be spending the day in bed sleeping, then playing computer games and listening to her music all night. Her ambition is to be a famous actress, but we doubt she can actually imagine her life very far into the future, and lacks the motivation to do anything about achieving her goal.

At the moment, the future is very uncertain, because Kate is so resistant to being helped, and has huge problems with communication. I guess most parents would be glad to have a teenager who won't use the telephone!

For me, the biggest sense of grief comes from the emotional deficiencies Asperger's entails. Kate doesn't 'get' why some things are so important to others, although she understands perfectly well in relation to herself: How devastated she would be to receive no birthday presents! But family birthdays, Mothers Day, Fathers Day can pass without comment or acknowledgement. She knows what is expected, but physically cannot act upon it. My mother finds it very hard that Kate won't speak to her on the 'phone. It's such a selfish syndrome – it really is 'all about me'. The temper outbursts are so convenient for getting out of anything she doesn't want to do, and I wonder how much of it is real. Is she pulling the wool over everyone's eyes? I feel guilty for having these thoughts, because although she can often appear to be absolutely fine, I know she's not. Just now and again, she will do something spontaneously, without being nagged, begged, bullied or chivvied endlessly, and it means so very much.

I often get angry and lose patience as we repeat the same battles over basic things like personal hygiene. Maybe this is as good as it gets, and for the rest of our lives we will be caring for and supporting an adult with the social skills and empathy of an eight year old. Is it right to keep pushing, trying to force self-sufficiency when it would be so much easier to say 'OK, just stay in bed' or 'Leave it, I'll do it.' Sometimes it's too tiring to fight, it only provokes another firestorm of shouting, stamping and slamming. Her persistent rudeness, aggression and spite make her hateful. Reprimands or shouting back push her into an autistic sort of 'shutdown mode' while the task required remains undone. Our frustration and despair at these times is incredible. We wonder why we ever became parents.

We sometimes wonder what Kate really needs from us now. It seems she doesn't want a Mum and Dad. There is little we can give her, emotionally, and we feel like the hired help. Even a hug has to be on her terms. Being close to my own mother, I'd looked forward to having the same good relationship with my daughters, but that's not going to happen. The precious, short, little-girl years which should have been so special were lost to tantrums and behaviour we thought was deliberately bad, and I wonder if the resulting arguments and punishments damaged Kate even more, putting our relationship beyond repair. We haven't been the parents we should have been, and have no right to say she isn't the daughter she should have been.

Our younger daughter Lucy, now twelve, was our hope, proof that we must be getting it right sometimes. She was a happy, easy child, readily forgiving the verbal and physical abuse Kate dished out, but that's changed this past year. Having had a rapid education about Aspergers, I tried hard not to 'see it everywhere', but had to admit that the indications were there with Lucy as well, although she is very different to Kate. So we are going through the assessment process again, and it seems likely we will be dealing with another teen with Aspergers. Maybe this time around we will be better at it!

Meanwhile we plod on, trying to get through each day's stresses and deal with whatever bombshell comes next. Each week brings a round of telephone calls, e-mails, appointments, meetings, all because of Aspergers. Sometimes it seems my whole life revolves around it. It has taken over and we cannot make any headway. At times we get overloaded, never want to hear the word again, want to run away and not deal with it any more. Aspergers has taken away the family we hoped for, and may ultimately wreck our chances of a secure future in this country.

When everyone is at home, the house is chaotic, like the Madness song 'there's always something happening and it's usually quite loud.' Mealtimes are like the Mad Hatter's tea-party. Kate loses no opportunity to 'have a go' at Lucy, who now retaliates, and neither will back down. Yet I still don't think we are that different in many ways to a 'normal' family – although obviously now, I realise, I'm not qualified to have an opinion on that! We certainly don't have the worries other parents may have over smoking, drink, drugs and bad company. The girls have somehow always found friends who are genuinely caring, who see beyond their strangeness. And of course, both have very firm views on what is wrong or right.

On bad days, I don't cope, and wonder how to keep going when things look so bleak. On good days, I like to believe that, although this time is difficult, it will get easier. Maybe my daughters will mature, fulfil the potential they both undoubtedly have and find their place in the adult world.

~

Liz's Story

My son's birth was traumatic, a fact I mention due to the amount of research suggesting that traumatic births may have some bearing on the development of autism. However, I can honestly say that until he was 3½ he was a quite delightful child, who only cried when he was hungry, or separated from his Mother. All this changed when we were on holiday in America in September 1991 and he had reached the age of 3½. He became a more and more difficult and demanding child, yet I was re-assured by friends and family that it was just a phase he was going through and all would come right in the end. I also blamed myself and decided that the fault lay in the way I was handling him. I could tell him repeatedly not to do something and he would carry on doing it, totally unaware, or uncaring of my disapproval.

Finally, having endured 2½ very difficult years, at age 6 I picked him up from a holiday club only to have them complain that he wouldn't stop hitting table tennis balls at the other children. The friend I was with, who happened to be a qualified paediatric nurse, said I must get help. I approached my GP's surgery and spent a totally fruitless year seeing a variety of psychiatrists, all female and all with English as a second language. They assured me he was a lovely little boy and I am sure they considered me a neurotic Mother. I went back to the GP, having read a lot about ADHD, and having decided this was what my son suffered from. I asked to see an expert at the Maudsley[1]. The GP took the trouble to 'phone me at home to say that he thought it would take a long time and he would refer me to a local diagnostic unit.

Tim had various tests and we finally saw a Consultant Paediatrician who spent several hours with me and said she considered he had Asperger's Syndrome. He was by then 8 years old, so it had taken 2 years from the start of my first quest for a diagnosis – far too long. You expect a diagnosis will lead to help but this, in my experience, is far from the truth. His primary school were reluctant to get a statement for him and, in fact, he did not have a statement or classroom assistant until he went into Year 6. He was a bright boy and I was constantly being told that he would have to go into mainstream education. There are no specialist schools whatsoever in our area. The classroom assistant was a rather nervous woman and my son ran rings round her. The Year 6 teacher finally said they could not cope with him and we were told to look for a special school. No help was given to us in this task and we had to do a lot of research and visiting to come up with a suitable placement. I might add that our local authority, one of the meanest in the UK in my opinion, initially refused a statement for our son and we had to threaten to go to Tribunal. They then backed down as at that stage they did not like having to go along that route. They are much more blasé now and I would say it has become even harder for parents in our borough to obtain the correct schooling for their

---

[1]   The Maudsley is a renowned London psychiatric hospital.

autistic children.

Tim was at his worst with me and could be violent towards me. However, we were never offered nor given any respite care. We had no family who would or could take him for a weekend so the whole burden fell on us. There were many incidents at school and, I would say, that the other parents showed a lack of understanding and tolerance. One Father even threatened to thump my son if he did not leave his son alone. Tim's threats to his son were totally verbal and not physical but the teacher had not sorted out the situation and only became involved at the bitter end.

We finally found a residential school in Somerset catering for children with dyslexia and Asperger's Syndrome. We were impressed with the school as a whole and when funding was obtained (another major battle) Tim was able to start just before his 11th birthday. Our first choice of school had been nearer to home, one where he could have returned every weekend, but they refused to accept him because of his behavioural problems. He was to return from the Somerset school for a long weekend every third week and for all school holidays – they had much longer holidays than the local state schools. Our social worker, with whom we had by then become involved due to the violence towards me, would telephone to tell me that she had the money for 9 hours help per week but no-one to give me the help, so on one long 9 week summer holiday break I had 9 hours help in 9 weeks!

I had tried to enrol Tim on a scheme for autistic children but they told me he was too challenging, which seems pretty incredible considering they were meant to be coping with all children on the spectrum. Tim was highly energetic and was finally, at age 16, diagnosed with ADHD as well as Asperger's Syndrome, a diagnosis that I, his Mother, had made at the age of 7! I enrolled him on normal activities which sometimes worked and sometimes didn't. I would often be told I had to pick him up immediately, or not to return with him due to behaviour issues. However, on the plus side he was very sporty – he did Judo with Brian Jacks and swam for a local club. Team sports, such as rugby, were not so good, but his total fearlessness meant rock climbing was a huge success, and they coped with him with no problems.

Academically he was coping well at his school and then the lease expired on their building and they had to find new premises. Funding was drying up for children with dyslexia to attend the school and they decided to move a few miles away and to cater only for those with AS. As you know AS children do not like change. Tim had become friendly with quite a few of the boys with dyslexia, so the change of location and the loss of his friends and pastoral worker combined to bring on depression. The school became increasingly anxious about his mental state and tried to get him admitted to a local adolescent psychiatric unit. They refused on the grounds that he was not a local child. By this time he was refusing to eat and had collapsed at school whilst out with one of his carer's. The school contacted us and he was sent home. They hoped he would be admitted to a suitable unit in our area that would treat his depression, and he could then return to the school.

The psychiatrist in charge of our local adolescent mental health facility is a man for whom I have no time whatsoever, an opinion shared by many, many parents of autistic children. His diagnosis at one time was that we were just bad parents. Tim remained at home with me for many months. Fortunately I work part time and my husband was able to take time off to be with him when I had to go to work. He just wanted to study and be cuddled, but could not be left alone at all. Two mental health nurses visited him and asked if he felt suicidal and when he said yes, they told me never to leave him but offered no help whatsoever.

He was finally admitted to a unit full of girls with anorexia. Some people with AS tend to copy those around them and by the time he left this unit – removed by us as we could stand it no longer – he weighed a mere 6 stone. The psychiatrist in charge of this unit had told Tim that 'if he wanted to commit suicide he would' a really helpful statement to make to a boy not yet 14 years old. I am not sure where the good psychiatrists are but they are most certainly outweighed by the really, really bad ones.

Tim was now back at home with me and would threaten and attempt to commit suicide on a regular basis. He would say he was going to run in front of cars, if we were out for a walk, or throw himself off the top of a car park if we went shopping. He had to be restrained from doing this on more than one occasion by my husband and myself. We finally had a referral to the Maudsley and he was put on medication. Following a visit to this unit, which seemed to go well, we returned home. I thought Tim was in bed asleep and got up to go into the hall to find him hanging from his judo belt. I called an ambulance and they talked me through the resuscitation procedure which my husband had been trained to do. Tim had actually stopped breathing when we cut him down. He was taken to a London hospital and put on a ventilator in the ICU (intensive care unit). No-one had any idea whether there was any brain damage or not.

He was transferred from there to a local adolescent psychiatric unit that we had tried, and failed, to get him admitted to before. They never left him on his own for a single minute for about 6 weeks, until they were certain the threat of him repeating his action was over. They had a school attached to the unit that he was able to attend and in time he became a day patient, attending the school and returning home to us in the evening. The only problem with the unit was that they specialised in boys with drug problems and Tim was introduced to cannabis. It was decided that a new school should be found for him - this is very difficult after a suicide attempt. One was finally found fairly close at hand, at least in the same county, but they seemed to have a very vague idea of what Asperger's entailed and in the end the placement failed before it had really commenced due, we felt, totally to the school. It would have been much fairer had they not agreed to take him in the first place.

There was then a very unfortunate incident at the unit, Tim became locked in a room with one of the drug using boys, of whom he was very scared, and encouraged to participate in throwing billiard balls at the staff. I was informed that he had to be removed from the unit and sent to a medium secure private facility in our area. I was made to feel that this was the only course of action open to anyone and duly signed the piece of paper which sectioned my son. The private unit sounded really nice but proved to be really awful, with no stimulation for the children, a very basic education, and very strict rules for the children and their parents, who were never made to feel particularly welcome when visiting. The only good to come out of this unit was that the doctor investigated schooling possibilities for Tim, but it took a long, long time and he remained in the unit for far longer than was necessary.

At last, at age 16, having had no formal education for 2 years (this was a child expected to obtain a large number of GCSE's) he was sent back down to the West Country to live in a house and go to a school owned by an organisation that coped, primarily, with children with behavioural difficulties, or from very bad family backgrounds. He then went, at their suggestion, to a College to study horticulture with a full time helper. We felt he would have been better doing something more academic and would have liked him to have continued to try and obtain more GCSE's. He had managed a few despite his lack of education for 2 years. He thoroughly enjoyed languages and attended an adult education class to study French and went to a Chinese tutor to learn that language, no mean feat.

The Horticultural College was a mixed success. He bonded with some of the students and not with others and was the victim of bullying at times. He would most certainly not have coped without his full time helper. Unfortunately a lot of the children at the College also smoked cannabis, not a good idea when you suffer from mental health problems, but he would never take that on board, despite our constantly imploring him to consider the effect the drug could be having on him. He completed the first year and obtained a pass with distinction.

Our local authority then decided that it was all too expensive and he needed to be re-located nearer to home. We applied for a place at a Horticulture College in the county, but not one that he could have travelled to from our home. The local authority said he would not be able to live in the student accommodation attached to the College as he required more help and supervision than they could provide. They then failed totally to find any alternative accommodation or help for him. College was due to start in September and at a meeting at the end of August the College said they could not accept him under the circumstances, because the local authority had not done their job.
We managed to get him back into the College down

in Somerset, a move he did not want. He had been looking forward to being near home, able to return every weekend, and be visited by us on a regular basis. However, we had no alternative. He was also able to return to the house in which he had lived before as they had not filled his place. He had, however, to have a different helper at College as his helper from last year had been re-assigned. They had had a very good working relationship.

Having failed to save money on the College front, our local authority decided, at the end of that year that they could save money on the accommodation front and they would move Tim to a flat on his own where he had limited support. This was a vulnerable child of not 18 years of age. However, when we put forward our worries we were told there was no option. He was given the top floor flat in a house with, at that time, one other occupant. He, of course, thought it would mean total freedom and all his friends visiting regularly but, in truth, he was really quite lonely. His psychiatrist withdrew his anti-depressants because she was worried about him over dosing with no-one responsible to oversee the medication.

He returned to us for the half term week in February and we had the best week together we had had in long time. He seemed happy and was nicer to me than he had been for ages. I even began to think we had got past the stage when he would attack me. He returned to the West Country on the Sunday and depression seems to have struck almost immediately. On the Monday night he tried to kill himself in his shower, but the man in charge of the house became alarmed by his behaviour and stayed the night to make sure Tim was safe. The next day he attended College and tried to hang himself in the grounds. His helper took him to his GP and he was admitted to a psychiatric unit. That was on the Tuesday and that unit appeared to be reasonable, but on the Friday the decision was made to move him to a much smaller unit, local to where his flat was.

This proved to be the worst decision that could have been made. My husband had gone down there and was staying in Tim's flat. He took him to the new unit and was alarmed when he returned to visit in the afternoon to find that Tim had cut both his arms really badly. He self harmed when agitated, but instead of finding out his worries the nurses just told him that was an unacceptable way to behave. He was put in a room as far from the nursing station as it was possible to be which contained at least 10 ligature points and he was left with his shoe laces. His level of observation was downgraded by the nurse, without any say so from a doctor.

He had been told in the first unit to ask for medication when he became agitated, but at 6.00pm when he asked for the medication, it was refused. The nurse said she would be along to talk to him in 10 minutes but never went. He actually asked the nurse whether she had any knowledge of AS and she said she had, this despite the fact that she repeatedly mis-spelt it in the medical reports.

The extent of her knowledge could have been written on the back of a postage stamp. He went to his room, removed his shoe laces, tied them round his neck and then round the knob of a wardrobe and hung himself. My husband arrived at 6.30pm to visit him. They had no idea where he was and as soon as they went to his bedroom they found him. It was too late, he was dead at aged 17. A life that could have amounted to something, came to an end because of an uncaring system and no knowledge of Asperger's Syndrome.

We employed a solicitor as we wanted to fight our case at his Inquest, but so did the Trust and they made their case with skill and half truth's and pretended to be caring. I had to sit and listen to what I considered to be a fabrication of the facts and I was not allowed to speak. The judge said his death could have been prevented but nobody was to blame. If it could have been prevented then someone was to blame.

I would advise all parents to consider carefully before putting their children in a psychiatric unit. At this particular trust, a man of 30 took his own life 15 months after my son, in exactly the same way. They have obviously not learnt any lessons and not remedied the things that could have prevented his death i.e. ligature points.

We took our local authority to task and after what was deemed an independent review of the case they were all found to have done everything they could have done. That in itself was a total farce but

I think their definition of independent and mine are two totally different things. The Trust where my son died came out of the whole situation as before. The Coroner made recommendations but there is no legally binding reason why any of them have to be acted upon.

Tim was our only son so you can possibly imagine what his loss means to us. Despite all the problems and worries we loved him dearly. He needed to be kept busy and my husband enjoyed going up to London with him and exploring the City. He had travelled abroad with us extensively, sometimes very successfully, at other times not so successfully. He told us he had suffered from depression since the age of 7 and that he didn't get the enjoyment from things that he should have done.

I miss him every single day and will do so until the day I die. My feelings are that an uncaring system failed him totally and that no lessons seem to have been learnt that will stop the tragedy being repeated.

~

Marie's Story

People with Asperger's Syndrome (some like to be called "Aspies") often say that they feel as if they are from another planet. I may understand how they feel because, as the mother of an Aspie, I sometimes feel like an alien, too.

How weird, I thought, that the articles in the "parent's" magazines didn't describe Emily, my new baby. Why the curious, sidelong glances from other moms, when I shared stories about my child? From what planet were they? Being different was difficult, for both of us. To start with, everything bothered Emily; the sunlight, the chill of a fresh blanket, even the smells of dinner cooking. But, in spite of the fact that the slightest sensation overwhelmed her, the conventional wisdom was that Emily would soon learn to soothe herself.

"Let her cry," my pediatrician said, "She'll stop after fifteen minutes. No baby cries for longer than that."

I told him that I had a clock, and that Emily did indeed cry for hours. He regarded me kindly, pitying my distress.

"It just seems like forever," he said.

We were on our own. Of course, I didn't "let her cry." I carried Emily while she howled, singing as loudly as I could. I don't know if it did her any good, but as long as I belted out tender lullabies, I couldn't get upset with her. She slept a bare five hours each night. I was delirious, but so what? I wasn't the one who was bawling. Emily's suffering was clearly greater than mine, and I was desperate to help her. But it was Emily, after all, who figured out what to do. At four months, Emily discovered that she could soothe herself by sucking her thumb. That's when she smiled for the first time, and I learned she had surprising resources.

Emily couldn't crawl. Instead, she'd scream as if stuck by pins every time I laid her on her belly. (Nobody believed me.) She couldn't tell me where she wanted to go, and the frustration made her frantic. When I pointed, she wouldn't look to where I was pointing, but instead her eyes followed my hand. She didn't seem to understand anything I said to her. So I lifted her up, and when her feet touched the floor her body became stiff as a board. That was fine, because if she could stand I could kneel behind her and rock her forward. Like a divining rod, she guided me to what interested her. All were amazed when she walked at nine months. (Emily finally did crawl, when she was a year old. She crawled to the nearest piece of furniture, desperate to pull herself up off the hated floor!)

Nursing was another comfort, so Emily nursed until she was three. When she screamed at pre-school, the teacher suggested that I bring her "comfort object." I had to confess that I was Emily's comfort object. Of course, I was given the advice properly given to the parent of a neurologically typical child: Stop coddling her. If I didn't detach from Emily, she'd be an emotional cripple. Nevertheless, I knew that Emily couldn't handle the "rough and tumble" of a room full of kids without an extraordinary amount of support. She cringed in the corner, sobbing, and the teacher was sure that Emily was being manipulative. We tried three different preschools after that, but never did find a place that was a good fit. That was when I accepted that my parenting experience was of another world.

At home, Emily was a smart, funny kid. But trips to the grocery store, the bank, or to the library brought on painful, screaming panic. Life outside the mother-ship seemed impossible. She was terrified of the squirrels on the front lawn. Their sudden movements were hard for her to track, and she seemed to think that they were about to scurry all over her. Hundreds of times, I assured her that the squirrels were far away, and that they would not hurt her.

Emily was failing kindergarten. "She doesn't understand what you're saying to her," I told the teacher.

"You should call the family into the kitchen for ice cream," her teacher told me, "and when she doesn't respond, and sees everyone with ice cream, you tell her she can't have any because she didn't come into the kitchen. That will teach her to listen."

"A simple instruction like that isn't the problem," I explained. "She comes when called. Emily can't keep up with multi-step directions."

"Then it's ADD," the teacher said. "We'll put her in the front of the room."

Sitting in the front, Emily seemed more confused than ever. "Put her in the back of the room," I suggested. "If she can see what the other kids are doing, she'll follow their lead."

Finally, to everyone's amazement, Emily did indeed

do better at the back of the room, with less instruction. But it was too late, too little. She lagged behind, crying throughout the day "for no apparent reason."

To explain why Emily did all the "wrong" things, I had only one insight from our years together: The hard things were easy, and the easy things were hard. (She could walk before she could crawl. Really. I know it's hard to believe.) Most second graders could walk through a crowded mall, but for Emily the aisles led through a spinning whirligig. Conversely, most second graders didn't like to read encyclopedias. Emily couldn't stop reading them. Emily was a slow processor. But "slow" doesn't mean "stupid." I discovered her giftedness when I enrolled her in a private special-ed school for children with "language-based learning differences." In the sixth grade, Emily scored at post-high school level for reading, science and history. But although she read Dickens, she still needed twenty minutes to stop and tie her shoe on a crowded street corner.

At last, a developmental pediatrician made the diagnosis. I learned the terms for what made Emily different: Asperger's Syndrome is a pervasive developmental disorder related to Autism, a "processing disorder." Emily has two of the most common processing problems for Aspies: Sensori-Integration and Auditory Processing Disorder. Sensori-Integration Disorder occurs when Aspies have to process sights, sounds and other sensations at the same time. The most innocuous things can overwhelm Aspies, the stuff neurologically typical people don't even notice. Certain lights, sounds, movement, and even textures are unbearable (Emily couldn't stand to feel pants on her legs. She wore dresses every day. She got lots of compliments.) Conversely, Aspies can feel calmed by activities that require focus, doing things normal people would find tedious and even stressful. When she was two years-old, Emily liked to line up pages of newspaper across the floor, perfectly abutted, end-to-end.

Emily also works hard to overcome Auditory Processing Disorder, that other common problem for Aspies. But her Sensori-Integration Disorder contributes to her auditory processing problem.
"Look at me when I'm talking to you," the teachers would say. "
But I listen better when I don't look at you," said Emily.
Emily can hear, but it takes a long moment for her to understand you. Auditory processing works both ways, so Emily needs time to come up with a reply. She listens with the concentration of someone mentally translating from another language. Most people don't understand her pauses and will re-phrase what they said, as if to simplify it for her. This just makes it more difficult, because now she has more to translate, and she wonders why the clarification was necessary…and so it goes.

As I've already said, sometimes someone suspects that maybe Emily isn't the problem. I'm not the first mom blamed for her child's symptoms. Frustrating as that is, I try not to take it personally. When autism was first studied, blame was put on "refrigerator moms," who caused the disorder because they were cold and distant to their children. That was forty years ago. Nevertheless, the idea persists that parents, especially mothers, are to blame.

Remember the conversation with the kindergarten teacher? According to her teachers, Emily didn't follow directions because she never suffered any consequences for not listening to me. I explained that Emily couldn't follow directions because she didn't understand what I was saying. How could I convince them? To them I was obviously a stubborn, ineffective mother. My understanding of the problem was just as apparent to me. Too much was going on in the class, all too fast. But the teachers wouldn't believe it. Any normal child would be able to do as she were told.

That's the most insidious problem for Aspies. Those who are high-functioning appear normal enough, and their moms seem to be looking for excuses for their odd behavior. These children are the absent-minded professors, the geeks. We have all witnessed the mistreatment of these children in school. Unfortunately, while we know it's wrong to laugh at any other disability, it's still okay to laugh at them. They are humiliated and even physically abused, but no one feels sorry for them. Their problems are annoying. Obliged to be compassionate to every disabled group, we now come to the end of the line, to the awkward people. I've noticed that the closer Aspies get to the end of the Autism spectrum, toward "normal" range, the more neurologically typical people just want to smack them on the head and say, "Snap out of it."

I must say this: If socially well-adapted "normal" people would spend just half the energy trying to understand Emily that Emily does trying to come to terms with them, it would make her life a lot easier.

What else would help? Keep it real. The biggest problem, as Emily sees it, is that people talk nonsense. She is a concrete, precise thinker, while most other people seem to say things they don't mean. White lies, false modesty, and other social niceties are not her style. A current theory is that Aspies are somehow unable to perceive social nuances, but I have Emily, my own expert, who offers a different explanation. Emily feels overwhelmed in social situations, so it is hard to feel empathetic toward anyone. She tells me that facial expressions flicker too quickly across the faces around her. She has trouble watching and listening at the same time, so it's hard to keep up with a quickly changing face while monitoring a tone of voice. But she has learned what even the most subtle expressions mean, if you show her a picture. It's an exhausting way for her to communicate, but she does try keep up with our incessant body language. Emily understands that, even though the "social smile" is a chore, it is a necessity. But really, wouldn't it be simpler if we all smiled only when we really felt like smiling, the way

Emily does?

Emily is my hero. Somehow, she manages to function on this alien planet. She is even happy here with us, as long as we appreciate her differences. I try to show her how things are done here, just as she is my guide on Planet Aspie. But I know I can't make her neurologically typical, any more than she can make me have Asperger's Syndrome.

That's okay, though. We are fellow travelers. Our journey takes us to a place where I can see my own world from a different perspective. It's a view I never would have had, since I don't think I have any special understanding. I just follow Emily because I love her, and I know she doesn't want be alone. Planet Aspie may be fascinating and full of wonders, but it looks like it could be a very lonely place.

~

Marie Gallagher's Story

I can't even begin to explain the elation Aaron and I felt when we found out our third child was going to be a boy. Both sides of the family were excited as well. Aaron's family was glad the Gallagher name would continue on and mine couldn't wait to have another nephew. We had our hopes and dreams too, like any other parents. There would be baseball in the yard, weekend football games and of course, like the girls, Ivy League college. Often Aaron and I spent the quiet evenings after the girls had gone to bed discussing what our son would be like. Aaron would ask if he would be as smart and outgoing as the girls and I would always answer "Of course!"

It was four thirty in the morning on Aaron's birthday when I woke him up with a few nudges of my elbow and a "Happy Birthday."

He groaned through his barely parted lips, "Go back to sleep," and I nudged him again. He repeated himself and turned over with a huff. When I shared with him that it wasn't just his birthday, he shot out of bed and we were off to the hospital. Chris was born an hour later at 5:32 in the morning only four minutes later than Aaron. We saw this as an omen that the two of them would be closer than any father and son alive. We relished every milestone, the first smile, babbling, sitting, standing, walking. It was a fairytale life with three wonderful children and a house in the 'burbs. Nothing could take this feeling away. Nothing until the flapping started.

Chris appeared to be developing normally. He started speaking at thirteen months and seemed interested in everything around him. He loved to be cuddled and chased around the house but then it seemed like things changed overnight. It was around twenty four to thirty-six months that the flapping and finger wiggling started. I'm sure there were earlier signs I missed but when I noticed this it made my heart sink. As a speech pathologist I was aware of autism, but at the time never worked with any of these students directly. I occasionally would visit the autism classrooms at work, and I knew some of the characteristics the children displayed. Initially I denied what I was seeing, hoping it would disappear on its own, but it didn't. Chris seemed to fall deeper and deeper into his own world. He liked spinning in circles, flapping his hands and wiggling his fingers in front of his face more than cuddling or playing with us. Extended family members and friends thought everything he did was just so cute. I'd smile at this comment and acknowledge how adorable he was overall.

One morning Chris picked up a red Matchbox car out of the toy box and began walking around with it. He held on to it all day and that night and the next and the next until a month passed. If we tried to take it away he would scream endlessly. Initially I thought what harm is it if he holds on to the toy; it's not like it will hurt him and it's not abnormal for a boy to like cars. The more I pondered the situation the more I realized it was hurting him. He was unable to function without this toy and he needed to learn how. One evening after he fell asleep I took the car away from him and hid it in my drawer. The next day all he did was cry, there was no consoling him. He didn't eat, he drank very little and he didn't want to be held. I tried giving him other toys but he rejected them. As hard as it was, I knew I couldn't give in and Aaron agreed; Chris needed to learn. We weren't always sure what we were teaching him but we knew it was for his benefit. The next morning Chris woke up happy and content as if the prior day hadn't even happened.

At Chris's three year check-up I discussed my concerns with his pediatrician. Chris not only obsessed on cars, but cried and tugged at tags when I put his clothes on, couldn't stand to have anything on his hands, he totally avoided finger foods, and ran crying out of the kitchen when the microwave beeped. I could only vacuum when he was asleep or out of the house. His doctor wasn't as concerned as I was; he felt Chris was developing nicely and spun and flapped out of excitement. I was told not to worry; he would grow out of it, and was sent home with a "healthy" child. With heavy hearts Aaron and I could see the doctor was wrong and would have to do something on our own.

Both my husband and I worked full time and like other working parents were exhausted when we got home. In addition, we had no idea what we were doing. Most of the figuring out process was up to me. So I started out using trial and error. If it existed, I pretty much tried it, if it didn't work I moved on to something else. It was a matter of unofficially analyzing results and going forward from there. As time went by and Chris showed steady progress, I became confident in my ability to help him and change his life for the better. We saw an increase in eye contact and his language was blooming; I felt like "the little train that could." Although one may not find the techniques I used in any professional text, tickling, massage, and repeatedly lifting him quickly up into the air, they worked. It wasn't until years later that I learned I had been addressing Chris's sensory needs. With work and progress came lots of praise, Chris seemed to thrive on this as well as roughhousing. Although many times I felt as if I was just "winging it," we appeared to be met with quite a bit of success.

When it was time for kindergarten Aaron and I thought Chris would do well in the same private school we enrolled the girls in, what were we thinking? The school was fast paced and required I.Q. testing and an interview before acceptance. Chris was tested and achieved the necessary criterion so we set up an interview. That's when it all went downhill. He became so excited he began to stim[1] and spin and that was followed by crying, lots of crying, by me. Rejected by the first school Aaron and I researched other possibilities and found another private school for typical and gifted

---

[1]   Stim. - to describe the self stimulatory behavior seen in individuals with autism (e.g. hand flapping, finger wiggling, rocking etc.)

children. The classes were small with twelve students and two teachers, the interview was informal and less stressful and Chris was viewed as inquisitive and observant. He was accepted on the spot and life seemed great once again. He had two wonderful years there, his academics were self-paced, his teachers were extremely positive and they embraced his individuality. Over this time Chris developed various obsessions involving Lego and nuts and bolts. Although his teachers didn't mind having these around, we limited his opportunities to take them to school.

During late fall of second grade, our family moved to New Jersey. Before buying a house we researched school districts in order to find one that would benefit all our children and remove the need to pay for schooling. We instantly fell in love with Chris's second grade teacher. She was caring and patient and also accepted Chris for Chris. Toward the end of January I attended a parent teacher conference to review Chris's progress. It was during this meeting that his teacher revealed he wasn't performing at grade level and quietly recommended we ask for services. As suggested I approached the Principal to discuss what was available to help my son. The conversation was a disaster; He gave me the runaround and told me outright lies. As I quoted the parental rights book to him, he yelled at me "What do you want from me!" I calmly responded "What my child is entitled to," and left.

That afternoon I faxed a letter to the child study

team requesting a meeting. A day later I received a response in the mail. As the evaluation process was underway, Chris developed rapid eye blinking. Not knowing what the cause was, I brought him to a neurologist. During this visit I didn't mention my concerns about Chris's development only the blinking and a new punching behavior. He was diagnosed with Tourette's syndrome and prescribed medication. The doctor wanted to see him in a month to see how the medication was working. During the revisit the doctor checked his reflexes, spoke with him and performed other neurological examinations. When she was finished she returned to her desk and flipped through his file several times. Unable to find what she was looking for she looked up at me and asked "You did tell me he had Asperger's, didn't you?" I was relieved to finally have a diagnosis, and with that in hand, I was ready for his classification meeting. The meeting itself went fairly smoothly. Chris was placed in a small class, taught by a special education teacher, for reading and math and received in-class support for social studies and science. Occupational therapy was not provided because "*he knew how to write.*" I didn't know at the time I should have fought for this invaluable service.

One of our biggest joys was when Chris told us he wanted to call his friend and presented us with a crumpled paper containing an almost illegible phone number on it. Nervous and excited at the same time I punched out the numbers on the phone and a beautiful Irish accent greeted me. After speaking for ten minutes or so I scheduled Chris's first play date. As I rang the bell holding Chris's hand, I didn't know both he and I would be meeting one of our best friends. Brigid opened the door with a big smile and welcomed us in. Ian welcomed Chris with a "Hey" and the two walked off. Over some tea Brigid and I got to know each other. I shared some of my concerns about Chris's ability to get along with others especially as he had recently started smacking his sisters as they walked passed him. Brigid just smiled warmly and said, "Show me someone who doesn't have any issues, and I'll tell you they're a liar." We both laughed and have been doing so ever since. The boys have grown up together and have many shared interests.

Even though I was relieved that Chris made a friend, I was developing many frustrations. I always helped my children do their homework when needed, but Chris needed my help every night, and it wasn't a small question here and there, it was for every assignment and it was taking two hours to complete. One night I became so aggravated that I began yelling at him and left the table crying. Aaron followed me upstairs to find out what was wrong. I told him that I didn't think I could do this any more. "Every day I sit with Chris and explain the work to him. He gets upset and I get upset and it takes two hours to finish. This is supposed to be homework, things he can do at home to reinforce what he learned. Evidently he hasn't learned it. He's only in second grade, am I supposed to do this until he graduates? I can't do this for ten more years!" Well those ten years are almost up, and somehow we've gotten through them together.

Our biggest struggle at this time was that Chris's services were reduced. Speech therapy fell from three individual sessions to one group. He received resource room for language arts and math instruction and was placed in a regular classroom containing a special education teacher for science and social studies. All his other classes took place in a regular sized, twenty-five to thirty student classroom with a regular education teacher. As sixth grade progressed Aaron and I realized that some of his teachers didn't even know Chris had Asperger's. I received phone calls, notes, and even attended meetings where teachers told me he was lazy and disorganized. When I told the staff he had Asperger's and explained the condition to them, they responded "Are you sure? He looks normal." That comment has followed Chris straight through his high school years.

The bullies fully welcomed Chris to school and their relationship has been a long standing one. I unfortunately didn't find out that Chris was being harassed during his eighth-grade year until he came home with a bump on his head and a blood encrusted nose. Chris readily told me what happened and informed me that the four boys who caused his injuries were bothering him all year. I became teary eyed as he told me how they teased him. When I asked why he didn't tell anyone, he told me he had. He told the teacher but after she told them to stop they'd just do it again. I then questioned why he didn't tell me and he stated that he was told to tell the *teacher* when a kid bothered him. That was the rule he formulated, get teased tell teacher. He never generalized this to get teased tell mom.

Soon after this incident my second daughter Mackenzie, who is two years older than Chris, decided on her own that other's needed to be made aware of autism. She saved the money given to her for her birthday and bought autism awareness items. She selected some shirts, a water bottle and a messenger bag that she used for carrying her books. The day after her order arrived, she was wearing a shirt to school. She received some comments about her shirt and classmates asked her about autism. She explained to them what autism was and even found others in her class who had siblings diagnosed with the disorder. Mackenzie watched out for Chris during his freshman and sophomore years. Now that she is in college, he's on his own in the hallways and still being taunted.

As of now many of the old challenges still exist. I run interference with his teachers, writing letters and speaking to them on the phone trying to educate them about his needs. I still hear the remark that "he looks normal" and cringe every time. I need to keep on top of him with regard to his assignments and personal hygiene. He doesn't read emotions well or discern tone of voice. We have sought out counseling for Chris and it has been of great benefit. The psychologist we found specializes in teens with Asperger's. He's not only been a guide for Chris, but for Aaron and me as well. Our current focus is addressing Chris's concreteness of thought.

It is important for anyone to play on their strengths, so we are trying to help Chris do this. He currently takes private art lessons to develop his artistic skills and foster emotional expression. Through this medium we have seen a building of self esteem and an increase in communication skills. An added unexpected benefit has been reduced stress levels. Chris lights up when his instructor arrives and talks throughout the session. They cover just about every topic under the sun. Many not related to the task at hand, but as the piece develops so does the conversation.

Chris wants to attend college like his older sisters and has even chosen computer graphics as his focus. Our search for the best school is in progress and we hope that we find the right fit. At the moment we don't think Chris will be successful living on his own or with a roommate so our journey will be a local one. I believe he will continue to need considerable assistance when organizing his schedule and assignments as well as keeping his personal effects in order. My biggest fear is that he will be taken advantage of and could lose his belongings; he is easily convinced to make uneven trades and unfair sales.

Our fourth child, Emily, was also diagnosed with Asperger's. I find the lessons I have learned from raising Chris help me in being proactive with regard to Emily, but as I look back at the last sixteen years there are many actions I regret. I am a yeller when I get frustrated. Some of my famous bellows include: "How many times do I need to repeat myself," "I've shown you this a thousand times," "You're grounded forever," "Stop yelling at me," and "I can't take you anymore." Of course I love my children dearly and never mean any of these things, however, when pushed to my breaking point this is my cry for help. Although I am surrounded by a loving supportive family, I can still feel alone in this battle. I just hope my children never do. I have learned to apologize and to choose my words carefully. Once I wished they weren't mine but realized immediately that I was really wishing they were normal. I still cry about their issues and I find it cathartic, but as soon as I think I'm through "grieving", something else pops up. They have taught me so much about myself and what is important in life. I'm now able to focus on their strengths and not harp on the weaknesses. I want my children to live a happy productive life, and I want society to see them as I do, intelligent and able.

~

Laura's Story

Another meeting in the Headmaster's office about another of Jack's misdemeanours had us all sitting in the cosy armchairs set around a coffee table but as always, in these situations, I could not have felt more uncomfortable, unwelcome and unwanted. On this occasion Jack had set fire to one of his detention letters with a bunsen burner in a lesson whilst the teacher had left the room. The teacher and headmaster presumed that Jack had done this as an act of defiance to deliberately destroy a detention slip that he resented. They were also understandably concerned that his behaviour was dangerous.

However nobody was viewing the situation as Jack did, which was frustratingly and inexplicably at odds with other people's. The headmaster described the incident in detail to us and then asked Jack to explain his actions. I can imagine in similar situations the pupil mumbles apologies and looks suitably repentant, even if not inwardly so, the uncomfortable meeting is closed and everybody gets back to everyday life with perhaps a lesson learnt by the offending pupil. Our meetings with the headmaster always followed a more lengthy and tortured pattern with minute details of the incident analysed, debated, and argued over until eventually everybody, excluding Jack, would lose the will to live and wonder whether the rest of their lives would be spent in this room.

Jack explained how he grabbed the opportunity of

the teacher leaving the room to experiment with setting fire to paper which happened to be the detention slip in his pocket. This was not an act of defiance as detentions were not a punishment that troubled Jack, proved by the reams of such slips that arrived home regularly.

But surely Jack would see that his actions were dangerous as the headmaster moved swiftly on to the safety implications of the incident? The headmaster vividly described the dangers of the fire spreading across the room but Jack retorted in his measured, even tone that he had ensured he had extinguished the fire before discarding the detention slip in the bin. By now the exasperated headmaster spluttered at Jack that had he not considered that the paper might have spontaneously combusted in the bin and left a pause for Jack to at last play the remorseful pupil. I desperately attempted to kick Jack under the table, knowing full well he would challenge the possibility, but Jack failed to get even this blatant message and turned to the headmaster quizzically saying 'spontaneously combust Sir?' eager to debate for as long as it may take the unlikelihood of this interesting scientific phenomenon.

With hindsight if Jack had only been diagnosed as having Asperger's syndrome during those crucial secondary school years, just maybe the teachers would have been more understanding of what they saw as at best inappropriate behaviour but at worst outright disruptive behaviour. Instead we worked for what seemed like endless years in a vacuum without this vital insight which made all of our lives incredibly difficult and stressful. A life of constant meetings such as these where you were made to feel the most inadequate parents in the world. Any effort you made to help Jack and his school life failed miserably and more likely spectacularly so and teachers either patronised us or humiliated us, very rarely having any empathy with our position at all.

Jack's consistent failure to respond to the rules and authority of the school which he viewed as a 'battle' of right against wrong resulted in continuous detentions, isolations, disciplinary meetings and fixed term exclusions. I would be regularly phoned at work and at home about the latest incident and felt utterly at a loss as to how to deal with Jack. We as a family had always held education in the highest regard. Jack himself had loved finding things out and reading books, although only reference books, from being a young boy so the way his secondary education was turning out caused deep pain as we could not help but feel the school were blaming us for Jack's attitude. However hard we tried to convey our frustrations to Jack we were banging our heads against a brick wall as Jack only saw each situation that arose from his own viewpoint and was totally incapable of understanding how his own behaviour was causing concern to us and the school because he did not perceive he was doing anything wrong.

~

Education

&

Behaviour

'He shows great originality which must be curbed at all costs'
~ an early school report on Peter Ustinov

During the preparation of this book I was privileged to learn the stories of hundreds of parents. It soon became apparent to me that a great many of the problems we seem to have with our children relate directly, or indirectly, to the process of trying to access a suitable education. I hadn't initially planned a section on education but as time went on I increasingly felt that there were potentially some important issues to be debated. I hope that this short chapter begins to stimulate a constructive discussion about finding imaginative, creative, flexible and financially viable solutions.

There is a tendency to assume that all people with Aspergers have the same needs. No two people are the same whether they have Aspergers or not. Frustratingly, when it comes to education this point seems to be forgotten. There will never be, and can never be, one type of school that will adequately provide for the varying needs of students with Aspergers. Flexibility, choice and creative solutions must be kept to the forefront. All too often the education system seems to be part of the problem rather than part of the solution. Schools are encouraged to 'straitjacket' children, trying to mould them to fit into narrow and culturally defined ideas of normality - ideas to which many of us do not subscribe.

As many as one in four children with Aspergers[1] are excluded from school (including special schools). If special schools with their teams of experts can't cope, what hope is there for our children's education. Quite evidently the current system is not meeting the specific needs of many of our children. The emphasis appears to be on inclusion, usually into extremely large comprehensives/academies[2]. Many children with Aspergers are unable to benefit from the extra facilities which these institutions can offer because they become disabled by the vast and complex environment which is overwhelming for them. When a learning environment is specifically adapted to them, they do learn and many excel.

Exam results would seem to be the principal criterion of assessment in mainstream schools. The present alternative to mainstream schooling is the special school where children, irrespective of their difficulties[3] and talents, are often clumped together in the same institution; this is, perhaps, not the best recipe for success (particularly academic). Additionally, the gifted children with Aspergers are frustrated that the only learning that is valued and available is exam-based and uninspiring, with little opportunity to discuss and challenge. Because of the dictates of the school timetable, it is particularly difficult for children with Aspergers (who frequently get obsessed by something) to suddenly leave a

---

[1] This figure comes from a UK source
[2] In the UK these are schools that are non-fee paying, usually non-selective and cover ages 11 up to 18
[3] Special schools cater for children with a wide variety of problems such as Down's syndrome and ADHD

subject that has captured their imagination. Many children with Aspergers who are currently failing to benefit from mainstream or special education could better be served by flexi-schooling, homeschooling with tutor and Internet support or small home-like education centres.

The 'bad behaviour' our children sometimes exhibit is often caused by inappropriate expectations and environments. When a child has hypersenstivity or sensory integration problems, expecting them to adjust to a sensory-overloaded environment is, frankly, cruel. The education of our children has become a one-size-fits-all system, where the measure of success is one dimensional. Square pegs must forcibly be rounded and jammed into a round hole. Atypical brain types must, if we wish to get the best out of them, be granted an atypical education. At the moment, sadly, conformity seems to be the unwelcome mantra *du jour.*

Finally, I don't think I would be forgiven by all the parents involved directly and indirectly in this book if I didn't raise the following issue. When applying for a place in a special unit or to get one's child any extra help, it is very easy for a novice to delude themselves into thinking that the authority is representing the interests of the child. We are variously advised that our children don't need to be statemented (assessed) because they have only minor problems[1]. This apparent delaying tactic merely serves to string out the time before the

---

[1]   I have been reliably informed that the situation is very similar in the USA and UK

authority's responsibility is finally taken on board. Being cynical, we believe a reasonable explanation for long delays and incomplete diagnosis is that either some professionals are incompetent or the decision is controlled by budgetary constraints. In other words, if there is no diagnosis, then no extra services have to be provided. We are expected to rely on the people appointed by the state to decide our children's future[1]. One cannot help but wonder how impartial they are able to be. Surely the link between the LEA and the diagnosis and assessment of provisions, needs to be broken.

For many, the system is experienced as being unnecessarily obstructive and, during the process of researching for this book, I began to see a parallel with the writings of Dostoyevsky, who, in my opinion, is the most astute observer and satirist of government processes. I also have rather uncharitably referred to the LEA (school district) as the 'Circumlocution Office'[2]

If one is fortunate enough to have an accurate diagnosis and appropriate assessment of needs, the next hurdle to be faced is not only to find the right school but to find one that has space. For many, getting to this point is only the start of the process. Families all too frequently have to

---

[1]   If the individual is inexperienced in Aspergers, the child may just be labelled as having conduct disorder.

[2]   The Circumlocution Office is a term used in ridicule by Charles Dickens in 'Little Dorrit'. It is a place of endless confusion. Forms need to be filled in to request permission to fill in more forms. Everybody tries to relegate every matter needing action to someone else.

persuade their LEA to fund a placement with absolutely no guarantee that any funding secured will be continued.[1] All too frequently this process fails leading to what one parent has termed 'Aspergers Education Syndrome' which she defines as 'the result of being forced to hop from school to school, never finding a good fit'. This same mother sagely notes that 'at every subsequent change the student becomes more anxious and troubled academically.'

We need educational establishments which can truly cater for the different abilities, personalities and interests of each child, and then, and only then, will we have the beginnings of a tolerant society. A society that embraces and uses difference to its advantage will surely ultimately benefit all its members.

'Most geniuses have Aspergers but most Aspergers are not geniuses'

A Parent

---

[1]   A number of parents I spoke, to both in the UK and Australia, have felt that the funding obtained for their child was not always used to benefit their child, often seeming to be misappropriated for other purposes.

Behaviour

This short section is the result of in-depth discussions with many parents about Aspergers, specifically regarding behaviour and discipline. There appears to be a discrepancy between how some professionals[1] view and review an episode and how we (the parents and child) see the same event. This discrepancy causes parents to feel that some professionals do not understand the complexity and subtleties of Aspergers and that they view us as indulgent parents, unwilling to discipline our children. Despite professionals confidently stating that they understand Aspergers, the way that many interpret and handle our children's less desirable behaviour would suggest otherwise. Many parents cite incidents at schools which were really trivial and minor but ultimately, through inappropriate handling, were allowed to escalate into incidents sometimes necessitating police intervention.

Society conditions us to take a very black and white view of behaviour. Bad behaviour equals bad parenting. When our children fail to respond to the normal strategies used to confront unwarranted behaviour then professionals generally fall back on the standard explanation that our children are therefore :-

- manipulative
- attention seeking

---

[1] Professionals could mean teachers, LSAs, psychologists, psychiatrists, medical staff, police, social workers etc.

- lacking parental boundaries

Almost all the parents I spoke to had been on the receiving end of this attitude and almost all vehemently refute that allegation. They believe that much of the children's undesirable behaviour is linked to sensory issues and an Asperger person's different view of the world (e.g. literal interpretation of language).

These children are not maliciously or wilfully breaking rules but reacting to situations they see from a view point totally at variance with the neuro typical. It is incredibly insulting to be accused of failing to set boundaries, especially for those parents who have successfully reared other neuro-typical children. But what concerns us even more than the personal attack, is that this view unduly influences the educational and medical approaches offered to our children.

Most of the parents, through experience, insight, careful observation and a good deal of discussion with our children, have learnt to search for the underlying reasons for any 'bad behaviour'. A child that has extreme sensory issues, a rigid understanding of the world, of language, of rules etc. will often see events in a totally different way. After punishment at school many of these children were unable to explain the sequence of events or understand the nature of the problem; in other words, appreciate what they had done wrong. This causes confusion for such a child and he or she will feel resentful. Feeling they have been unjustly accused frustrates and angers them, in which case we are punishing a child for an offence of which it has no concept. It is often mistakenly assumed that, because many of our children are highly intelligent and look normal, they are deliberately choosing to behave 'badly.' People forget that they are wired differently, Aspergers traits originate at the brain level. The brain is simply another part of the body that can go wrong and at such times its performance is not within our control. We don't tell a diabetic to control their pancreas so why do we think a wrongly wired brain is any more controllable.

Punishment does not serve its purpose if the child does not understand what it is being punished for. If a young baby is feeding itself chocolate pudding we do not reprimand it for its table manners, as we all understand that it is not coordinated enough to eat neatly. Developmentally it has no concept of polite behaviour or the social need to be clean. The same is true of any behaviour - if one person does not understand or accept a situation in the same way as others, then their response to that situation may be at variance to the norm. The reasons behind all behaviour need to be investigated and what tends to happen is that we apply our preconceived notions of correct behaviour and then are so intent on correcting any deviations that we fail to investigate and determine the underlying reasons for the perceived problem.

Perhaps the best way I can explain what parents are expressing is with a selection of real life scenarios which they have provided. Two of these examples are taken from the text and the third one from correspondence with a parent.

Example One

This illustrates sensory integration and language processing difficulties.

Emily has normal hearing and speech but she has trouble in processing verbal language. She also has trouble interpreting body language and coping with multiple stimuli. When someone asks her a question, she has to interpret it as if it were a foreign language. This causes a delay in her response, which in turn leads the questioner to conclude that she has failed to understand their question, so they rephrase the question. Poor Emily now has two pieces of information to process and recall, plus the overload of sensory stimuli and body language to interpret. This is clearly an exhausting process which can on occasion lead to frustration and anger. The professionals involved in this case believed that she was deliberately not listening!

Example Two

This illustrates sensory hypersensitivity.

Johnnie is hypersensitive to sound, smell and light. During one family lunch he asked for the kitchen strip light to be turned off; his brother and sister, who were reading, wanted it left on. His mother explained that for the moment it needed to remain on. Johnnie then asked for the extractor fan to be turned off because the noise was so loud. His mother mentioned that as he had complained about the cooking smells when he first joined them at the table she felt it should stay on. Johnnie then started to cover his ears and close his eyes yelling 'stop, stop it – it's hurting'. The mother feels that he is manipulating the circumstances and that his siblings' needs should be considered too.

After a few minutes Johnnie can no longer bear the over-stimulation of sound, smell and sight and becomes aggressive because nobody has responded to his distress and request. In order to understand Johnnie's behaviour, one has to appreciate the way he experiences his senses is many times more intense than for normal people. In this particular example, his mother - under the guidance of the psychologist - interpreted his outburst and request as manipulative and trying to dominate his family, totally discounting the child's genuine distress. He had no desire to manipulate and control the situation, his motivation was purely to stop the stimuli that caused him distress.

Example Three

This illustrates the literal interpretation of language.

Many children with Aspergers have communication problems. James tended to understand language in very concrete and literal terms. He was being assessed by an educational psychologist who asked him to 'read this' and handed him a page of script. James sat silently, staring at the page. He had followed the instructions to the letter, and had read the piece to himself, not out loud as the psychologist had intended. The psychologist had interpreted his apparent non-response as 'insolence'. In reality the assumed bad behaviour was nothing of the kind. The psychologist had failed to understand the necessity to communicate his instructions in an unambiguous way – "Read this out loud please".

The most important lesson to be drawn from our experiences is that both the child and the parents need to be the key source of information. This invaluable resource can be used to draw up an individual care and education plan. During the first weeks at a new school incidents need be discussed with the parents and probable causes identified to provide helpful insight to others. Initially carers e.g. LSAs need to involve parents in the solution to problems which arise throughout the school day. When the children in this book were in environments which failed to accommodate their particular neurological differences, severe problems arose. During the teenage years some even ended up in police custody. These events are nearly always avoidable. And this has been proved, for when these same children attended a school with a true understanding of difference they all, without exception, dramatically improved. An inappropriate environment causes inappropriate behaviour. If I take an animal wired to be a loner (a bear for example) and force it to live in a group, I will be providing an environment that is at odds with its wiring. When the animal displays aggression and undesired behaviour towards other animals, it is my lack of understanding of that animal which has caused that behaviour. The bear is not 'BAD'.

It is so easy in theory to talk about managing 'a situation', we know only too well how hard it can be to understand these children. The reality is that a teacher in a class of thirty (or more) cannot realistically remain hyper-vigilant to the autistic child. It is a tall order to expect a teacher to remain calm, work out what triggered a problem and take the necessary time to consider how to respond. But in smaller settings it can be done and if our governments are truly committed to the concept of inclusion, then they need to limit the size of some senior schools. Inclusion seems to work for those with physical disabilities because in these cases, what is required is easily identified and fixed by modifications to a building. It is not so easy to cater for children with sensory and communication problems. It seems to many parents that when it comes to psychological differences the onus is on the child to change and, as many can't, it fails.

It is perhaps misguided to believe that a single school environment can ever give us all equal opportunities. Take the city academies which on the surface make sense. Large academies, it is reasoned, enable more children to enjoy better and more extensive facilities but such an environment does not afford all its members equal opportunities. An introvert, for example, may well feel absolutely overwhelmed by the sheer number of students and the resultant 'hustle and bustle' to such an extent that they cannot function. However, an extrovert would, in all probability, thrive on the very things which would disadvantage the introvert. But what the advocates of large settings seem to forget is that for introverts, autistic children, people with sensory issues, children with ADHD and anxious individuals, such large settings are experienced as overwhelming environments and for many it can be impossible to function in them, so they are actually disadvantaged by a supposedly enriched, inclusive environment.

Anna Van Der Post et al

Our Survival Tips

My Survival Tips - For what they're Worth!

Living with any problem over a prolonged period tends to strip life down to the bare bones of existence and from there you find out what really matters. I have learnt not to expect too much from life. I have learnt not to feel obliged to follow normal societal rules/conventions if their purpose is unimportant. Too many people persist in trying to make their child fit into normal family ideals causing distress and friction for everybody. Once you let go of unnecessary conventions the tensions dissipate overnight. I have learnt not to ask my son to be somebody which he is not.

He is himself and he is good enough as he is. I have learnt to take ecstatic pleasure from the little things like an electric blanket welcoming me to bed and warming my feet, offering comfort. My first cup of tea of the day is bliss and I always take it back to bed with me. A book that makes me think or laugh. True friendships – the meeting of minds both intellectually, emotionally and philosophically. Humour - I laugh a lot, sometimes with friends but even more when I am alone. I laugh at myself and with myself. I come up with funny little paradoxes and oxymorons or observations on life, and I laugh. A surprise package of chocolates from a friend who knows when I'm struggling. These gestures are invaluable, not for the present itself (although chocolates are always welcome-preferably dark!) it is the effort, love, kindness and understanding that they extol which makes every single bite a pleasure. Each chocolate strokes and heals the bruises with the kindness of one human to another.

Hope – I always have some premium bonds[1] because if I hit the jackpot, I could buy James a house in 'the sticks', he would be happy away from me and away from CCTV cameras, surrounded by his servers. I could find some peace then and who knows maybe even begin to live a little. I know it won't happen but the dream helps me. Fantasy is great too, if you can't live the life you want to, you can pretend. One friend and I have alter egos and we sometimes e-mail each other in character and it is such fun to be this other person, just for a while. Even eye contact and a smile with a stranger can be uplifting. Love – my love for others and their love for me.

These are the things which matter to me now, not material possessions, certainly not what others think, not holidays, flashy cars or prestigious careers – they are nothing to me and never will be.

Lilly

---

[1] Premium bonds – a government run savings scheme which guarantees the original stake. The interest is distributed in the form of a monthly lottery, with a top tax free prize of a million pounds and many smaller prizes.

Ways To Cope

Bringing up a child with Asperger's Syndrome not only leaves you and your child socially isolated, but also placed in this strange alien existence where very few others speak the same language.

These are some of the ways that help me to survive:-

My daughter will bombard me with a stream of consciousness, language that ranges from surreal fantasies to endlessly and teeth grindingly repetitive topics to which you are expected to supply exactly the right answers at exactly the right bit as you have done hundreds of times before. I employ a sort of über-voice/mantra inside my head which tells me to just do it, this will pass, it will be all right etc. etc. even though the real me wants to SCREAM terrifyingly loudly till my throat bleeds and to SMASH my head against a hard wall again and again and again. I can't do this, so I treasure like the most perfect pearl from the deepest ocean, those very rare times, like right now, when I am completely alone in the house apart from the patient and quiet dog. It doesn't matter that the reason I am alone is because I am ill and I have a chest infection. I don't have to talk at all. I don't have to supply the right answer over and over again. It is quiet. I am not talking to anyone at all. I am not going to be interrupted. My head feels soothed and calmed and I am breathing deeply.

I love my daughter to the deepest core of my soul.

With a savage intensity I protect her and fight for her and must survive for her. But only, only the parent of another ASD child could understand these thoughts.

I find calm and solace in nature and the natural world. Walking our gentle Labrador through the woods and fields gives me solace and times for my mind to catch up with itself. I'm always surprised at the Zen-ness of the thoughts my walks give me and the little mantras that flicker into my head.

Ten years ago when my husband and I were at our lowest ebb and trying to climb back from the precipice of a relationship break-up, his sister introduced me to Reiki. This is a Japanese-based form of spiritual balance and energy work which has come to be part of my everyday life. I've gone on to work quite deeply within it and it has really helped to give me balance and some serenity. Its very precepts- e.g. just for today, let go of worry- are invaluable to bring to mind when you are traipsing around Toys'r'Us with a 17 year old girl who wants to look at plastic figures of cartoon characters for at least half an hour and it really is one of the last places on earth you want to be in right then and you've done this regularly since she was about three.....Just for today...breathe........

Sex and drugs and rock and roll have their place, too, though not the sex so much these days. My husband and I are usually too exhausted and our daughter has those enhanced senses common to ASD people, so nothing is very private in our house. Drugs? Not easy for teachers like us to come by and we have to be so responsible and grown-up these days. There's alcohol but we can't afford, in the mental sense, to both be affected - just in case. Kicked the cigarettes two years ago and miss them like mad.

But the rock'n'roll still hits the spot and I can lose myself in my music.

The love and friendship of my husband who can still make me laugh till I cry.

Our animals. Our cats and dog who we give voices to and who supply us with much interesting conversation in this way.

The love and support of a few- a very few- good friends. Don't see them very often but they know.

Jane

*

Conclusion

I began this book because I needed it and if I needed it I felt sure that others did too. I wanted parents to feel less alone and I very much hope that I have met my objectives and they now feel part of something bigger. The strength and comfort that can come from a shared experience cannot be underestimated.

I also wanted professionals to appreciate the true impact, both positive and negative, their behaviour has on us. We can take away the good bits and continue working together to give our children what they individually need.

The many cases I read in preparation for this book were equally notable both for their similarities and differences. As autism is a spectrum disorder, it covers an enormous range. That is why none of us can ever afford to be complacent or to delude ourselves that we have fully grasped the condition and found one-size-fits-all solutions. Each child with Aspergers is unique and many of the children present with additional problems, such as OCD or ADHD. In an ideal world we could tailor our care and education to the child, taking into full account their wishes, personality and unique range of problems, without losing sight of their many, and often exceptional, assets. Most of us try to accept our children as they are. We want them to do the best with what they have and to be happy and confident. We just want a society with a broader concept of normality, one able to be more tolerant and even to embrace difference. So many of our concepts of standard, correct behaviour are in fact culturally dictated, and what is considered normal in one country or era would be labelled aberrant in another.

We have seen that the public can be very judgmental and how society as a whole has a tendency to blame the parents for a child's deviant behaviour. Politicians, too, tend to blame families for poorly behaved children; *ergo* as our children frequently behave badly, it follows that we must be bad parents. This is unbelievably demoralising and shows an ignorance and over-simplistic view of the causes behind all behavioural problems or, more dangerously, the resultant cures. As you have now witnessed, the families I have featured could not, in all fairness, be classified as poor parents. Many have successfully reared other children without any major troubles. The problems our children face are probably due to a genetic variant, perhaps differences in their brains and brain chemistry. They are each different and therefore what they need is frequently different. When a severely autistic child becomes aggressive, it is generally accepted that they can't help it and therefore they are not excessively disciplined or prosecuted. But because the children in this book are more obviously cognitively able, the temptation is to assume that they can use this intellect to modify and control their behaviour.

This results in both professionals and laymen perhaps having false expectations. When our children lose control they get labelled as bad or we get labelled as inadequate disciplinarians. It is a bit like the Dark Ages, when an epileptic was deemed to be 'possessed;' ignorance, sadly, allows us to make horrendous and deeply flawed judgements. If they cannot control themselves or fully understand our world, how culpable are they?

In order to comprehend the behaviour of someone with Aspergers, it is necessary to understand that they are wired differently and consequently the way they experience the world is at variance to neuro-typical people. If society cannot put themselves into the mind-set of the Asperger person, then we will persist in providing an inappropriate environment and communication style which, not surprisingly, triggers outbursts. Once we understand their perspective and sensory experience of the world, then their outbursts can no longer be judged as bad behavior; it becomes an appropriate and explainable response to the stimuli.

It seems to me that a great deal of bad behaviour is actually more a reflection of bad management and inappropriate expectations. When we fail to read the early warning signs of stress and to adequately modify the environment, tensions inevitably build, sometimes over days, with the resultant easily avoidable outburst. Many meltdowns are, in fact, triggered by the child misunderstanding the world and the way we communicate.

A number of the criticisms that have been directed at professionals are, I feel, to some extent our fault. In our desperation we sometimes have naïve expectations that there is a saviour out there who can make everything better. We think that being an 'expert' or 'professional' is synonymous with having all the answers. We need to re-educate ourselves, to have realistic expectations of what can be achieved. Most of the strategies offered we will have already tried for desperate parents are, in my experience, very creative and usually well read. The reality is that for all the expertise out there the extremely severe cases, at the moment, are usually only contained, controlled and managed. Sadly, few reach their full potential as individuals ready to take a full and productive role in society. As parents we need to work together with the professionals on equal terms trying to find individual solutions. Some professionals need to come down from their pedestal and admit they are often stumped; they need to listen when we challenge them, rather than hide behind the standard retort of 'well, I've had years of experience.' For, it has to be said, years of experience amounts to nothing if we repeatedly do the same thing, and fail to learn. Professionals are there to help us, but all too often inadvertently they add to our problems by wrongly assessing and judging the child and parents. The result is that so often we are made to feel ineffectual and despairing.

Before I compiled this book I felt very low and very alone. I felt like a leper, tolerated, but on the periphery of normal life. I had not appreciated the extent to which this sentiment was experienced by others. The isolation that many of us feel is widespread and even when we are surrounded by friends and family, we are still alone - because of our experiences. In carrying out research for this book I have read numerous poignant stories and this has had a very unexpected result. For the first time in many years I feel alive inside. I hadn't realised just how grey my life has been, merely existing, getting through yet another miserable day. I now have a renewed energy which has come from knowing that others have endured similar struggles and felt similar emotions. I hope that this book has done the same for you. I feel that we need to support each other. Our children need a flexible approach to their care and education but current policies are so focused on large institutions, exam results and conformity, to the exclusion of a more flexible, individualised and open education. When things are not right, together we need to communicate in order to ensure that the governments listen and respond to our collective experience and knowledge. Together we can be a powerful force for change and for good and therein lies our hope for the future.[1]

We end our stories during the teenage years, the most notorious time for problems. The contributors' feelings are inevitably coloured by the additional challenges that rearing a teenager with Aspergers brings. It may well be that once our children have reached their twenties, some of the more severe behaviours we have experienced will diminish and more reasonable young adults will emerge; only the passage of time will tell. The stresses and

---

[1] We have a website - see appendix - which is designed to enable us to use our collective voice to lobby for change. Alone we are powerless together we can be a real force.

difficulties of rearing a child with Aspergers can be so intense that we forget to focus on the future. We naively see the teenage years as the dénouement of our parenting role but sadly, for some, the issues we confronted during childhood will never resolve. Many of us hope and believe that by the age of 18 our children will somehow have changed and matured to the point where they can cope in society on their own. Whilst this may be achievable for some, we should not lose sight of the reality, that there are many adults with Aspergers still highly dependent on the protection of parents[1]. As many of our children may still need support it is important that we all start planning to ensure that there are appropriate facilities put in place for their futures.

Finally, it seems to me that it is us and the education system that needs to adapt. Perhaps we should ask our children what they want and need. Sometimes the answer is as simple as that!

*

---

[1] A conservative estimate in the UK is that around 40% of adults with Aspergers live with their parents.

Appendix

List of key Asperger Traits

Aspergers is a sub-group of autism. People with Aspergers tend to have three key areas of difficulties:

1. Difficulties in communicating – problems interpreting non-verbal communication and facial expressions
2. Difficulties in social relationships – although they usually speak fluently, their use of language may be rigid and literal. Making jokes, metaphors etc. can be hard for them to grasp. They may sound pompous and speak with a slightly strange tone. It is common for them to fail to sense when they are boring or offending someone. Difficulty in connecting with others.
3. A lack of imaginative and creative play – they are often extremely good at collecting facts and figures but may find abstract thought difficult so the study of literature can be hard. This lack of imagination can also make it difficult for them to understand how someone else may be feeling. They often have obsessive interests on which they are able to concentrate for phenomenal lengths of time.

Besides the above key traits many people with Aspergers often have other associated difficulties such as extreme oversensitivity of the senses, depression, obsessive compulsive disorder, anxiety problems, dyspraxia etc.

Children And Teenagers With Aspergers

Aspergers is a life-long developmental problem believed to be caused by physical dysfunctions in the brain. It is **not** caused by emotional deprivation or the way a person has been brought up.

*

Girls With Aspergers

It has been said that there are 9 boys for every girl with Aspergers. This figure has recently been called into question and it is now believed that because girls present differently, they are not always being picked up.

- Girls are often considered to be more verbal and more compliant than boys in educational settings and therefore might show better compensatory learning.
- Stronger desire to connect with others and more socially adaptable than boys
- They may be heavily dependent on one or two people and can be shielded and escape scrutiny due to this close relationship
- They may be passive, quiet and compliant
- They are more prone to eating disorders and can become obsessed with counting calories
- They may have tomboy traits and fail to be interested in more girly pursuits eg. Make up and clothes
- Often relate better to normal males who

have a more linear, step-by-step thinking and conversation. Men are also less bothered by manners.

- Lack instinctive understanding of social behaviour which comes naturally to most women
- Prolonged social contact can be exhausting for them
- Girls with Aspergers report feeling profoundly different and find it a terrible strain to conform to social expectations
- Tend not to like physical contact and this can complicate relationships later in life
- Girls have less motor impairment
- Girls have a broader range of obsessive interests and they are less strange eg. Horses and their obsessions tend to reflect those of normal girl's interests
- Better at copying mannerisms, behaviours and dress code than boys.

Suggested Reading

The following books were recommended by the contributors of this book.

Ellis, Albert, and Harper, Robert *A Guide To Rational Living* **(Image Book Compay)**

Atwood, Tony, *The Complete Guide to Asperger's Syndrome* **(Jessica Kingsley Publishers 2006)**

Tancredi, Laurence, *Hard wired Behaviour: What Neuroscience Reveals about Morality* **(Cambridge University Press 2005)**

Dacey, John S, and Fiore, Lisa B, *Your Anxious Child* **(Jossey-Bass Publishers)**

Shriver, Lionel, *We Need To Talk About Kevin* **(Serpent Tail 2006)**

Dacey, John S and Fiore, Lisa B *Your Anxious Child: How Parents and Teachers Can Relieve Anxiety in Children,* **(Jossey Bass 2000)**

Baron-Cohen, Simon *The Essential Difference: Male and Female Brains and The Truth About Autism* **(Basic Books 2004)**

Mark, Steege and Shannon, L. Peck *Sex Education for Parents of Children with Autism Spectrum Disorder* **(Steege Publications)**

Elbow, Peter, *Writing Without Teachers* **(Oxford University Press, 1998)**

Teri Dowty; *Free Range Education* *(Hawthorn Press Ltd 2003)*

Goodyear Bill; *Coaching People with Asperger's Syndrome* *(Karnac Books)*

*

Useful Addresses

National Autistic Society (UK)
393 City Road,
London
EC1V 1NG
UK
www.nas.org.uk

Autism Society of America
7910 Woodmont Avenue,
Suite 300,
Bethesda,
Maryland 20814-3067
U.S.A.
Www.autism-society.org

Autism Society Canada
Box 22017,
1670 Heron Road,
Ottawa,
Ontario
K1V0C2
Canada
www.autismsocietycanada.ca/

Anna Van Der Post et al

Education Otherwise - A charity offering information
and support on home education
Education Otherwise,
PO Box 325, Kings Lynn,
PE34 3XN.
www.education-otherwise.org
A charity offering information and support on home
education

A link to a well-designed site run by a teenager for
teenagers is available from our website
www.asteens.co.uk.

Our Web Site

This book is website linked.

The website has been set up by Rachel and Anna. Many of the contributors have had and will continue to have an active role in its content. It has two functions:- to support parents and to research the key issues that we need to campaign about. We are all powerless on our own but, together from the website we can become a powerful, united voice for change.

If you found the stories in this book interesting, you can find more and submit your own story on our website. There are extensive questionnaires which we need you to fill in so that we can compile reports as the basis for lobbying governments.

There is a contact e-mail – we would love to hear from you.

Pay us a visit www.asteens.co.uk.

Lightning Source UK Ltd.
Milton Keynes UK
18 August 2009
142808UK00001B/8/P